A Black Arts Poetry Machine

Bloomsbury Studies in Critical Poetics

Series Editor: Daniel Katz, University of Warwick, UK

Political, social, erotic, and aesthetic—poetry has been a challenge to many of the dominant discourses of our age across the globe. Bloomsbury Studies in Critical Poetics publishes books on modern and contemporary poetry and poetics that explore the intersection of poetry with philosophy, linguistics, psychoanalysis, political and economic theory, protest and liberation movements, as well as other art forms, including prose. With a primary focus on texts written in English but including work from other languages, the series brings together leading and rising scholars from a diverse range of fields for whom poetry has become a vital element of their research.

Editorial Board:
Hélène Aji, University of Paris Ouest-Nanterre, France
Vincent Broqua, University of Paris 8 - Vincennes/Saint Denis, France
Olivier Brossard, University of Paris Est Marne La Vallée, France
Daniel Kane, University of Sussex, UK
Miriam Nichols, University of the Fraser Valley, Canada
Peter Middleton, University of Southampton, UK
Cristanne Miller, SUNY Buffalo, USA
Aldon Nielsen, Pennsylvania State University, USA
Stephen Ross, University of Warwick, UK; Editor, Wave Composition
Richard Sieburth, New York University, USA
Daniel Tiffany, University of Southern California, USA
Steven G. Yao, Hamilton College, USA

Titles in the series include:
A Black Arts Poetry Machine, David Grundy
Affect, Psychoanalysis, and American Poetry, John Steen
City Poems and American Urban Crisis, Nate Mickelson
Lyric Pedagogy and Marxist-Feminism, Samuel Solomon

Forthcoming titles:
Queer Troublemakers, Prudence Chamberlain

A Black Arts Poetry Machine

Amiri Baraka and the Umbra Poets

David Grundy

BLOOMSBURY ACADEMIC
LONDON • NEW YORK • OXFORD • NEW DELHI • SYDNEY

BLOOMSBURY ACADEMIC
Bloomsbury Publishing Plc
50 Bedford Square, London, WC1B 3DP, UK
1385 Broadway, New York, NY 10018, USA

BLOOMSBURY, BLOOMSBURY ACADEMIC and the Diana logo are trademarks of
Bloomsbury Publishing Plc

First published in Great Britain 2019
Reprinted 2019

Copyright © David Grundy, 2019

David Grundy has asserted his right under the Copyright,
Designs and Patents Act, 1988, to be identified as Author of this work.

For legal purposes the Acknowledgements on p. ix
constitute an extension of this copyright page.

Cover design: Eleanor Rose
Cover image © Getty Images

All rights reserved. No part of this publication may be reproduced or transmitted
in any form or by any means, electronic or mechanical, including photocopying,
recording, or any information storage or retrieval system, without prior
permission in writing from the publishers.

Every reasonable effort has been made to trace copyright holders of material
reproduced in this book, but if any have been inadvertently overlooked the
publishers would be glad to hear from them.

Bloomsbury Publishing Plc does not have any control over, or responsibility for, any third-
party websites referred to or in this book. All internet addresses given in this book were
correct at the time of going to press. The author and publisher regret any inconvenience
caused if addresses have changed or sites have ceased to exist, but can accept no
responsibility for any such changes.

A catalogue record for this book is available from the British Library.

A catalog record for this book is available from the Library of Congress.

ISBN: HB: 978-1-3500-6196-5
        ePDF: 978-1-3500-6197-2
        eBook: 978-1-3500-6198-9

Series: Bloomsbury Studies in Critical Poetics

Typeset by Integra Software Services Pvt. Ltd.
Printed and bound in Great Britain

To find out more about our authors and books visit www.bloomsbury.com and
sign up for our newsletters.

Contents

Abbreviations	vii
Acknowledgements	ix

	Introduction: Amiri Baraka, the Umbra Workshop and the Writing of Literary History	1
	Baraka and Umbra	1
	'A populist modernism'?: Umbra and the politics of form	14
	'A conspiracy to blow up New York'	22
	Black arts legacies and chronologies of mourning	27
	Chapter summaries and methodology	30
1	'A Tale of Two Cities': Umbra, Internationalism and the Death of Lumumba	35
	'This is the time!' On Guard for Freedom protest the UN	35
	'A new perspective opens up': On Guard after the Lumumba protest	41
	Ishmael Reed's 'Patrice' and aesthetic distancing	46
	Rights and riots: Lorenzo Thomas's 'A Tale of Two Cities'	48
	'Cry Freedom': Askia Touré	54
	'There's no hiding place in a horn': A word on music	61
	Conclusion	65
2	'Poems That Kill': Amiri Baraka's Magic Words	69
	'Black Dada Nihilismus' (1963): 'A cult of death'	70
	'Black Art' (1965): A politicized objectivism	84
	'Black People!' (1966): Magic and the law	90
3	'Space of a Nation': David Henderson Writes the City	99
	The poetry of David Henderson: An introduction	99
	'Harlem to Lower East Side'	101
	'Keep on Pushing'	107
	'Yin Years'	116
4	Language, Violence and 'the Collective Mind': Calvin C. Hernton	125
	Calvin C. Hernton: An introduction	126
	'The Gift Outraged'	129

	'Jitterbugging in the Streets'	131
	'On Racial Riots in America'	133
	'Dynamite Growing out of Their Skulls'	136
	'The psychology of the damned'	139
	'Manhood' and gender	143
	Conclusion	149
5	'Home Is Never Where You Were Born': Calvin Hernton's 'Medicine Man'	151
	Umbra poets and the South	151
	'Chattanooga Black Boy'	156
	'Medicine Man'	158
	'Dressed at last to kill'	159
	Gris-gris	163
	'Thirty times ten removed'	164
	'To those residing in evil bite': Cannibalism and incorporation	165
	'*Singing in that rock!*'	169
	Conclusion: Mourning, melancholia and shame	171
6	'Return to English Turn': Tom Dent	175
	Tom Dent: An introduction	175
	New York to New Orleans	179
	'Return to English Turn'	189
7	Memory and Myth in Lorenzo Thomas's 'The Bathers'	197
	Introduction	197
	Umbra and Birmingham	202
	'The Bathers'	207

Conclusion: 'If Our Heads Are Harder'   219

Notes   233
Bibliography   236
Index   256

Abbreviations

Works by Amiri Baraka

Autobiography	*The Autobiography of LeRoi Jones/Amiri Baraka*
BM	*Black Magic: Collected Poetry, 1961–1967*
BF	*Black Fire: An Anthology of Afro-American Writing*
Conversations	*Conversations with Amiri Baraka*
Fiction	*The Fiction of Amiri Baraka/LeRoi Jones*
H	*Home: Social Essays*
TDL	*The Dead Lecturer*
SP	*Selected Poetry of Amiri Baraka/LeRoi Jones*

Works by Others

DMOH	David Henderson. *De Mayor of Harlem*
EM	Lorenzo Thomas. *Extraordinary Measures: Afrocentric Modernism and Twentieth-century American Poetry*
FOTSF	David Henderson. *Felix of the Silent Forest*
MM	Calvin Hernton. *Medicine Man: Collected Poems*
TB	Lorenzo Thomas. *The Bathers*

Other Abbreviations

BAM	Black Arts Movement
BART/S	Black Arts Repertory Theatre/School
BLM	Black Liberation Movement
BPP	Black Panther Party for Self-defense

CAM	Caribbean Artists Movement
COINTELPRO	Counter Intelligence Programme (FBI)
CORE	Congress of Racial Equality
CPUSA	Communist Party of the United States of America
FLN	*Front de Libération Nationale* (Algeria)
FST	Free Southern Theater
HUAC	House Un-American Activities Committee
KKK	Ku Klux Klan
LES	Lower East Side
NAACP	National Association for the Advancement of Colored People
NOI	Nation of Islam
RAM	Revolutionary Action Movement
RNA	Republic of New Afrika
SCLC	Southern Christian Leadership Conference
SNCC	Student Non-violent Coordinating Committee (renamed Student National Coordinating Committee in 1969)
UPC	Union des Populations du Cameroun

Acknowledgements

First of all, I wish to thank my PhD supervisor, Michael Hrebeniak, for his encouragement and support during this project's initial emergence as a doctoral thesis. Thanks also to my examiners, Paul Gilroy and Alex Houen, for their extremely useful comments on my work: their advice helped immensely in its transformation into a book. Many thanks to Daniel Katz, series editor at Bloomsbury, for his invaluable advice, and to the external readers for their comments on the manuscript. Thanks to Michael Tencer and Eben Wood for sharing archival material on Amiri Baraka and on Umbra. I am also grateful to the AHRC, BAAS, Robinson College, Cambridge, and the Faculty of English, Cambridge, for their financial support. Thanks, too, to the staff of the following libraries: University Library, Cambridge; British Library, London; University of Sussex Library Special Collections; the Fales Library, NYU; the Berg Collection, New York Public Library; and the Manuscripts, Archives and Rare Books Division, Schomburg Centre for Research in Black Culture, New York Public Library. Portions of the first chapter were presented at the BAAS Annual Conference in Canterbury, 2017, and the ALA Annual Conference in San Francisco, 2018; of the second, at Princeton University and Cambridge University in 2013 and at the ICA, the Centre for Marxist Education in Massachusetts, and the Bay Area Public School in Oakland in 2014; and of the fifth, at Cambridge University in 2015. My thanks to the organizers, and to the other participants, for discussion. For permissions to reprint material, thanks are due to SLL/Sterling Lord Literistic Agency/Grove Press and the Schomburg Centre for Research in Black Culture for work by Amiri Baraka, Antone Hernton for work by Calvin Hernton, and Aldon Nielsen for the estate of Lorenzo Thomas. All other quotations fall under the category of fair use.

In the composition of a book about the relation of poetry to the social, friendship has played a key role. I want to extend thanks to those with whom this work has been discussed and shared. They include Janani Ambikapathy, Tom Allen, Lucy Beynon, Sean Bonney, Christina Chalmers, Peter Gizzi, Ian Heames, Rosa Van Hensbergen, Owen Holland, Tobias Huttner, Lisa Jeschke, Justin Katko, Frances Kruk, Richard Owens, Neil Pattison, Luke Roberts, Hillary Taylor, Laurel Uziell, Mike Wallace-Hadrill and Tomas Weber. Above all, all my love to Gizem Okulu.

Introduction:
Amiri Baraka, the Umbra Workshop and the Writing of Literary History

Baraka and Umbra

From 1962 until early 1964, the New York–based group variously known as the Umbra Poets' Workshop, the Society of Umbra or, simply, Umbra organized a dynamic series of workshops, readings and publications.[1] A large collective of almost exclusively African-American poets, the group named among its ranks such writers as Lloyd Addison, Art Berger, Steve Cannon, Tom Dent, Ree Dragonette, Ray Durem, Al Haynes, David Henderson, Calvin Hernton, Rashidah Ismaili, Joe Johnson, Leroy McLucas, Lorenzo Thomas, James Thompson, the brothers William and Charles Patterson, Raymond Patterson, Oliver Pitcher, N.H. Pritchard, Maryanne Raphael, Ishmael Reed, Archie Shepp, Cecil Taylor, Askia Touré (Rolland Snellings) and Brenda Walcott. (The list is by no means exhaustive.[2])

Umbra was a bold and provocative force in predominantly white New York poetry scenes: in a later reminiscence, from which this book's title is taken, Calvin Hernton would describe the group as 'a black arts poetry machine' (Hernton 1993, 581). Yet the group effectively lasted for only two years, suffering a fractious and protracted split during late 1963 and early 1964. As Dent notes, 'though David Henderson has published several issues of the journal since 1966, the Fall of 1963 marks the end of the zenith of Umbra as an integral group – a period of a little over a year' (Dent 1980B, 108). Literary histories of the period tend to relegate Umbra to the prehistory of the Black Arts Movement (BAM), mentioning the group only in passing when introducing the work of the BAM. Though members such as Askia Touré played crucial roles in shaping the Black Arts aesthetic, Umbra's own work has received strikingly little critical attention, particularly when compared to the other focus of my study, Amiri Baraka, long acknowledged as one of the BAM's principal architects. This study aims to correct the balance through discussion of the work of Dent, Henderson and Hernton (the editors of the group's magazine) alongside Lorenzo Thomas, with additional reference to poems by Durem, Raymond Patterson, Reed and Touré.

Baraka was not a member of Umbra, though he knew many of its members from their shared inhabitation of the thriving artistic scene in New York's East Village. Hernton, Thomas, Henderson and Touré were all published in Baraka's landmark 1968 anthology *Black Fire*, as well as appearing alongside him in various little magazines during the early mid-1960s, and a piece by Baraka appears in the delayed third issue of *Umbra* magazine. Baraka and many members of Umbra inhabited similar political and aesthetic circles in New York at the time. As I show in the book's first chapter, between 1960 and 1962, the groups On Guard for Freedom and, to a lesser extent, Baraka's own Organization of Young Men laid the ground for Umbra: most notably, through a highly visible 1961 protest at the death of Congolese Prime Minister Patrice Lumumba at the UN building in New York. Umbra writers would also participate in Baraka's Black Arts Repertory Theatre/School in 1965. Personal relations between Baraka and individual Umbra writers – relations which mapped onto political disagreements – were sometimes tense, particularly given Baraka's growing literary fame, and his knowledge of Umbra's activities was somewhat limited and belated (*Autobiography*, 198, 218; Baraka 1984c). For their own part, Umbra writers, while acknowledging Baraka's status as a crucial influence on radical black poetics, were suspicious of his status as virtually the only younger African-American poet visible on the national stage. In his autobiography, Baraka humorously recalls his first encounter with Ishmael Reed and Calvin Hernton. Fresh from the success of *Blues People* (1963), his first book from a mainstream publishing company, Baraka was on his way to becoming a major figure in the white literary world. As he recollects:

> One later afternoon, as was my wont, I wandered into The Five Spot. The one on the corner of St. Marks and Third Avenue. I'm sitting there sipping and probably glancing at a paper or something when two bloods come up to me. [...]
>
> But one guy says to me, 'You LeRoi Jones?' I probably just nodded or grunted. One of these dudes is sort of big-headed and bulky, the other taller, with midnight-dark glasses and a rough complexion of skin stretched tight in what I'd have to call an ambiguous smile. The big-headed one says, 'I like your prose. I don't like your poetry.' The other guy just continues smiling like he knows a secret.
>
> 'Oh?' I left it pointed up like someone had let a pigeon shit on my shoe, but said no more. But the big-headed one wanted to go on and he did, saying some

other things. But then he introduced himself and his companion. 'My name is Ishmael Reed. This is Calvin Hernton.' And so I'd met Ishmael Reed and Calvin Hernton, but I didn't know them from Adam's house cat. Though it did seem that Hernton's name rang some kind of bell, someone had mentioned it or I had seen it. But the introduction seemed to me like some challenge, I didn't know, casual or not. But I took it as such, the way you had to deal with these various ersatz would-be artsy gunfighters roaming around the Village who thought that confrontation in the name of art was the highest form of hanging out.

(*Autobiography*, 181–2)

Despite Baraka's somewhat ungenerous characterization of Reed and Hernton as 'ersatz would-be artsy gunfighters', Baraka and Reed in particular would establish more cordial relations as time went on. Reed and Lorenzo Thomas visited Baraka in Newark in 1967, an experience memorably described in Thomas's *Extraordinary Measures* and 'Lorenzo and Ish' feature in Baraka's Newark-based short story 'Answers in Progress', dated March 1967 and published in *Umbra*'s third issue (*Umbra Anthology*, 39). More recently, Reed has charted his relationship to Baraka over a period of more than forty years in a moving but unsentimental article written for *Transition* magazine after Baraka's death (Reed 2014).

While Reed himself has attained literary renown nearly comparable to that of Baraka, Umbra as a whole has not. Named for the innermost and darkest part of a shadow, within which an observer experiences a total eclipse, Umbra indeed remains in the shadows. Such neglect is inextricably associated with the group's chosen forms of production and documentation. Umbra had a relatively short lifespan, during which only two issues of the group's magazine were produced. The first issue is simply dated 'Winter, 1963' and does not list a month of publication but appears to have come out by April, as attested by a review that appeared in *Liberator* that month; the second is dated 'December, 1963' (*Umbra* I, 2; *Umbra* II, 2; 'Umbra', 13). Though three subsequent issues, containing many of the same contributors, appeared under the editorship of David Henderson in 1968, 1970 and 1974, their appearance was subject to lengthy temporal gaps, and the group no longer functioned as a regular workshop (*Umbra* 1968, 1971, 1974).

As Lorenzo Thomas notes in an unpublished essay: 'Members of Umbra can be considered precursors of, and participants in the Black Arts Movement of the 1960s and 70s; but it is also clear that these writers seem to have established something of a distinct, if yet undefined, personal and group identity' (Thomas 198, n.p.). Developing in New York, but refusing to treat the city as disconnected from the rest of America or, indeed, the world, Umbra's aesthetic was simultaneously local and internationalist. Umbra's concerns were as politicized as Baraka's but emerged before the more widespread and public impetus of Black Power, and its members subsequently dispersed from New York across the United States and beyond. Yet, even after its dispersal, group members' activities paralleled and participated in the unprecedented achievement of the BAM as a movement at once local, national and international in its reach. As Kalamu ya Salaam argues, Reed's and Henderson's works in California during the 1970s form one of the earliest articulations of what would come to be known as 'multiculturalism' in the United States (ya Salaam 2016, 88). Along with Thomas's and Tom Dent's invaluable fostering of Black Southern writing, these activities were hugely significant features of the African-American literary landscape both during and after the zenith of the BAM. Umbra's neglect arises partly from its genuinely collective ethos; the group created a climate neither of individual achievement nor of a coterie poetics. Many contributors to the magazine published their only poems in its pages, including photographer and film-maker Leroy McLucas, best known for collaborating with the poet Ed Dorn on the non-fiction book *The Shoshoneans*, and exiled Civil Rights leader Robert F. Williams, while musicians Cecil Taylor and Archie Shepp did not publish with *Umbra* but were frequent attendees of group discussions. Furthermore, as the biographies in *Umbra*'s first issue note, though Hernton, Dent, Addison and Raymond Patterson were all in their early thirties when the issue appeared, Touré was in his mid-twenties, Henderson was twenty and Thomas was just eighteen. An enterprise in which the work of very young poets was set alongside older but barely known poets such as Hernton, Addison and Raymond Patterson and veteran Civil Rights activists such as Williams and Lerone Bennett, editor of *Ebony* magazine, Umbra refused distinctions of age and prestige. These would be hallmarks of Baraka's Black Arts aesthetic, exemplified in the anthology *Black Fire* (which contains contributions from more than seventy-five writers, from veterans such as James Boggs to complete unknowns) and were determined refusals of the established hierarchies of the time.

In his groundbreaking *Black Chant* (1997), Aldon Lynn Nielsen called for further work to be done on Umbra. Two decades later, Nielsen's call has yet to be widely answered, though Eben Wood's unpublished dissertation lays valuable groundwork, and Jean-Phillipe Marcoux's book on Umbra is forthcoming. Much of the work that has been done consists of self-documentation by the group's own members (Thomas 1978; *EM*; Dent 1980B; Rogers; Kane; Panish). Michel Oren's lengthy narrative account of the group, meanwhile, concentrates on a factual reconstruction of organizing activity, rather than on readings of the poetry itself (Oren 1984, 1986). Drawing on extensive interviews, Oren's piece has drawn criticism from group members, such as Reed, for perceived distortions and misrepresentations. Indeed, its narrative approach arguably risks sensationalism, even as it carefully attempts to map often-fractious social dynamics onto broader theorizations of collective organization.

Similar problems occur in the proliferating range of Baraka criticism. Significant work has been done on Baraka's relation to predominantly white avant-gardes (Epstein) and on his role in the BAM, whose growth sprang from his establishment of the Black Arts Repertory Theatre/School in early 1965. Indeed, when Baraka began BART/S in April 1965, it was to Umbra that he turned (*EM*, 143; Riley); at the three-hour launch event, Umbra poets Hart LeRoi Bibbs, Albert Haynes, David Henderson, Calvin Hernton, Charles Patterson, Ishmael Reed and Lorenzo Thomas read alongside Baraka, Larry Neal, Ojijiico and Steve Young. In his review of the event for *Liberator* the following month, Clayton Riley notes:

> The humor, fire and frequently awesome power of their individual works kept a large gathering rooted in the house for nearly three hours [...] It was an urgency of the sort that attends a jazz *set* when musicians are 'into something,' when that undefinable thread of connective tissue we sometimes refer to as *rapport* is established with the listener. All of which is to say that poets were there, deep in a *thing*; I was *there* digging, and, baby, it cooked. (Riley, 19)

Riley's review vividly suggests the dramatic intensity of Umbra's highly diverse but invariably politicized work: Umbra's collective aesthetic, often likened to that of a jazz group, manifested as much in performance as in publication, and the much-vaunted turn to performance in the work of Baraka and the BAM had already been established in their work for a number of years. Members of Umbra's 'nationalist' faction, whose growing anti-white rhetoric had precipitated the group's own split, were important participants, most notably Touré and William and Charles Patterson, all of whom were present at the founding meeting, along with Larry Neal, Muhammad Ahmad (Max Stanford) of the Revolutionary Action Movement (RAM) and others (Smethurst 2014, 14). (For BART/S, Calvin Hernton co-directed Charles Patterson's play 'Black Ice', which would appear in *Black Fire* (1966E, 6).)

Yet because Umbra's main activities predated the movement, it has received comparatively little attention. This book responds to such neglect in two ways, through its linked focus on Umbra and Baraka. One of the principal contentions

I make is that, while Umbra as an organization effectively lasted for under two years, its influence was felt for decades afterwards in the individual careers and collective endeavours of its writers. 'Umbra' is not simply the group as it existed in New York during a brief but formative period but the afterlife of that group, as it feeds into the BAM and beyond. The book thus addresses both collective production during this initial period and the overlooked work of individual writers both during and after this period, covering the formation of Umbra in the early 1960s through to the demise of the BAM in the early 1970s and subsequent activity, principally in the American South, during the mid- to late 1970s. But not only in its organizational activities, the *literary* work of the Umbra poets in many ways refuses traditional, linear models of history. It is impossible to discuss Umbra without reference to earlier periods – as seen below in my readings of Calvin Hernton's early poems of the 1950s – and to later work – as in Tom Dent's work on New Orleans in the later 1970s. This is what Jerry Ward, in his afterword to the recent *New Orleans Griot: The Tom Dent Reader*, calls an 'invisible history', and conventional models of literary history do not always suffice (Dent 2018, 499). Thus, the book ends on a poem by Lorenzo Thomas written in 1970, not published until 1975, and dealing with events surrounding the Birmingham Civil Rights protests in 1963. Likewise, Hernton's and Dent's poems of the South, both published in 1976, reckon with their childhoods there in the 1930s, written through the prism of Umbra and the BAM, and political debates about Black Southern writing and its neglect.

As Dent notes, Umbra's members have produced over forty books (Dent 2018, 489); to chart every member of the group, and its complex, often controversial histories of organization, publication and activity in their entirety is beyond the scope of a single book. (The beginnings of such a history will be provided by Jean-Phillipe Marcoux's upcoming work focusing on the five issues of the group's magazine.) Thus, though the majority of the writers in this study emerged from the Umbra workshop, this is not a cultural history of the workshop. Instead, I provide linked close-readings of individual Umbra poets' writings, referring back to the formative moment associated with Umbra and how it crucially shaped their work but expanding outwards to consider their subsequent careers. Because such work insistently addresses contemporaneous political events, such as the UN protest at Lumumba's death, the Harlem and Newark Riots, and the Birmingham Civil Rights campaign, these events will be addressed, as well as the trajectories of collective organizational involved in Umbra. However, my main focus will be not on the magazine the group produced, nor the complex networks of organization in the New York milieu of the early 1960s, but on their writing.

My argument is not that these writers – as individuals – had a sphere of influence as wide as that of figures such as Baraka. The Umbra poets flourished and must be understood in the context of collective production. Yet the very absence of careful readership of their individual works and their reduction to brief mentions within the contexts of collective activity also make paying attention to what those individual works do a necessary task of recovery. The techniques of close-reading and of addressing the work of individual writers on its own merits are ones frequently applied to 'great writers' (particularly white). I argue that we can – and must – do this to marginalized writers, not to subsume them to close textual analysis but to show how their work, often understood merely contextually, also repays this attention and to give it the attention it deserves.

In 'Kindred: Origins of the Black Avant Garde', Lorenzo Thomas argues that 'the Umbra Workshop was an avant-garde group that did not produce a collective style – not even in the sense that the Beats, the New York School, or the Black Arts Movement did' (Thomas 2001c, 63). Both as their work relates to 'Umbra' and as it extends beyond it, what bound these writers together were ties of friendship and, despite their often very different individual writings, their sense – though diverse and sometimes even divisive – of a shared, politically inflected aesthetic project. As well as the contextual links provided by Umbra, what productively links these studies of individual writers – Baraka, Hernton, Henderson, Dent and Thomas – are their poems' address to particular political issues – in particular black internationalism (exemplified in the first chapter), the racialized spaces of New York, often figured through urban insurrection (Baraka, Henderson and Hernton), the spaces of the South (Hernton, Dent and Thomas) and, more generally, the writing of non-proscriptive but intensely politicized work. Such work develops and continues the earlier work of politically committed African-American writers – of which valuable studies have been provided by James Smethurst, Michael Denning and others – as well as anticipating and feeding into what would become known as the Black Arts Movement. While Umbra opposed certain trends in the reception and production of black cultural work, their place within a broader – though disrupted – continuum is also key.

Given this, the date range covered in this book is far broader than that of Umbra's brief existence as a collective. Umbra functions in these writers' works as a motivating moment of collective shared inhabitation, whose influence extends far beyond the specific nature of 'Umbra' as magazine or as workshop. In this book, we see how parallel trajectories in shared political moments, friendship and collective activity were followed by linked but diverse responses to the changing literary and political climate. The trajectory of each chapter reproduces, on a smaller scale, the implicit argument of the book. Beginning with the writers' work during the Umbra period, I move on to their later work. I argue that Umbra has to be understood not only as an organization at a particular time but as a shaping influence that fed into many diverse strains of writing which themselves feed into the BAM and which emerged from previous strains of black radical writing and activism.

One of the principal difficulties of writing about Umbra and similar groups, as suggested by the paucity of previous scholarship on Umbra, is that this is a period of often violent personal disagreement, often with strong ideological inflections. But what ties them together, as the title of the book makes clear, is the 'Black Arts'. Whether or not this is the 'Black Arts Movement' per se, commonly understood as dating from 1965, or whether we can see Black Arts as starting earlier, during the Umbra period, or perhaps – as Smethurst's and Kalamu ya Salaam's valuable studies suggest – a combination of both, Black Arts (or, to use Smethurst's useful term, 'the Black Arts matrix') as a concept encompasses diverse ideological positions with a common emphasis on a politicized writing that is not tied to the dictates of form. The sheer diversity of the Black Arts makes it resistant to monolithic readings, and this argument is reproduced on a macro level in my examination of the complexities and contradictions of individual writers' work.

While I also address work by Ishmael Reed, Askia Touré, Raymond Patterson and Ray Durem, my principal focus besides Baraka will be on the three Umbra editors: David Henderson, Calvin Hernton and Tom Dent. Henderson's prolific early work saw others regard him as one of the most naturally talented of the group, and his career across poetry, music writing and cultural organizing manifests Umbra's diverse and collective ethos. Of the three editors, Hernton took principal responsibility for the arrangement of material and section titles (Dent 1980B, 108). Dent calls him:

> [O]ur strongest and most mature voice [...] Calvin produced a lot of material, and dominated just about everything we did with the salt of his personality [...] He is a writer whose work deserves a lot more attention than it has received. (Dent 1980B, 107)

Dent himself was the group's organizational pivot: the workshops were hosted at his apartment, and he was one of the most active of the Umbra poets in organizing workshops and readings, both during the Umbra period and on his return home to New Orleans. Dent's passionate and sustained engagement with Southern writing adds an often-ignored Southern dimension to the Umbra ethos. Finally, I consider the work of Lorenzo Thomas: though, like Henderson, he was extremely young when Umbra formed, Thomas remains important not only as a poet but for his vital scholarly work *Extraordinary Measures*, a history of twentieth-century 'Afrocentric modernism' which includes Umbra, Baraka and the BAM. Through linked close-readings, the first four chapters of the book broadly deal with the experience of New York, principally through Thomas's, Baraka's, Henderson's and Hernton's poetry of urban alienation and insurrection, and the last three chapters with the American South, via Hernton, Dent and Thomas, who all moved to the South in the post-Umbra period. My analyses of these poets will be set throughout against contextual readings of the political events which shaped Umbra, most notably the 1961 pro-Lumumba protest at the United Nations (UN), the 1964 Harlem Riots and the 1963 Birmingham Civil Rights campaign.

Alongside my focus on work by Henderson, Hernton, Dent and Thomas, the book's second tactic is to use Baraka as a linchpin around which to frame discussion of the Umbra poets. In this way, it hopes to cast fresh light on Baraka's work. During this period, Baraka was not alone in reckoning with the difficulties of writing engaged political work that went beyond simple 'protest poetry'. Addressing Umbra writings which emerged from the 1961 UN protest informs the analysis of Baraka's writing on riot; likewise, as I show in the following chapters, Henderson's and Hernton's writings on urban insurrections form a valuable correlative to those of Baraka addressed in the second. This approach will provide a comprehensive picture of the range of subjects and analytical frameworks deployed within a thriving African-American poetics which includes, but extends beyond, Baraka. Situating Umbra alongside Baraka shows how they anticipated his more canonized post-1965 work and gives us a greater sense of their achievement. It also makes sense from the perspective of cultural history: though Baraka was not present at Umbra workshop meetings, he was perhaps *the* major figure in black radical writing at the time. In that sense, his *poetics* is a part of the poetics of the Umbra group: including his work here produces a mutually productive exchange between their work and an expansion of our sense of both of their aesthetic projects.

Baraka's treatment as an isolated exemplar may, in part, result from his own strategies of self-presentation. As James Smethurst notes: 'Baraka himself sometimes overemphasised the whiteness of [New York's] downtown bohemia so as to make the story of the break with it more powerful' (Smethurst 2014). Baraka was famously the only black contributor to Donald Allen's *The New*

American Poetry, and the list of 'young wizards' whom he identifies as his poetic comrades in his statement for the anthology includes no black poets (Baraka 1960). Baraka would later serve as an important mentor to younger black poets, writing the preface to Henderson's *Felix of the Silent Forest* (1967). However, his earlier magazines *Yūgen* and *The Floating Bear* printed very few black writers, as he later noted:

> I was 'open' to all schools within the circle of white poets of all faiths and flags. But what had happened to the blacks? What had happened to me? How is it that only the one colored guy? (*Autobiography*, 157)

Baraka's status as 'King of the East Village' – as he was dubbed by the *New York Herald Tribune* in 1964 – was predicated, in part, on his enhanced visibility as the sole African-American in a predominantly white scene (Eberstadt). Though he was involved in numerous projects with Baraka, whom he considered a friend and comrade, Askia Touré in a 2004 interview reacted with some exasperation to what he saw as the excessive focus on Baraka in histories of the BAM and its predecessors.

> What is the root of this seeming obsession with Amiri Baraka? Is this an unconscious aspect of a Personality Cult? Do you realize that you've never asked any questions about Larry Neal, Sonia Sanchez, Hoyt Fuller, Dr. Carolyn Fowler, Haki Madhubuti, Sarah Fabio, 'Umbra,' Ishmael Reed, Tom Dent, Lorenzo Thomas, Calvin Hernton, my mentor John O. Killens? Only Baraka, Baraka, Baraka? (Touré 2004)

Though neither Touré nor I underestimate Baraka's immense significance, I concur with these claims about the neglect of a whole host of writers who contributed to what was a *movement*, not simply the career of one major figure and his followers. Though I do not address all the writers Touré names, this book will attempt to correct the balance through new scholarship on Touré, Henderson, Hernton, Dent, Thomas, Raymond Patterson and Reed.

Wherever the responsibility lies, isolating a single figure as representative of an entire range of literary traditions contradicts Umbra's communal mode of organization. As Dent notes:

> We talked a lot about [...] the 'one writer of the times' syndrome. We were very conscious of that as an obstruction. The group idea of presenting many voices was a conscious attempt to break that down and to attack the idea that there was Wright who passed the mantle on to Ellison who passed the mantle on to Baldwin who passed the mantle on to, it was grabbed by, LeRoi Jones. (Dent 1981, n.p.)

More polemically, Reed caustically comments: 'There's always a seat up for grabs, and every faction in the establishment has its token darkie. What happened was that Baraka courageously walked away from it; Calvin Hernton walked away from it. You're supposed to stay in New York when your book is published and be exploited. Calvin Hernton went to England' (Reed 1995, 21). By contrast, as the foreword to *Umbra*'s first issue noted:

> UMBRA is a group project. The magazine grew out of Friday night workshops, meetings and readings on Manhattan's Lower East Side [...] and out of the need expressed for it at those meetings. (*Umbra* I, 4)

Joe Johnson would later provide a memorable description of the atmosphere at such meetings, 'on Fridays in a hot small room on second street on the lower east side (first floor, first apt. to the left)':

> Tom [Dent] on couch, Askia [Touré] in chair, David [Henderson] pacing, Art [Berger] holding the wine, Norman [Pritchard]'s head nodding, Nora [Hicks] with legs folded, Charmie [Charles Patterson] with his head to the side, Ish[mael Reed] seeing, Lennox and Maryanne [Raphael] listening, Al's head back, Lorenzo [Thomas]'s back back, Jamie [Thompson] eyes counting, Steve [Cannon] on his way, and Joe Johnson standing on the wall. (Hernton 1976, 5)

Umbra succeeded in translating this more intimate space of friendship into a highly visible presence within New York poetry scenes. In stark contrast to the apparent absence of black readers suggested by literary-historical accounts, the group would often 'read eight or ten at a time' (Oren 1986, 181). Hernton recalls:

> We became famous on the Lower East Side for our readings [...] We behaved like a dynamic, well-rehearsed black arts poetry machine [...] We would form a line across the front of an audience – in a bar, church, living room, auditorium, theater, on a street corner or pier. (Hernton 1993, 581)

Likewise, the group did not aim at inclusion within a literary mainstream which would dilute the radicalism of their content for fear of losing financial backing. The editorial's polemical rejection of 'perennial "best sellers"', 'the commercial press' and 'accepted journals' also opposes tokenist inclusions of individual 'spokesmen of the race situation' (*Umbra* I, 3). Within such an atmosphere, some in the group felt incidents such as Hernton's signing of a book contract with Doubleday to be a betrayal of its collective ethos (Oren 1986, 201).

Baraka's break with New York's integrated literary culture was undoubtedly significant. However, moving beyond Baraka's autobiographical self-figurations provides a more nuanced view of how poetry and politics intersected during this period. For instance, the increasing adoption of Black Nationalism by African-American artists tends to be attributed to Malcolm X's death in February 1965, an account fostered by Baraka's own 'conversion narrative' in which he recounts the moment Umbra member Leroy McLucas burst into a reading in a Village bookshop to announce Malcolm's death, triggering Baraka's own move from the Village to Harlem and the establishment of BART/S (*Autobiography*, 200–1; Sell, 238). Yet, while Malcolm's assassination acted as the most visible trigger, tensions concerning nationalism already existed not only between black and white artists but between nationalist and non-nationalist wings within African-American writing communities such as Umbra (*EM*, 142).

The nationalism espoused by some Umbra writers is generally adjacent to that associated with the BAM. (See, for instance, Touré's critique of Baraka's anti-white bias in 1968 (Touré 1968, 304).) The Nation of Islam (NOI) creation myth forms the basis for Baraka's 1966 play *A Black Mass*, and Malcolm was a central figure in Black Arts eulogy (Baraka 1969B). Though Malcolm was also eulogized by Umbra poets such as David Henderson and Raymond Patterson, Calvin Hernton actively disparages NOI ideology in 'Another Man Done Gone', an essay written after Malcolm's death, arguing that Malcolm's move towards Pan-Africanism and his ability to speak to the lumpenproletariat were his key virtues (1966D, 97–104). Hernton is wary of the use of nationalist ideology for hypocritical ends – what Touré called 'porkchop nationalism' (Touré 2004) – as indicated by his satire of the Republic of New Afrika in the 1974 novel *Scarecrow* (1974, 189). While Dent moved towards a Pan-Afrikan Nationalist position, concerned with black political control and representation in the political institutions of New Orleans (Wood, 315, 349), the focus on the 'black nation' in his later works strongly tends to the psychological and spiritual, rather than material (Dent 1985), in contrast to Baraka's 'Whas Gon Happen' ('Land/will change/hand/s' (*SP*, 160)). Likewise, in a 1966 symposium on Black Power organized by Harlem CORE, Thomas argued:

> Our attempts to think out loud have often been taken up by the news and represented to the nation as our plan of action. Black Power for instance. Forget Black Power. There is more to life than that, and our life might perhaps become the truth of the moment we seek without the need of slogans. In times past people were content to *experience* their lives, but today one is not really living unless one has a programme. (Quoted in Cruse 1967, 198)

In this regard, Thomas would later develop a conception of 'Afrocentricity' as 'positional, rather than polemical' (*EM*, 100).

Though poets like Dent and Thomas themselves later developed more open-ended versions of nationalism, it was the question of nationalism that led to Umbra's own protracted split, from November 1963 to early 1964. The immediate cause was a controversy over the proposed publication in the magazine's third issue of a prose piece by Ray Durem (Oren 1986, 181). Durem, some years older than the other Umbra poets, had fought in the International Brigades during the Spanish Civil War but turned away from Communist organizations due to their neglect of racial issues, authoring a series of anticipatory nationalist poems and essays until his death in 1963. The text in question, 'A Decoration for the President', is a bitterly satirical epistle highly critical of John F. Kennedy's foreign policy in Cuba in which the president is presented with the charred hand of a Cuban orphan killed in the bombing of a Cuban housing project: 'fourteen years old, the same age as Emmett Till, when he was murdered' (Durem, 24; Ramey, 246). The piece is dated April 1961, the month of the Bay of Pigs invasion. However, its proposed appearance just after Kennedy's own assassination sparked such fractious debate within the editorial collective that the proposed issue never emerged, and the group itself slowly fell apart. Following the split, Tom Dent handed the editorship of the magazine to James Thompson, before handing it back to David Henderson, who edited all subsequent issues of the magazine (Oren 1986, 182). Yet, despite occasional plans to reform, and barring retrospective gatherings at readings and conferences, Umbra transitioned from being a workshop which met regularly to being an occasional magazine in which the diverse participants who attended the workshop and published with Umbra were united through a textual, rather than material space.

Umbra's insistence on political and aesthetic non-alignment, while not precluding individual members' involvement with organizing – from the workshop itself to On Guard for Freedom, Baraka's Organization of Young Men and In/Formation and the emergence of BART/S – also meant that competing ideological and aesthetic strands sometimes could not find resolution. It is not my intention here to provide a definitive account of the split. Umbra's address to this political moment was based not on a monolithic ideological or political programme but on collective engagement. What emerges here is a context, parallel to that of Baraka and the BAM, equally concerned with issues of media- and self-representation, urban political struggle, and debates surrounding violent and non-violent resistance. Challenging existing models for the figuration of history per se, Umbra's work explicitly addresses the political moments in which it was written: from Birmingham to Harlem, New York to the Congo, its 'positional' Afrocentric focus recovers founding traumas and neglected traditions, engaging in nationalist-inflected imaginings of a post-revolutionary future. As Touré wrote in 1963, '*We are not invisible men*' (Touré 1963, 11). It is high time for Umbra to emerge from the shadows.

'A populist modernism'?: Umbra and the politics of form

In what follows, I situate Umbra within the hostile, conservative climate of the McCarthy era and suggest ways in which the group created a forum that was both formally adventurous and politically motivated. I then move on to outline some of the dynamics of the New York climate from which Umbra emerged. These sections will provide a contextual framework which will inform much of the subsequent enquiry. In 1964, the English novelist and critic Walter Allen wrote a sceptical review of Baraka's anthology *The Moderns* for the *New York Review of Books* (*NYRB*). Allen's piece provoked Baraka to wryly comment in a letter to his friend Ed Dorn: 'Guess you saw Walter Allen's little piece in NYReview about Moderns? How you like them apples??' (Pisano, 176). In his introduction, Baraka had discussed 'a continuing tradition of populist modernism that has characterized the best of twentieth-century American writing', and this term forms the theoretical framework to Werner Sollors's 1978 study of his work (Baraka 1963D, xvi). Allen, however, had insisted that the term was a contradiction in terms. Distinguishing between what he characterized as a Whitman-derived populist tradition and a French symbolist-derived modernist tradition within American literature as a whole, Allen argues that any convergences between these two strains are 'more apparent than real', appearing to unite the two 'only because of the nature of their content' (Allen, 11). This dismissive formalist analysis discounts Baraka's insistence on the political significance of subject matter and voicing, removing both populism and modernism from political and social life. Nowhere more does Allen's demotion of 'content' blind him to the political import of these works than when he mistakes the location of Baraka's pieces from *The Moderns*, excerpts from his then in-progress *The System of Dante's Hell*. Baraka is not 'recreating Harlem scenes of his childhood' but those of his birthplace, Newark, New Jersey, and Allen's casual elision of the two, seemingly as generic stand-ins for the black 'ghetto', is telling.

During this period, as Al Filreis has shown, mainstream literary criticism sought to limit the political effectiveness of avant-garde writing, both by at once claiming it as a depoliticized aesthetic space and criticizing it for political hypocrisy or naivety. Such arguments were put forward even by such nominally leftist thinkers as Renato Poggioli, as well as by more obvious conservatives (Filreis, 47). Though the *NYRB* would become known as a leftist publication (it was described by Tom Wolfe as 'the chief organ of radical chic'), it prided itself at the time on what David Riesman, in a 1963 article on Kennedy's assassination, called a 'non-partisan' intellectual liberalism, rejecting the 'excesses' of both 'right-wing abusiveness' and the attempt 'to overthrow "capitalism" by worker or other militant action on the intoxicated left' (Riesman, 3). Riesman manages to slur and elide both the activist Left and, by implication, the generation of drunken bohemians suggested by the use of the term 'intoxicated'. It is exactly this kind of wild mishmash of targets which Lorenzo Thomas debunks in his poem 'A Tale of Two Cities', published in *Umbra*'s first issue and examined in the first chapter. Satirically responding to a racist *New York Times* article by war correspondent Homer Bigart, and ironically portraying black activists as 'New York beer-drinkers', Thomas shows the pitfalls faced by politically committed artists and activists in a climate of near-overwhelming hostility and condescension. Discourses such as those of Allen, Bigart and Riesman were not simply misplaced; their authors were often actively involved in the repressive activities of the American State. During the early 1940s, Riesman, author of the popular study of social alienation, *The Lonely Crowd* (1950), had served as assistant deputy attorney in Manhattan, where he prepared briefs for the Rapp-Coudert committee hearings, which barred Communist party members from teaching positions in New York public colleges. Riesman was also a member of the militantly anti-Communist, CIA-funded Congress for Cultural Freedom, a group of public intellectuals whose secret government funding belied their claims to non-partisan neutrality. In this intellectual climate in which even ostensibly liberal fora were often hostile to left-wing activism and thought, the work of Baraka and the Umbra writers assumed a potent political edge. Likewise, within the academy, the dominance of the Southern Agrarians reinforced a stultifying racial hostility, obliquely registered in Calvin Hernton's first published poem, 'Remigrant', from 1954. Hernton reappropriates the lyrics to *Dixie*, themselves the title to the Southern Agrarians' 1930 manifesto: 'I'll take my stand' becomes 'I'll make my stand [...] As an equal man' (Hernton 1954). Shortly after the poem was published, Hernton found himself subject to the attentions of the FBI.

Following his high school studies in Chattanooga, Tennessee, Hernton had won a scholarship to Talladega College, Alabama. A historically black college, the college employed an interracial faculty, who, as Hernton notes, were 'nearly all [...] considered radical' (Hernton 1996, 149). During the McCarthy era, the college was under frequent surveillance, and several professors received summons to appear before House Un-American Activities Committee (HUAC). 'Not unflatteringly, in those days Talladega College was often referred to as the "back door of the Kremlin"' (Hernton 1996, 149). After graduating from Talladega with a BA in sociology in 1954, Hernton attended Fisk University, Nashville, in order to study for a Master's degree. In March 1955, while at Fisk, Hernton was himself briefly placed under government surveillance (Maxwell, 104, 148–9). Significantly, it was the Communist sentiments apparently espoused by his poetry, as much as his attendance at Talladega, or his supposed association at Fisk with a suspected Communist activist (the names are redacted from the record), that gained the FBI's attention (United States Department of Justice). Hernton's poem 'The Lynchers' (1955) is, ironically, accessible only in the FBI files and reads as a reaction precisely to this climate of suspicion in which race-based activism and Communism were elided as they had been in the earlier Red Scare. As the activist Nelson Peery noted:

> The concrete expression of anti-Communism in America was anti-black [...] If you spoke out for equal rights for the African-American people, you were a communist. If you murmured anything about women's equality, you were a communist. If you spoke for peace (and were not wearing the cloth), you were a communist. The intellectually independent African-American was a communist.
>
> (Peery, 16, 124)

Hernton's poem is framed through the racially charged motif of lynching: the phrase 'the summoners ... summon' strongly suggests the activities of HUAC, and the poem ends on a list of slurs uniting racial activists with the culminating, ultimate slur, 'Red'.

> Once more the lynchers reach out.
> The victims vary:
> A lawyer, a preacher ... a worker,
> Novelist, poet ... or a professor
> at a southern university.
> But the rope is there, the rope is always there.
>
> the rope of an editorial ... political, religious rope,
> economic.
> Lynch by smear, hatred, by creed and fear [...]
>
> Once more the summoners ... summon. The recallers
> recall. The cash-register of a lying tongue
> rings.

> Once more the historic word, the slogan ... the cyanide
> lables [sic] that have bloodied man's record for progress
> through the years:
> Barbarian! Christian! Jew! Anarchist!
> Abolitionist! Socialist! Red!

As an African-American with a criminal record from a poor Southern background, Hernton was already open to suspicion. The FBI agents questioned Hernton not only on his poem, and his associations with activists, but on his earlier encounters with the police, at a time when initial incarcerations for petty crime could see African-Americans trapped within the penal system for decades. (Hernton had been convicted on two counts of breaking and entering while at high school in Chattanooga in 1949 and sentenced to six years' probation.) Hernton details his relationship to the police in the later essays 'Chattanooga Black Boy' (1996) and 'Between Paranoia and Me' (1998) and in passages of his semi-autobiographical novel *Scarecrow* (1974). Growing up in Chattanooga and Tullahoma, Tennessee, Hernton's early childhood was shaped by the specific dynamics of racism in Southern small towns and by the wider events of the Great Depression and the persecution of the Scottsboro Boys on false charges of rape. He had encounters with the police from the age of seven, when he was picked up for walking beside a white female schoolmate. As he writes in 'Chattanooga Black Boy':

> I was taken home to my grandmother where the police warned us about the 'crime' of a 'Nigraboy' playing with a 'Whytegurl'. After the policeman left, my grandmother cried, and warned me of the danger of getting lynched or sentenced to life imprisonment for rape, 'like what happened to the Scottsboro boys', she said. (Hernton 1996, 143)

Like Hernton, his close friend Ishmael Reed was born in Chattanooga and dates his own experience with the police to the age of three (Reed 2000A). Such experiences shadowed the police brutality both writers would experience during the Umbra period in New York and form the background to Hernton's poem on the Harlem Riots, 'Jitterbugging in the Streets' (1965), and his essay 'Dynamite Growing out of Their Skulls' (1968), addressed in the fourth chapter. Reed's uncollected poem 'If I were Icarus, Come Down Crashing' (1965) is dedicated to Hernton and details an incident from the preceding year in which Reed was arrested and beaten by New York City police. Reed recalls the incident which inspired the poem in a later essay detailing his encounters with the police over the years. As he writes, in 1964, 'about a month after one of the first demonstrations against the Vietnam War had taken place in Times Square', he, Hernton and sociologist Duncan Roundtree III were walking down 10th Avenue in New York. On seeing two policemen carrying paper bags out of a bar, Reed jokingly alluded to the police corruption recently exposed by the Knapp Commission: 'they're taking bribes in low places'. The policemen responded by arresting the three men, and Reed was beaten while in police custody (Reed 2000A). Reed's poem, full of characteristically vituperative energy, and a furious despair that recalls Hernton's own work, ends with an image of a bottle flying into the face of a cop that echoes Hernton's own 'Jitterbugging'.

> I mourn my people.
>
> No wonder they are throwing beer bottles
> at helmets which cluster together like a bunch of
> grapes, dangling from the great rectum of the world.
>
> If i were Icarus, i would come down crashing on
> Lennox Ave. The whole sky
> a bottle factory.
>
> (Reed 1965)

The political edge of much Umbra writing was shaped not only by their more recent experience of the Harlem and Newark Riots, or the violent response to the On Guard protest, but by a lifetime at the receiving end of police brutality, state surveillance, and anti-Communist and anti-black hysteria. In such a climate, the writing they produced could never be 'non-partisan'. Writers like Walter Allen or David Riesman could claim that 'politics' had no place in 'aesthetics' or that political engagement was an abstract concept – even as Riesman's own career had seen him actively participate in legal measures associated with McCarthyism and with intellectual groups funded by the CIA. But for Reed, Hernton, Baraka and others who faced constant police harassment, politics was lived experience, whether in the South or North.

While Hernton would remain politically engaged, it appears that the FBI did not subsequently maintain serious surveillance, in contrast to Baraka's voluminous FBI file, though the forty-four-page file on Hernton does note his association with the 'new literary magazine', *Umbra*, copies of which were provided to investigating agents in October 1963. (The final entry on Hernton from the file is a 1969 cutting of a review of his book *Sex and Racism* from British socialist newspaper, *The Morning Star*.) But Hernton's surveillance does see him join company with such major writers as Baraka, Ralph Ellison, Richard

Wright, Larry Neal and W.E.B. Du Bois, as charted in William J. Maxwell's excellent study *F.B. Eyes*. Such surveillance links the anti-Communist hysteria of earlier decades with the state response to black radicalism during the Black Power era and indicates Umbra's own lineage, not only in terms of political and aesthetic activity but of State perception and persecution of such activity. Indeed, Ray Durem was surveilled for over twenty years until his death in 1963, a fact ironically registered in the posthumously published poem 'Award (A Gold Watch to the FBI Man Who Has Followed Me for 25 Years)' (Hughes 1963, 33).

Umbra writers forge work which determinedly resists McCarthyite suppression. Yet their work, while always politically inflected, resists the models of 'vernacular' or 'protest poetry' prevalent among Popular Front conceptions of 'ethnic writing' which impose standards limiting form and subject matter. Challenging previous poetic models, Umbra emerged in parallel, but often with very different emphases, to such widely known groupings as 'Black Mountain', 'Beat' and the 'New York School', forging its own distinct mode of what Thomas describes as 'Afrocentric modernism'. Thomas was involved with Ted Berrigan's workshops and 'New York School' circles, but Umbra in general had fewer connections to the white avant-garde than did Baraka. Indeed, though the group had two white members, and whites were free to attend the workshops, their whole ethos was based on establishing a new space specifically for black writing.[3] As Tom Dent notes:

> We didn't know Ginsberg and people like that, but we knew what they were about, and we were absorbing the same atmosphere and so forth. Where we were different was in the fact that we were Black, and we were consciously black and conscious of the fact that we had to figure out how to get our voice out either through publishing or through readings. (Dent 1981, 6)

White poets like Ginsberg, Berrigan, Ed Sanders and Tuli Kupferberg – whose little magazine *Birth* likely provided the source for Thomas's 'A Tale of Two Cities' – may in some sense have been kindred spirits, likewise insisting that aesthetic experimentation was tied to political engagement and rejecting the formal conservatism of earlier poetries of both a conservative and a leftist bent. But the ideological hurdles which the Umbra writers had to face were different, and we should set them alongside African-American writers such as Langston Hughes and Ralph Ellison (with whom Umbra members conducted a group interview) and organizations such as the Harlem Writers Guild, the Association for Women of African Heritage, On Guard, CORE, the SNCC, NAACP and the RAM – with all of whom they intersected – rather than seeing them as an adjunct to white avant-garde poetry circles of the time.[4]

In early 1962, Dent, Hernton, Henderson, Touré, Joe Johnson and Charles Patterson attended initial meetings of an LES group organized by artist Aldo Tambellini but grew frustrated with the broadness and vagueness of its objectives. Instead, as Dent notes in his valuable essay 'Umbra Days', they were 'interested in a group that could meet our needs as black writers. We felt it imperative that we have a device that could deal with race, that could serve to bring us together, that could be a vehicle for the expression of the bitterness and beauties of being Afro-American (as we called ourselves at the time) in this plastic land' (Dent 2018, 54). In Kalamu ya Salaam's words, Umbra represented the 'conscious decision to be a black writer in the context of community, and not just as an individual' (Dent 2018, 49). Umbra developed out of twin impulses: the sense that the galvanizing, leftist-nationalist activism of On Guard lacked an aesthetic parallel and the sense of the need for an explicitly African-American collective, arising from what Dent calls 'a growing sense of alienation from the white literary world'. Dent insists:

> This was not a negative development born of rejection by the white literary establishment, but a healthy development […] The only way we could say certain things as black artists – the things that needed saying – was to recognize that we constituted a separate world […] distinct […] from the main body of American literature […] We discovered that to survive we had to protect, in fact advocate and encourage, our distinctiveness. How else could we possibly know who we were? (Dent 2018, 57)

Insisting on linking Third World anti-colonial struggles to their own struggles as African-Americans, and on the political work that non-linear, disjunctive aesthetic practices might do, Umbra sought to expand the narrowing audiences for such work not only through their own magazine but through other small-press publication, literary journals and radical newspapers. Their poetry was mobilized within contexts generally devoted to more pragmatic political argument, attesting to the increasing intersection between black radical politics and aesthetics which reached public prominence through the BAM. Work by Umbra writers was published in leftist and countercultural journals such as *Evergreen Review, Masses and Mainstream, Peace News, Revolution* and *Streets*, as well as emergent, African-American-controlled journals with an internationalist bent, in particular, *Liberator*.

The foreword to *Umbra*'s first issue – likely written by Calvin Hernton in collaboration with fellow editors Dent and Henderson (Dent 1980B, 108) – firmly states the group's sociopolitical intentions.

> UMBRA is not another haphazard 'little literary' publication. UMBRA has a definite orientation: 1) the experience of being Negro, especially in America: and 2) that quality of human awareness often termed 'social consciousness'. (*Umbra*, I, 3)

However, the editors go on to qualify this statement.

> UMBRA will not be a propagandistic, psychopathic or ideological axe-grinder. We will not print trash, no matter how relevantly it deals with race, social issues, or anything else. We are not a self-deemed radical publication; we are as radical as society demands the truth to be. We declare an unequivocal commitment to material of literary integrity and artistic excellence. (*Umbra*, I, 3–4)

What this suggests is that the poetry printed in *Umbra* was bound neither to a prescriptive set of political positions nor to a single literary style. Nonetheless, as Thomas noted in a 1981 interview, any 'personal' elements in the poems he would present to or publish with Umbra were always oriented towards an intensely politicized analysis, whatever their style.

> It was very clear that one of the major purposes of the group was to use poetry and fiction to address the socio-political situation that black people found themselves in the United States. So you will not find poems in the issues of *Umbra* that are dealing with my relationship with my woman, with my parents, with my child unless there is also an aspect of that poem of what that relationship means in reference to the social and political situation of black people in the United States. (Thomas 1983, 6)

Given Umbra members' involvement in activism, it should be no surprise that the magazine printed poems by activists such as Robert F. Williams and CORE's Robert Brookins Gore. Indeed, the first issue printed an advertisement for Williams's controversial *Negroes with Guns*, on whose title Art Berger riffed in his piece on the workshop for *Mainstream*, 'Negroes with Pens' (Berger 1963).

But, as Thomas later put it, the group 'was not a [political] party. It was a workshop' (Thomas 1983, 6). For Umbra, the tokenistic acceptance of 'political' African-American writing – worthy versions of 'protest poetry' that would be well received by white liberals – was inadequate not only aesthetically but politically. As the foreword notes:

> We do not exist for those seemingly selected perennial 'best sellers' and literary 'spokesmen of the race situation' who are currently popular in the commercial press and slick in-group journals [...] The subject matter of accepted journals is too often dictated by the fears of backers, and of readers whom those journals fear to lose. (*Umbra* I, 3)

Umbra's editors oppose themselves not only to the 'perennial "best-sellers" and literary "spokesmen of the race situation" who are currently popular in the commercial press and slick in-group journals' but also to 'haphazard "little literary" publication[s]'. The desire to avoid the positions, of either being 'official' and compromised 'spokesmen' in the media or an ill-formulated 'underground' in-group, suggests the delicate course which politically aware but formally experimental African-American poets might have to negotiate.

As much as they sought to avoid 'ideological axe-grind[ing]', the *Umbra* editors understood aesthetics not as separate from 'politics' or 'society' but as *in itself* political. A central part of Umbra's mission was the attempt to find new literary forms that would neither be tied to preconceived ideas of racial identity nor crowd out any sense of identity through what Thomas calls 'white Anglo Saxon northeastern conceptions of what literature was that did not fit their everyday reality of identification as black people' (Thomas 1983, 7). The material printed in the magazines varies widely from Leroy McLucas's satirical alphabetized lists to Julian Bond's pithy couplets, Lloyd Addison's wildly inventive punning, Ray Durem's aggressive and direct proto-nationalist pieces, and Ishmael Reed's fusion of esoteric studies and tropes from American popular culture (*Umbra* I, 9, 24–6, 39; *Umbra* II, 5–6, 29–32). Whether in the way the group was run, or in the work that was produced under its auspices, Umbra functioned as a shared political-cultural project, open to various conceptions of form: truly a 'populist modernism'.

'A conspiracy to blow up New York'[5]

As Thomas notes in *Extraordinary Measures*, the New York context, out of which both Umbra and, later, BART/S emerged, was one of Harlem street parades and street-corner orators (see Henderson's 'Marcus Garvey Parade' and Baraka's 'Street Protest'), musicians (Henderson's 'Boston Road Blues', Dent's 'Ode to Miles Davis'), Lower East Side (LES) urban deprivation (Hernton's 'The Gift Outraged'), the 1964 Harlem Riots (Hernton's 'Jitterbugging in the Streets' and Henderson's 'Keep on Pushing'), and the ever-present memory of the harsh conditions of the American South (Touré's 'Floodtide') (*DMOH*, 31, 39; *FOTSF*, n.p.; *Home*, 98–9; *Umbra* I, 23–4, 28–31; *MM*, 83–6, 109–114). Though, as we'll see, the 'space of a nation' between Harlem and the LES was a source of conflicted feeling for many of these writers, they were energized by Harlem through its connection, both to black culture and to geopolitics, as the scene of Malcolm X's and Nikita Khrushchev's meetings with Fidel Castro at the Hotel Theresa in September 1960.

Likewise, the following year, the formative On Guard for Freedom protest took place at the UN building, a short distance north of the East Village and south of Harlem: activists such as Calvin Hicks and Baraka interrupted from the gallery while the UN was in session, provoking widespread arrests and media coverage. This important event, addressed in the book's first chapter, physically manifests the link between African-American and Third World struggles against racism and imperialism, occupying and disrupting official space in order to interrupt the narratives of apology, racism and red-baiting manifested in the speech by US representative Adlai Stevenson's speech which the activists interrupted.

In their workshops and collective readings in the bars and coffeehouses of the LES, the members of Umbra refused the boundaries separating the enclosed, private spaces of literary activity from a public presence, and they were intensely engaged with their urban environment both in their organizational work and in their poetry. Umbra developed within the bohemian scene of New York's LES, a place remembered with affection by Hernton, Thomas and Dent not only as the seat of a non-conformist rejection of American mainstream values, and of a vibrant and dialogic artistic community, but also as a seat of intense poverty and sharply visible tensions relating to race and class (Thomas 1978; Dent 1980A; Hernton 1993). Baraka would famously castigate the political inadequacies of this milieu as relating to an overtly white and bourgeois aesthetic and ideology, yet Umbra's work demonstrates the presence of an explicitly black – and highly politicized – avant-garde which thrived in this scene and whose activities prefigured those of the BAM. That said, Umbra's collapse as an organization attests to the difficulties of maintaining such a collective enterprise not only within the heightened racial climate of the time but also within a bohemian milieu whose relation to politics tended towards enthusiasm rather than a longer-term programme of protest, diagnosis and resistance. Given this, as Norma Rogers suggests in her introduction to a 1993 *African-American Review* feature on the LES, Umbra should be read neither as part of a 'romanticize[d] history' nor as a test case for the political inadequacies of bohemian culture (570). Rather, it can and should be understood as a crucial exemplar of a mid-century African-American avant-garde, formed as it was in a 'multiethnic and multicultural neighbourhood,' out of a combination of 'the old left, the new music, experimental theater and the beginnings of black theater, experimental visual artists and filmmakers' (598).

As Thomas notes, the LES was a complex space of negotiation, suspicion, hostility and subtle shades of class and ethnic tension, as well as of a mutually productive creative and political atmosphere. There was an 'uneasy truce' between various ethnic groups: older Jewish communities, European immigrants fleeing war-torn Europe, African-American artists and the Puerto Rican population who were gradually taking over from the Jewish community as the environment's predominant inhabitants. In such an environment, educated artists such as those involved with Umbra were viewed with suspicion by older inhabitants whose prospects were far more limited:

> [T]he black and white collegians and dropouts appearing on their streets would not be doomed to stay there. 'Every ten years,' Mike Gold wrote in 1930, 'there has been a new population on the East Side. As fast as a generation makes some money, it moves to a better section of the city'. The difference in 1961 was that the young people moving into the East Side began with options that the earlier successive waves of immigrants often never achieved in lifetimes of hard work. (Thomas 1993, 575)

Likewise, in a review of Calvin Hernton's 1976 Collected Poems, Tom Dent wrote:

> The LES was the ethnic basement of New York – Jews, Eastern Europeans of all nationalities, Chinese, Russians, avant-garde white artists, Puerto Ricans, leftist whites, new blacks had all somehow ended up there. We struggled for identity amidst this unmelted conglomeration; each nation, each people twisting slowly in the tight noose of a rope made from tarnished dreams. There was little social intercourse between peoples, each existed on separate islands; we passed each other like ships in the night [...] Possibly they sensed we were only temporarily on the scene and hated us for being free to come and go, for being conscious, for speaking out. (Dent 1980A, 247)

Yet there were gradations within LES bohemianism. As Umbra member Rashidah Ismaili notes in her 1993 memoir 'Slightly Autobiographical', the significant African-American presence in the LES artistic community marked a less overtly bourgeois predecessor to the more widely known activities around venues such as the Electric Circus that took place there in the later 1960s.

> The 'flower children' of the 'counter-culture' took over certain streets. And the documentation of the privileged (i.e., privileged to) revolt has obfuscated much of 'our' involvement in the events of the '60s. Accounts of the impromptu be-ins of St. Mark's Place abound. But where are we to read of the old building of rickety stairs and high ceilings that housed the Negro Ensemble Company and served as a home to Black playwrights, actors, directors, and arts administrators for years. (588)

The 'underground' cultural scenes of the LES have frequently been celebrated for their establishment of new and experimental forms of literary community.

Yet Umbra's position on the LES, a complex meeting point of immigrant and bohemian communities, was fraught with complication. As we've seen, the Umbra writers reacted against the McCarthyite conservatism of dominant literary discourses which attacked both aesthetic experimentation and politically radical subject matter. They were also confronted with the dilemmas facing mass political organization – and the role of politically engaged art – following the decimation of the Old Left during the 1950s, dilemmas that played themselves out in debates around Marxism, nationalism, armed struggle, electoral politics, music, the use of the vernacular and the politics of gender. Recent scholarship by James Smethurst, Cary Nelson and others has convincingly argued that alliances between African-Americans and the Communist Left during the 1930s were fruitful on both political and aesthetic grounds, extending well beyond the usual trajectory of Hughes, Wright and Ellison (Nelson 1989; Smethurst 1999). In 1928, the Communist Party of the United States of America (CPUSA) had adopted the so-called 'Black Belt South Thesis', which argued that the African-American population in the Southern states was an oppressed nation with a right to self-determination. (This thesis would be taken up once more by Amiri Baraka in the 1970s.) The policy, which was passed into the Comintern through the efforts of 'Black Bolshevik' Harry Haywood, combined with large-scale organizing around the Scottsboro Trial, sharecroppers' unions, and the anti-Fascist efforts of the International Brigades (in which Ray Durem had served), suggested that links between black radicalism (including Marxist forms of Black Nationalism) and the official left might be real (Haywood, 391–415). Yet the subsequent growth of McCarthyism saw a large-scale suppression of both Communist and black radical activity, bolstered by government-funded attempts to use art as an anti-Soviet weapon in the Cold War, the brutality of continuing Jim Crow reflected in US imperial intervention, and by internal Communist Party (CP) factionalism following Khrushchev's 'secret speech' and the Soviet invasion of Hungary in 1956. In addition, the party's dropping of the 'Black Belt South Thesis' in 1935, and dissatisfaction with the leadership of Earl Browder, had long formed a source of particular discontent for party members such as Harry Haywood (Kelley, 49–50; Haywood, 529–627).

Nonetheless, Umbra writers maintained links to those traditions which McCarthyism sought to suppress. Thomas observes that various members of Umbra 'had been exposed to alternative (i.e. reliable) versions of recent political history by poets such as Art Berger and Henri Percikow, an experienced trade unionist' (*EM*, 142). Thomas and Henderson were involved in a writers' group organized by Percikow, many of whose members were unionized garment workers, and which was an early source of funding as well as inspiration for Umbra itself (Thomas 1983, 7–8). Likewise, many figures associated with Umbra – most notably, Calvin Hicks, Archie Shepp and Berger – had strong connections to Communist organizations, and the first significant piece of criticism on Umbra – an essay by Berger entitled 'Negroes with Pens' – appeared in *Masses and Mainstream* which, as James Smethurst notes, was 'more or less the official cultural journal of the CPUSA in the 1960s' (Berger 1963; Smethurst 1999, 252, n.10). As Tom Dent recalled, 'most of the money for the original magazine's two issues was raised at fund-raising parties at Advance, the Communist Youth Organization, at 80 Clinton Street. The parties were widely attended and helped to popularize us throughout the LES' (Dent 1980B, 108). Other connections include Southern Civil Rights activism (Dent's work with the NAACP and Touré's with the SNCC) and the generation of the Harlem Renaissance and the Popular Front, principally Langston Hughes, who was supportive of the group, printing a number of Umbra writers in his 1963 anthology *New Negro Poets USA*. In Askia Touré's words: 'Langston Hughes was our Umbra mentor. He used to speak w/our Umbra writers & editors weekly. He was our living Role Model. He critiqued our work, and got us published in many international anthologies' (Touré 2004). Indeed, it was at a series of readings for younger black writers organized in Harlem by Hughes's secretary, Raoul Abdul, that a number of the Umbra writers met, and he was an important influence on David Henderson in particular (Dent 2018, 50).

Umbra was also influenced by a mode of Black Nationalism emerging from movements such as Garveyism the NOI, and the Five Percenters. As Thomas wryly puts it:

> [T]he cultural black nationalism of the 1960s and 1970s did not spring forth from inspiration of the New York Times or the late news. It was a result of continuing tradition, transmitted as naturally as possible under the circumstance of a specifically malicious and aggressive white American culture that overshadowed the integrationist ideologies of the NAACP and the Urban League. (*EM*, 141)

This tradition was as much artistic as it was political, equally encompassing the 'vernacular', esoteric mysticism, political radicalism and engagements with European and American modernist art. In his discussion of black sign painters – most of them still unacknowledged – Thomas describes conversations ranging from the 1940s WPA mural projects to the Bauhaus and the Communist propaganda art of Diego Rivera (the latter an influence on Touré's early visual art studies in New York (King, 220)). For Thomas, these sign painters are part of 'an artistic underground group', stretching from the 1920s to the 1960s, who 'maintained a cultural alternative within the black community' that involved 'explicitly political scholars of Marxism, leftover Garveyites, and Pan-Africanists' (*EM*, 140). Other important figures were the older Harlem poet Hart LeRoi Bibbs, 'a true scholar of the street's traditions of rapping and strolling', and the poet-musician Sun Ra, whose work appears in *Umbra*'s third issue and whose studies of Egyptian mythology were crucial for Thomas and Henderson. Ra had emerged from an environment of earlier street-corner radicalism in Chicago's South Side, rubbing shoulders with Marxists, Black Nationalists and jazz musicians while simultaneously instigating what John Corbett calls an 'African-American grass roots *intelligentsia*' and beginning an initially private rehearsal band which would go on to become his Arkestra (Corbett, 5). Ra's background in vernacular auto-didacticism, his involvement with the jazz tradition and his participation in the BART/S, all suggest a lineage for the writing of Baraka and Umbra. So, too, does the relation of Umbra writers to Langston Hughes, Ralph Ellison and Richard Wright, both of whom had been to a greater or lesser extent involved with the CPUSA.

Umbra can thus be located among traditions of urban oratory, rapping and street-corner wit, Communist politics, vernacular nationalism, the 'New Thing' in jazz, and the Harlem Renaissance. Though this diverse mix of influences can be overlooked in accounts of the developing 'counterculture', it was a vital part of Umbra's collective ethos. Negotiating the complex, ethnically diverse communities of the LES, the black epicentre of Harlem, histories of Marxist and nationalist activism, and the relation between politics and aesthetics, Umbra provide a stunning counter-example to the contemporaneous dismissal of the American avant-garde as elitist and one-dimensional and a crucial chapter in the history of what Cedric Robinson calls the Black Radical Tradition.

Black arts legacies and chronologies of mourning

In the era of McCarthyism, Umbra emerged from a period characterized by the experience of defeat, drawing on underground traditions that still persisted despite active attempts at their erasure.[6] Yet the collective possibilities that flared up within and outside their work from the mid-1960s to the early 1970s were themselves defeated, sometimes leading to a growing despair, even nihilism, that characterizes, in particular, elements of Hernton's work. In the light of this, rewriting history, even very recent history – Thomas's 'The Bathers' is a case in point – assumed a crucial function. This rewriting applies not only to the cultural work done by Baraka and the Umbra writers in their poems, essays, novels and criticism but to the work the literary critic brings to bear on this enterprise. Approaching movements left out of conventional historical accounts and thus rewriting that history are tasks fraught with complexity in which the issue of narrative framing – what story to tell and how to tell it – is of key importance.

Umbra had ceased to exist as a formally constituted grouping by the time the BAM began, and while it was crucial in helping its members to find their voices as poets, it was not until well after the group's demise that much of their work appeared in collected, widely distributed form. (While smaller-scale pamphlet publications by Oliver Pitcher and Calvin Hernton appeared in 1958 and 1964, respectively, no book-length collection of poems by any of the Umbra writers appeared until Raymond Patterson's *26 Ways of Looking at a Black Man* in 1969.[7]) The fugitivity and ephemerality of much of this work attest to the particular difficulties facing collective groupings within literary and political frames subject to dispersal and disappearance. The poems by Hernton and Thomas addressed in the book's fifth and seventh chapters illuminate this further. Both are the title poems to collections of work which, though they did not appear until 1976 and 1981, respectively, contain material dating back, in Hernton's case, to the early 1950s. Hernton's 'Medicine Man' was written during the 1960s but did not appear in print until 1976, while Thomas's 'The Bathers', written in 1970, remained uncollected until 1981.

Bearing this in mind, such work seems to mourn not only the lost moments of political and aesthetic possibility found in the Black Arts and Black Power movements but those inherent in the period of Umbra's official existence (1962–64): the presence, however fragile, fugitive or brief, of a non-prescriptive, yet politically committed, mode of writing pre-dating the Ron Karenga–influenced nationalism exemplified by Baraka's Black Arts writing of the later 1960s and early 1970s. Examining Umbra both during and after the 1962–64 period not only gives us a new, more complex lineage for the development of BAM writing but moves beyond Baraka as the sole filter for the historical and stylistic shifts associated with different phases of the movement.

In 'Ten Years after Umbra', a mournfully retrospective poem first published the same year as Hernton's 'Medicine Man' and dedicated to his fellow editors Hernton and David Henderson, Tom Dent celebrates the workshop's heyday in which 'something in us/burst [...] free like/a flash fire', lamenting the subsequent 'drag of too many jammed years' in which that moment 'fades into dream/and so without touching/our hurting' (Dent 1976A, 21, 1980B, 114). In its republication in a feature on Umbra, edited by Dent for *Black American Literature Forum* in 1980, the poem is juxtaposed with Alvin Simon's 1963 photograph of the younger, Umbra-era Dent reading from a sheaf of papers in front of a stock of wine bottles at one of the Umbra gatherings, emphasizing its oral address and the collective space of friendship and discussion from which it emerged: a space which the poem itself nostalgically addresses as a moment of lost possibility, yet which it argues might once again be kindled. In Hernton's words:

> Physically, as a cohesive, functioning entity, Umbra existed for only a couple of years. But in terms of its impact on my work and my life, the two years of Umbra's physical existence constituted a lifetime; its influence on my writing and its meaning for my life through the years are immeasurable and timeless. (Hernton 1993, 581)

Yet what is instructive in Umbra's case is not simply its success but the very factors that destroyed it. Pinpointing the exact reasons for the split – the moment at which what Dent calls a 'flash fire' of collective creativity began to die out – remains a contentious issue. Nonetheless, as James Smethurst argues:

> The sort of rupture between different moments and modes of black radicalism seen here was one repeated many times, in many places, carrying a symbolic importance and emotional charge that goes far beyond the often apparently small issue or event (the publication of a single poem or the control of a small amount of money) that appears to have precipitated the break. (Smethurst 2005, 149–50)

Indeed, for Smethurst, it is precisely the political-aesthetic tensions which precipitated the split – those attendant on the encounter between a more prescriptive mode of Black Nationalism and looser, more traditionally left-wing varieties of black radicalism – which later flared up within BART/S and the BAM.

> Intense conflicts were potentially if not absolutely inherent to the complicated matrix of political and cultural radicalism out of which the [Black Arts] movement grew. These conflicts not only contributed to the decline of the movement but also to how we remember and interpret the movement today. (367)

Likewise, for Dent:

> The members of Umbra […] anticipated the Black Arts Movement, in fact anticipated all of the black cultural directions that were to develop a few years later. Really, we went through every crisis, every form of confrontation over direction, every emotional attitude that black cultural groups went through during the Sixties and Seventies. (Dent 2018, 58)

As much as their earlier work in particular provides a thriving sense of new collective possibilities, the often fraught figurations of contemporaneous political flashpoints also lead to a sense of mourning associated with the political and aesthetic tensions that contributed to the demise of both Umbra and the BAM; whether in Dent's 'Ten Years after Umbra', Hernton's reckoning with the legacies of misogyny in 'Medicine Man' and *Scarecrow*, or Thomas's negotiations with both the recent and wider historical past in 'The Bathers'. The second half of this book allows us to see Umbra work from a later period as a useful reflection on and illumination of their own earlier writing: a form of memory, mourning and retrospection that resists historical erasure and envisages a transformed future.

Chapter summaries and methodology

This book is broadly chronological. However, bearing in mind the complexities of Umbra's existence as a collective and its members' publication records, as well as their combination of insistent address to contemporaneous political events with a non-linear approach to history, each chapter should be understood not as an isolated stage in a linear historical progression but as part of a series of parallel narratives, histories and connections which both demand and resist shoehorning into any singular contextual narrative. As noted above, they are studies of the work of individual writers which emphasize the importance of analysing their work in formal terms, not simply as contextual background to cultural history. That said, the majority of these chapters centre around poems emerging from specific events – the 1961 UN Protest, the 1963 Birmingham Civil Rights campaign, the 1964 Harlem Riots and the 1967 Newark Riots. The book is organized around a series of key texts with each work constellating into and out of the complex literary-historical and political contexts from which it initially emerged. Through this, I show how the form of these texts intersects with a literary-historical account of Umbra as a group existing at a specific moment in time, as well as the movements of melancholy, nostalgia and exemplary strength drawn from periods of historical possibility and historical defeat. Given Umbra's existence as a literary collective in early 1960s New York, a revisionist focus on the neglected role of race in the city's LES poetry milieu is important – and I hope that this book might contribute towards a growing body of scholarship in this field. However, to focus solely on personalities, publishing and personal connections risks leaving unanswered the question of *why*, precisely, we might focus on the qualities of the work itself. By close-reading work not usually close-read – let alone discussed at all – I argue that Umbra's importance inheres both in textual form and the circumstances of literary production.

My first chapter focuses on five poets – a collective voice which charts Umbra's emergence out of On Guard. Each of the subsequent chapters focuses on a single poet: Amiri Baraka, David Henderson, Calvin Hernton (two chapters), Tom Dent and Lorenzo Thomas. This focus reflects what Kalamu ya Salaam calls 'a jazz paradigm for artistic development, i.e. individual development within a collective context' (Dent 2018, 466). The introduction and first chapter serve as something like thematic statements with those that follow as 'solos' which always refer to ensembles of various kinds – other writers, other histories – manifesting the jazz interplay of spontaneity and pattern, tradition and innovation, history and the present.[8] Throughout, the critical accounts of Tom Dent and Lorenzo Thomas in particular serve to retrospectively explain and reflect on Umbra's initial flowering.

Umbra emerged at a transitional moment. Valuable scholarship by James Smethurst on the BAM and Cheryl Higashida on Black Internationalist Feminism shows that existing chronologies for black radical writing at this period are inadequate (Smethurst 2005, Higashida). Rather than a transition between Old Left models which subordinated race to class and the subsequent rise of nationalism, both authors show the continuance of a vital tradition in activism and art which exemplified a tradition of black internationalism or what Higashida calls 'nationalist internationalism' (Higashida, 19). My first chapter draws out this context. Addressing figurations of internationalism in poems by Thomas, Ishmael Reed and Askia Touré, with briefer reference to poems by Raymond Patterson and Ray Durem, it begins by addressing Umbra members' participation in the 1961 On Guard for Freedom protest at the assassination of Patrice Lumumba. In so doing, I shift the conventional starting point of studies on black radical poetry of the 1960s – the death of Malcolm X in 1965 – showing instead that Baraka and the Umbra poets were equally politicized by Lumumba's death in 1961. Following an account of the protest, and of Umbra's development out of On Guard, I focus on two poems emerging from the protest by Reed and Thomas published in *Umbra*, alongside another by Askia Touré published in *Liberator*, and shorter readings of poems by Raymond Patterson and Ray Durem. Doing so illuminates the political and aesthetic negotiations faced by the Umbra writers at a time of complex Cold War politics and emergent Third Worldism and continues the work done in the introduction to contextualize Umbra in a history of black radicalism. The chapter ends by focusing on the importance of music in Umbra poet's figuration of internationalist anti-imperialism. Touré's use of music – as with Henderson's in the third chapter – predates Baraka's more publicized embrace of black popular culture in such works as the highly influential essay 'The Changing Same' (1966). Baraka's ideas – as with Larry Neal's in his totemic 1968 essays 'The Black Arts Movement' and 'And Shine Swam On' – were strongly influenced by those of Touré in particular.

My second chapter moves on to Baraka himself, examining the shifting presentation of violence in three of his most controversial poems, dating between 1963 and 1967: 'Black Dada Nihilismus', 'Black Art' and 'Black People!'. I focus on these poems for several reasons: because they are the most frequently cited examples of his political commitment; because of the ways they were mobilized within politicized contexts of reading and reception; because of their role in charting his own aesthetic and political development; and because of the way those developments mirror broader trends within the developing BAM. My focus here is two-fold. I provide a detailed close-reading of the poems, examining their frames of reference and linguistic ambiguities, which both trouble and reinforce their polemical force. I also provide a historical account of the poems' publication and reception history to show how they participated in, influenced and were influenced by political action. Setting three of Baraka's most widely cited poems alongside Umbra helps us to see these not as exceptional or unprecedented outbursts, as many critics have taken them. I begin with Baraka's 'Black Dada Nihilismus', exploring its mystical and political references, alongside Lorenzo Thomas's contemporaneous poem 'The Unnatural Life'; I trace the often-ignored literary lineage behind 'Black Art', and its social context in Harlem, through Thomas's own later criticism; and I conclude by focusing on 'Black People!', contextualized through Thomas's account of visiting Baraka in Newark with Ishmael Reed and Baraka's trial for weapons possession in 1968.

My analysis of Baraka sets up the following chapter on David Henderson. One of the youngest members of Umbra, he co-edited the magazine's first two issues with Hernton and Tom Dent, assuming sole editorship thereafter. One of the few Umbra poets to be born in New York, Henderson's 'documentary' poems provide vivid catalogues of what he called the 'space of a nation': between uptown Harlem – where he had grown up – and downtown LES, where Umbra had formed. Addressing Henderson's figuration of invisibility, and setting it alongside his responses to the 1964 Harlem Riots, I suggest that Henderson, among the Umbra poets, is one of the most acute writers of the New York experience. Influenced by Harlem Renaissance predecessors such as Langston Hughes – himself energized by recent currents in black radicalism, including contacts with the Umbra writers – and participating in the nascent BAM,

Henderson's 'Keep on Pushing' (1964) and 'Yin Years' (1965) are two of the major poems of the 1960s.

In the fourth chapter, I turn to Henderson's close friend, Calvin Hernton. Once more examining responses to urban deprivation and unrest, I focus on his early poems of the LES and his own poem of the Harlem Riots, 'Jitterbugging in the Streets' (1965), before moving on to his incendiary essays on urban insurrection, which appeared from the mid-1960s onwards. In particular, I focus on 'Dynamite Growing out of Their Skulls', published in Baraka's anthology *Black Fire* in 1968. While Hernton's essay, in the wake of the works by Baraka, Touré and Henderson previously examined, appears to exemplify the new militancy of the period, there is, as I show, a conflict between imaginings of a revolutionary upsurge and a focus on negativity and pathology as imbricated parts of this upsurge. I then address questions of gender, setting Hernton's account of urban insurrection in relation to the BAM vocabulary of 'manhood', the Moynihan report, and gender relations within Umbra, anchored in Rashidah Ismaili's autobiographical account of workshop meetings and Hernton's own later critique of the gendered discourse of the mid-late 1960s. I conclude by examining the dilemmas of defeat when the rhetoric and strategy of insurrection fail to produce the change they seek, via Hernton's novel *Scarecrow* (1974).

Hernton's work is in many ways the fulcrum on which the book turns, linking the New York experience crucial for Umbra in its formative stage to that of the South addressed in the remaining chapters. Though Umbra was formed and based in New York, the majority of its members came from outside the North, often from the South, and many moved South following the group's dissolution. Thus, while the first four chapters of the book focus on urban unrest in New York and nearby Newark, the final three chapters focus on the South, via Hernton, Dent and Thomas, illustrating how Umbra lived on beyond its initial moment and extending the New York–centric focus of much writing on the BAM. In the fifth chapter, I turn again to Hernton. Beginning by outlining writing of the South in early issues of *Umbra*, I set Hernton's autobiographical essay 'Chattanooga Black Boy' (1996) alongside a close-reading of the long poem 'Medicine Man' (1976), tracing its figurations of gender, hoodoo, the South and the political role of memory.

Tom Dent's writings of the South – in particular, the major poem 'Return to English Turn' (1976) – form the basis of the following chapter. A key organizational presence in Umbra, as his fellow editor Hernton was a key aesthetic presence, Dent was born in New Orleans, and his career manifests a deep engagement with black Southern writing. As I show, Dent's time in New York with Umbra helped him to grapple with his own conflicted sense of Southern identity; his subsequent career in New Orleans, with the Free Southern Theater, *Nkombo*, *Callaloo* and numerous other initiatives, exemplifies Umbra's continuing impact into the 1970s, while also extending our sense of the BAM's regional scope. 'Return to English Turn' emerges as a poetic instantiation of his organizational goals and of his political and aesthetic ethos. Dent's critical writings provide a point of reference throughout the book, and his aesthetic work demands the same attention.

In the book's seventh and final chapter, I return to Lorenzo Thomas, focusing on his important long poem 'The Bathers' (1970). Written on the eve of his departure to Vietnam, where he served in the Navy, the poem takes as its subject a famous photograph by Charles Moore, depicting the water-hosing of Civil Rights protesters in Birmingham, Alabama, in 1963. Like Hernton and Dent in the previous chapters, Thomas addresses issues of generational disjuncture, ancestral memory and political action. Addressing itself to what Cary Nelson names as 'revolutionary memory', the poem attests to diaspora and defeat yet seeks to find collective possibilities even within these conditions (Nelson 2001).

Developing in New York but refusing to treat the city as disconnected from the rest of America or, indeed, the world, Umbra was simultaneously local and internationalist. In my conclusion, I suggest ways in which Umbra's work might readjust our conceptions of literary history and African-American self-figuration during this crucial period of political and aesthetic unrest, excitement, ferment and fervent struggle. These include the growth of black internationalism, figurations of urban insurrection, poetry's reckoning with the melancholy of defeat and its capacity to mobilize modes of current resistance. The book ends, fittingly, with a poem, Tom Dent's Ten Years After Umbra a coda to the Umbra experience which also serves as a summation of some of its achievements and suggests the group's vital and continuing significance today.

1

'A Tale of Two Cities': Umbra, Internationalism and the Death of Lumumba

'This is the time!' On Guard for Freedom protest the UN

On 17 January 1961, Patrice Lumumba, the first democratically elected prime minister of the newly independent Congo, was murdered while in the custody of troops loyal to anti-Communist, Belgian- and CIA-supported Katanganese secessionists. On 15 February 1961, the day after the official announcement of Lumumba's murder, a group of around sixty African-American activists loudly interrupted Adlai Stevenson's inaugural speech as US representative at the UN building in New York in protest at Lumumba's death. Meanwhile, four hundred other activists picketed the building from the outside. Among these groups were Baraka and many future members of Umbra, participating both as part of On Guard and Baraka's own Organization of Young Men. Chaos ensued with the police and UN security guards violently moving in on the protestors, and a number of the activists, including Baraka and On Guard's leader and future Umbra member, Calvin Hicks, were arrested. The *New York Times* characterized the protest as 'the most violent demonstration inside the United Nations headquarters in the world organization's history'; for the first time, the UN's outside gates were locked while a meeting was underway, and the building was closed to the public for the next two days to prevent further disruption ('Riot in Gallery', 1; Philip Benjamin, 18). In Hicks's words, 'we tore the place up' (Tinson, 18). As Baraka later recalled: 'I found myself marching outside the UN in demonstrations, while others, mostly blacks, took off their shoes and threw them down in the gallery as the gallery guards were called in to toss the demonstrating blacks out. Sisters were bashing the guards in the head with their shoes and throwing the shoes down in the gallery' (*Autobiography*, 181).[1]

The event emerged from and served to foster new links between a disparate group of New York–based intellectuals, activists and artists, proving crucial for the emergence of Umbra and for Baraka's own increasing political commitment. It was on these picket lines that Baraka met Askia Touré, later both a member of Umbra and an important participant in BART/S and the BAM. The protest also caused highly visible disruption to a building of globally significant symbolic and administrative value, unavoidably registering a militant, internationalist African-American activist presence which linked anti-colonial politics to the more militant wings of the domestic Civil Rights Movement.

In contrast to the brief narratives of this event given by Jerry Gafio Watts and Komozi Woodard in their books on Baraka, my account stresses its emergence from an organizational climate to which Umbra would soon provide an aesthetic parallel. Instead, I build on the work of James Smethurst and Cheryl Higashida, which emphasizes the vital tradition of black internationalism – particularly on the part of female activists – in the protest (Smethurst 2005, 118–19; Higashida, 54–5). Moving beyond characterizations of On Guard as a confused and prefigurative stage in the development of Baraka's own singular political career – fostered in large part by the account of Harold Cruse, himself a member – a closer examination of the Lumumba protest alters our histories of New York's black radical climate at the time. Following a more detailed history of On Guard and the UN protest, I will examine poems emerging from this event by Ishmael Reed and Lorenzo Thomas, published in the first two issues of *Umbra*, and by Askia Touré, in *Liberator*. This analysis enables us to see Umbra in a tradition of black internationalism on which the poets reflect both critically and in solidarity.

Though tracing the exact trajectories of the group's formation is complicated by gaps in the archival record, it appears that On Guard was in large part the initiative of Calvin Hicks and Sarah E. Wright. Hicks, a journalist and writer whose mother had been a member of the CPUSA, had worked for *Time* magazine, undertaken independent research work in the South following the Montgomery Bus Boycott in 1956, and, following his move to New York in 1957, worked on a weekly local newspaper in Harlem alongside Tom Dent (Flynn; Dent 2018, 50, 441). He was also executive director of the Monroe Defense Committee in support of Robert F. Williams, and the Fair Play for Cuba Committee, with whom Baraka had visited Cuba in 1960. Wright, who had visited Cuba in the same delegation as Baraka, had published poetry in the *Daily Worker* and other left-wing periodicals beginning in the late 1940s and joined the Harlem Writers Guild in 1957, alongside Maya Angelou, John Henrik Clarke and others. Galvanized by a demonstration outside the Hotel Theresa in Harlem during Fidel Castro's visit in September 1960, Wright and Hicks began to plan a newspaper devoted to what Wright called 'the anti-colonial struggle, abroad and at home' (Wright, 594). In January 1961, Wright wrote to African National Congress (ANC) Deputy President Oliver Tambo and to the London office of the National Democratic Party of Southern Rhodesia outlining the plans for the newspaper, characterizing it as 'a new periodical by which we hope to inform our people of the struggle for liberation going on not only in our own country, but in Africa as well' (quoted in Wood, 162). The same month, another letter credited to the organizing committee (and handwritten by Wright) announces a fundraiser that February at which 'our very own beloved' Max Roach and Abbey Lincoln would perform and describes *On Guard* as 'a new kind of newspaper – a fighting newspaper – which we hope will help do the job our other organizations and newspapers *won't* do' (quoted in Wood, 163).

The group's undated constitution (likely written the same month) proclaims their intention to 'act as an educational and action organization' (On Guard, n.p.). On Guard oppose the pacts made by the US government with 'undemocratic, racist, dictatorial governments all over the world' and place their struggle 'in the tradition of Nat Turner, Denmark Vesey, Gabriel, Toussaint L'Ouverture, Frederick Douglass, Harriet Tubman, Soujourner Truth, W.E.B. Du Bois, Paul Robeson, Patrice Lumumba, Sekou Toure, Kwame Nkrumah, Antoine Gizenga, Jomo Kenyatta, Juan Almedia [and] Robert Williams'. Listing among a series of victims, Emmett Till, the Scottsboro Boys, the unknown victims of lynching, and Thomas Russ, Amiri Baraka's grandfather, they proclaim their 'ultimate goal' as 'self-determination and independence'. A supplementary 'Declaration of Grievances' anticipates arguments for reparations that would come to increasing prominence through organizations such as the Republic of New Afrika and through the efforts of former CPUSA and future RAM member Queen Mother Moore, who formed a Reparations Committee of Descendants of U.S. Slaves, Inc., in 1962, demanding 500 trillion dollars to be spread over the next four generations (Kelley, 119). Thus, the fifth grievance states: 'Actual slavery existed for 400 years and Black Men have never received reparation for the free labour that helped build this country.' Though it is primarily a political document, the constitution also emphasizes the importance of art, arguing that '1/10th of the total population of the United States are Negroes. No American art or cultural contribution can be divorced from the influence of the Black American.' As such, it indicates the involvement of members who defined themselves equally as writers and activists and suggests the aesthetic direction from which Hicks, Wright and other members of the group emerged and which would pave the way for the emergence of Umbra.

While On Guard's constitution is fairly broad in its concerns, from the start, the Congo was a clear focus. Cuba and the Congo are given as examples of 'the legitimate resurgence of nationalism and free-thinking', and Lumumba appears in the roll call of names in whose tradition 'we intend to carry on our struggle'. A galvanizing figure for black internationalism throughout the 1960s – he is part of the pantheon of heroes and martyrs in Baraka's 'The Revolutionary Theatre' and was frequently mentioned by the Black Panther Party for Self-defense (BPP) and other activist groups – Lumumba was head of the independent Congolese Trade Union and founder of the Congolese National Movement Party. Elected by an overwhelming majority in the first elections held in the newly independent Congo in 1960, his displacement in an anti-Communist coup and subsequent murder became a locus for internationalist activism. Many black radicals believed that Eisenhower had ordered his murder, and pro-Lumumba protests served as a means to unite struggles against racism in the United States with struggles against imperialism across the globe (Reed 2000B, 105–6; Peery, 200). Even before Lumumba's death, the situation in the Congo had become a key issue for the nascent activities of On Guard. The first of the group's two newsletters appeared in early February 1961, very soon before the official announcement of Lumumba's death on February 13, and contained an article, 'What Means Independence in the Congo', which opened with an eerily prophetic warning that, 'with the rapid change continually taking place in the Congo, it will be no surprise if within a very few weeks Prime Minister Patrice Lumumba will be returned to power or be dead' ('What Means Independence', 1).

When Lumumba's death was finally announced, nearly a month after it had occurred, it set off an outraged reaction: there was widespread fury at the refusal by both the United States and the UN to support Lumumba after he had appealed to them and speculation as to CIA involvement in his death. On February 15, demonstrations took place worldwide and across America in Washington, DC, Chicago, San Francisco and Houston. In New York, activists associated with On Guard, the Harlem Writers' Guild and other organizations – including Hicks, Sarah E. Wright, Daniel Watts and Robert F. Williams – planned to cause maximum public disruption at the UN building in New York. The aforementioned interruption to Adlai Stevenson's speech was decisive and bold. Wearing black armbands and veils which had been prepared at the home of singer and activist Abbey Lincoln, the activists who interrupted the speech included members of the Cultural Association for Women of African Heritage (Lincoln, Wright, Maya Angelou and Rosa Guy), Daniel Watts's Liberation Committee for Africa, Baraka's Organization of Young Men, On Guard, and the Harlem Writers' Guild. Rosa Guy, a member of the Harlem Writers' Guild and an important participant in On Guard's early organizational activity (though she was never an official part of the organization) stood up when Stevenson defended US foreign policy with regard to the Congo as a means of avoiding 'the jungles of internecine warfare and internal rivalry', and disorder began when guards rushed for her. Guy recalls: 'I began injecting myself. You'd think I was one of the delegates. We began to yell "This is the time! This is the time!"' (Wood, 165, 173). As the *Times* report noted, this intervention turned the tables: the UN representatives were turned 'from actors to audience' as African-American activists took centre stage ('Riot in Gallery', 1). Having been expected to 'wait', to watch, to be the audience, the protestors now intervened in a highly public arena, ensuring that their images appeared in the media and in front of a cast of world leaders.

As with the wide variety of artists, intellectuals and political activists who had met with Fidel Castro at the Hotel Theresa the previous year, the UN protest involved a disparate group of protestors from differing political backgrounds. James Lawson, president of the United African Nationalist Movement (UANM), stated that at least fifteen organizations had taken part in the demonstration. When the event was reported in the mainstream media, it was predictably stigmatized as a 'riot'; uncertainty as to who had organized and coordinated the protest, and rumours spread by representatives of the US government, set off panicked invocations of the twin fears of Communism and Black Nationalism. One such response in the *New York Times* played on fears of international Communism, citing rumours spread by unnamed US officials that 'Communist agitators had stirred up pro-Lumumba demonstrations around the world' ('Riot in Gallery', 1). This rumour spread even more wildly by the California-based *Lodi News-Sentinel*, whose February 15th edition denounced the protest as a 'Communist inspired [...] riot' by 'screaming demonstrators', placing a photograph of Calvin Hicks's arrest under the banner headline 'Mobs Rampage Around World in Lumumba Protest' ('Mobs Rampage', 1). Though some protesters, such as Daniel Watts, editor of *Liberator* and founder of the Liberation Committee for Africa, identified as nationalists and explicitly not as Communists, the members of On Guard possessed a definite leftist orientation ('U.N. Rioting Laid to Pro-Africans', 11). Calvin Hicks would later argue, using Cedric Robinson's term, that 'the understanding, or the lack of understanding, of On Guard, coming from the Lower East Side, was a kind of Black Marxism' (Wood, 181). Likewise, Umbra member Rashidah Ismaili characterizes On Guard as 'working-class oriented, [...] cultural workers, and [...] leftwing politically' (Wood, 169).

Such left-wing sympathies invited a predictably paranoid media response – even if On Guard's orientation tended more towards the non-aligned politics identified with Castro, Lumumba and the 'Bandung World' than to the Soviet Union. These reactions had uncomfortable echoes of the 1919 Red Summer in which the spectre of black bolshevism was used to justify large-scale campaigns of terror conducted against black neighbourhoods, and African-American commentators were quick to point out the links between the situation in the Congo and the conditions they faced in the United States. In the *New York Times Magazine*, the month after the protest, James Baldwin sarcastically demolished media arguments which stigmatized left-oriented self-organization by African-Americans as part of a Communist plot.

> According, then, to what I take to be the prevailing view, these rioters were merely a handful of irresponsible, Kremlin-corrupted provocateurs. I find this view amazing. It is a view which even a minimal effort at observation would immediately contradict. (Baldwin, 103)

Linking conditions in Harlem to the anger felt by the protestors at events in the Congo, he argued that the protest represented African-Americans' refusal to 'wait' or 'adjust themselves to the cruel racial pressures of life in the United States [...] The American Negro can no longer, nor will he ever again, be controlled by white America's image of him. This fact has everything to do with the rise of Africa in world affairs' (103). As Baldwin's comments suggest, On Guard's solidarity with Africa was not tokenist Afrocentrism – a charge frequently levelled at the Black Power and Black Arts Movements – but a conscious and active response to the realities of geopolitics, imperialism and domestic racism. The connections between African-American demonstrators expressing their solidarity with anti-colonial struggles were more than merely symbolic. Rosa Guy, due to her fluency in French, had played a key role in establishing connections in New York for the Congolese delegation to the UN, who spoke little English, and received news of Lumumba's death before it was officially announced through contacts in the Congolese diplomatic corps (Angelou 1981, 170; Smethurst 2005, 118). Moreover, the choice of location for the protest was tactical and precise. The UN building formed part of a key symbolic geography which demonstrated the growing links between African-Americans and visiting representatives from Third World governments, particularly in Harlem, as with Fidel Castro's stay at the Hotel Theresa. Four miles north of the Lower East Side and six miles south of Harlem, the UN building was within walking distance of Baraka's and Umbra's base. As with the later Harlem and Newark riots, an occupation of public space emphasized the links between representation, topographies of power, and domestic and international politics.

'A new perspective opens up': On Guard after the Lumumba protest

In some ways, the UN protest represented the group's most visible entry into public life, and On Guard's activities continued for a further year following the protest. But it also appears that the group's organization subsequently changed from its initial, more collective ethos towards a model which gravitated towards Hicks as leader, as he put it, 'more approaching the Soviet model' (quoted in Wood, 167). At this time, the group included many future Umbra members such as Calvin and Nora Hicks, Tom Dent and, from Baraka's Organization of Young Men, which merged with On Guard after the protest, Leroy McLucas, Archie Shepp, A.B. Spellman and Joe Johnson. On Guard published a 'Declaration of Conscience' in support of Cuba in the *New York Post* in April 1961 alongside W.E.B. and Shirley Graham Du Bois, Abbey Lincoln and Maya Angelou ('Cuba: A Declaration', 9). The group's second and final newsletter was published the following month with Calvin Hicks listed as editor and Dent as managing editor. Hicks's headline article, 'Cuba and the Struggle for Afro-American Liberation', sets out On Guard's internationalist perspective, linking black American struggles with Third World revolutions taking place across the globe – a view which would become increasingly prominent in the circles around Umbra, *Liberator* and the RAM, notably in Askia Touré's important essay 'Afro-American Youth and the Bandung World' (Touré 1965A).

Received accounts of this period tend to focus on Baraka's famous essay 'Cuba Libre', first published in two parts in *Evergreen Review*. Reflecting on his visit to Fidel Castro's Cuba with the Fair Play Committee for Cuba in July 1960 – a delegation which also included Harold Cruse, Robert F. Williams and Sarah E. Wright – Baraka's open-ended conclusion has not yet found a clear politics. Baraka still identifies himself as an American, alienated by the policies of his government, but unable yet to find a meaningful means of solidarity with Third World revolutionaries such as those he had met in Cuba. Stating that 'the rebels among us have become merely people like myself who grow beards and will not participate in politics', he argues that there is no alternative 'not inextricably bound up in a lie [...] not part of liberal stupidity or the actual filth of vested interest' and that 'the Cubans, and the other new peoples (in Asia, Africa, South America) don't need us, and we had better stay out of their way' (*H*, 78). Baraka's account sidelines the valuable work done by writers involved with On Guard, most notably Wright, dismissively characterized as a 'professional Negro wife [...] who wrote embarrassingly inept social comment-type poems', though Wright's political analysis was already far in advance of Baraka's, and she had been following developments in Cuba from 1952 (*H*, 25; Karageorgos, 136-9, 146-9).

By contrast, Calvin Hicks's 1961 article for *On Guard*, produced from and addressed to a predominantly black political collective, suggests more concrete alternatives. As Baraka would later note, Hicks was a far more experienced organizer than he at this stage (*Autobiography*, 168). Both this and the galvanizing effect of the UN protest – a demonstrable expression of solidarity with Third World struggles – explained the clarion-call clarity of Hicks's article and began to convince Baraka, too, that there *were* palpable alternatives to 'liberal stupidity or the actual filth of vested interest'. For Hicks, opposition to US anti-revolutionary politics in Cuba – notably, the failed Bay of Pigs invasion of April 1961 – and to other imperialist interventions in the Third World was indelibly linked to the 'century long struggle against segregation and lynch justice', manifesting in the current Civil Rights Movement. Given this, Hicks writes:

> A new perspective opens up. Our struggles are no longer national. Nor are we now the only ones concerned with them. They are hemispheric, international …. All liberation struggles of Asia, Africa and Latin America are interrelated with white supremacy and the myths of white superiority from which we suffer. (Hicks, 1)

Hicks links CIA activities and US-backed invasions in Cuba, Guatemala, Costa Rica, Nicaragua and Laos to African-American struggles in the United States with the ghost of Lumumba ever present. Because of the United States' role in suppressing anti-colonial struggles, Hicks argues, African-Americans struggling for their own liberation within the United States must of necessity be linked to those struggles. As well as emphasizing covert and overt American intervention in the Third World, Hicks emphasizes resistance movements such as the Algerian *Front de Libération Nationale* (FLN) and forces in South Africa and Angola.

But the task of putting theory into practice was far from straightforward. Hicks's article emerged not at the beginning of On Guard's publishing and organizational history but towards its end. On Guard had collapsed by 1962 as its members moved onto other aesthetic and political activities. As an organization, it was, like Umbra, short-lived, and it has often been retrospectively characterized as something of a failure. In his autobiography, for instance, Baraka writes that the group had collapsed due to 'obvious contradictions' concerning its members' interracial relationships (*Autobiography*, 197). Likewise, in his highly influential *The Crisis of the Negro Intellectual* (1967), Harold Cruse – himself a previous member of the group though he was not part of the UN demonstration – characterized On Guard as a confused mishmash of Communism, Liberalism and nascent Black Nationalism. Cruse saw the group as an emblem of the 'new breed of Afro-American nationalist' exemplified by Baraka, committed to violence and supported primarily by young intellectuals and artists (Cruse, 32). Yet, for Cruse, On Guard was limited because of its ties to a 'downtown' politics overly influenced by a 'psychology of political interracialism' derived from white Communism and white liberalism (Cruse, 365). This account is severely flawed. Seeing On Guard simply as an unsuccessful predecessor to more overtly nationalist organizations like BART/S, Cruse renders the group simply an appendage of Baraka's political development. In doing so, he promotes both Baraka and himself to prominent leadership roles and downplays the collective ethos behind such organizations.

Indeed, Cruse's retrospective account reproduces the media coverage of this event, which, as we've seen, played on the twin fears of Communism and nationalism. Unfortunately, Cruse's reductive characterization has been uncritically reproduced in much scholarship on the period, resulting in factual confusion, to which the present study is a necessary corrective. In his highly problematic biography of Baraka, Jerry Gaffio Watts relies solely on Cruse's account of On Guard as Baraka's creation. Watts's brief, critical account focuses on the politics of interracialism and gender and dismisses the group as possessing, 'in some respects, no political purpose outside of addressing the idiosyncratic needs of some black intellectuals to "do something"' (Watts, 494, n.5). While less simplistically dismissive, Komozi Woodard also downplays the group's activities. In his important book on Baraka and Black Power politics, Woodard's account of the UN demonstration relies exclusively on the *New York Times* article, giving the names of Daniel Watts and Fair Play for Cuba's Richard Gibson as the 'leaders' of On Guard and omitting any discussion of the organizational networks involving members of Umbra such as Hicks and Dent (Woodard, 58–9). Such accounts factually distort On Guard's membership and activities, presenting the group simply as a confused predecessor to Baraka's later political organizing. There are parallels to the neglect of Umbra's aesthetic production: both groups are often literally reduced to a footnote. This is symptomatic of a broader trend. By ignoring and distorting the recent histories out of which the Black Arts emerged, particularly in New York, we receive a history of black aesthetic radicalism which downplays its origins in collective struggle and debate. This is not to say that such struggle was without often divisive tensions; yet to attribute value to collectives based solely on longevity is to distort the way that literary and political history actually operate, ignoring the difficult groundwork that precedes, and in some cases provides more nuanced versions of, more publicized endeavours.

Working out who exactly was responsible for attempting to coalesce the shared currents around the Harlem Writers' Guild and the Cultural Association for Women of African Heritage, into On Guard, and for initiating the UN demonstration, as well as the shifting leadership structures and subsequent tensions within the group, is a difficult process. The documentary evidence is often scant and contradictory, and though they gave some oral testimonies, most of the main participants are now deceased.[2] Given the exclusions which have been repeatedly performed on African-American women such as Maya Angelou, Rosa Guy and Sara E. Wright in histories of this period, it does appear that their role has been under-emphasized in existing accounts: as Cheryl Higashida has argued, such accounts have all but obliterated the role of women such as Angelou, Guy and Wright in not only participating in but *initiating* such movements (Higashida, 54, 194, n.87). Indeed, as Higashida notes, Guy and Angelou, who met with Malcolm X the day after the UN demonstration to question him as to why he had not participated, can be credited with opening his developing political awareness – in Guy's words, 'forc[ing]' the men of the time to 'grow' (Higashida, 54–5; Angelou 1989, 229).[3]

What we can say, however, is that the participation of members of On Guard was crucial to the protest, that the protest itself galvanized them and that both galvanized what would become the Umbra Poets' workshop. Likewise, while acknowledging the complexities of competing racial, sexual and political dynamics within the organization, and the retrospective sidelining of female activists who in fact played a major role in its inception, it is key to emphasize its significance as an exemplar of the attempt to create a viable black internationalism at a time of intense geopolitical upheaval. On Guard, and its extension into the aesthetic project of Umbra, created the space for a productive debate on tactics, ideology and aesthetic production. Indeed, the new spheres of production and discussion set up in Umbra may have allowed for a more nuanced take on fractious political debates. Umbra's complex literary production served as a useful reflection on ideological confusion, rather than simply presenting ideological positions as a *fait accompli* which jarred with the tasks of organizing on an aesthetically and politically non-aligned basis. As Michel Oren notes, the literary activities of Umbra members had begun to intersect as early as 1957, most notably in Raymond Patterson and Calvin Hernton's reading at Patterson's Lower East Side apartment in 1957, Patterson's organization of a series of six readings at the Market Place Gallery in Harlem in 1960, and Umbra poets' correspondence with the Dutch editors Paul Breman and Rosey Pool for the anthologies *Sixes and Sevens* and *Beyond the Blues* (Oren 1984, 168), both published in 1962. Around this time, these writers were also politically active through the activities of On Guard. By the summer of 1962, On Guard had ceased to function as an organization – in part, as Tom Dent suggests, because of tensions between the activist focus of some members and the desire to form a writers' group among others.

> There were a lot of problems because when we put out one issue of the journal, there was an indecision within the organization about whether it would be some sort of activist community group or a publication, or writers' group. We actually never had a writers' workshop, and some people wanted a more activist situation where they would actually do something […] Those of us who were interested in writing decided we need to develop another organization. On Guard wouldn't do it […] We consciously started Umbra out of On Guard for those people who were more interested in writing.
>
> (Dent 2018, 442–3)

As Kalamu ya Salaam notes, 'Prior to the Black Arts Movement, most aspirant black writers chose either journalism or fiction as their focus. Even Langston Hughes made his mark as a journalist while producing fiction' (24). The tensions within On Guard – the sense that a focus on activism and journalistic writing excluded an aesthetic dimension – manifested a broader transition for which Umbra was keenly placed: what Dent sees as an 'intermediary, transitory stage', from earlier models of black journalism and activism, and a tradition of 'naturalist protest writing' in the vein of Richard Wright, to a more experimental approach (58). Dent had moved to the Lower East Side from Harlem in January: in August or September, he, Hernton and David Henderson sent out a call for young black writers, beginning Umbra as a regular series of Friday night workshops, based at Dent's apartment (Dent 1981, 2). Umbra members would continue to participate in political organizing, both individually and, more occasionally, as a group. Several members attended the 1963 March on Washington as a group, carrying weapons to protect themselves in the event of racist attacks, and both Dent and Askia Touré were heavily involved in activism with the SNCC and the NAACP during the mid-1960s (Art Berger, 21). While some members of Umbra were more involved in On Guard than others, the organization was crucial in forging the politically engaged, ideologically complex field they would negotiate. The reverberations of On Guard and of the UN protest in particular are indicated by the fact that Lumumba's death appears in a number of poems by Umbra writers, to which this chapter now turns.

Ishmael Reed's 'Patrice' and aesthetic distancing

Perhaps the best-known writer to emerge from Umbra, Reed would go on to develop his influential 'Neo-HooDoo' aesthetic in a series of vital poems and novels such as *Conjure* (1972), *Mumbo Jumbo* (1972) and *Flight to Canada* (1976). Distancing himself from the ideological rigidity of elements of the BAM, he would also fiercely reject the stereotypical roles forced on black writers and has dedicated his subsequent work in California to nurturing a multicultural aesthetic through the Before Columbus Foundation, an important example of how Umbra's collective ethos continues to manifest long after its initial demise. Reed was, as Dent notes, a member of the group's 'second phase', attending workshop meetings following his move from Buffalo to New York later in 1962 (Dent 2018, 56). Though not a participant in On Guard, he shared a background in journalism with Dent, Hicks and others, while in Buffalo, he had served as a correspondent for the *Empire Star Weekly*, a black community newspaper, and as the co-host for a local radio programme that was cancelled after Reed conducted an on-air interview with Malcolm X (Fox, 624). As Reed notes, 'all of my early attempts at poetry were lost in an old car abandoned on the freeway while I was enroute to New York' (Reed 1972A, vii). Likewise, he sees the new poetry he began to produce while part of Umbra as apprentice work, written under the influence of Pound, Blake and Yeats. As he sardonically put it in 1972: 'Excuse me. I know that it's white culture. I was a dupe, I confess' (Reed 1972A, vii). This approach is perhaps exemplified by the poem 'Time and the Eagle', a kind of parody of Yeats which opens *Umbra*'s second issue, figuring history as a cyclical and 'interminable ceremony' of violence out of which some sort of dialectical resolution is sought.

> The shackled black, being torn in innocence;
> Molded his advent through cyclical time [...]
> Begatting contraries which fuse and breakaway
> like fire, water, wood and metal. [...]
>
> Victims, seaweed in their hair,
> Victims; dangling from dark trees a mob
> Hurrah in memory.
> Victims; who have forgotten the snake
> And do not know the past nor present [...]
>
> An interminable ceremony.
> (*Umbra* II, 5–6)

Appearing further on in the issue, Reed's 'Patrice' more explicitly addresses itself to contemporaneous politics. One of his first published pieces, it has never been reprinted. Only five lines long, the poem's reflection on Lumumba's death extends the critique enacted in the On Guard protest within the sphere of the aesthetic – and, importantly, in terms of *aestheticization*. The poem reads in full:

PATRICE

Patrice is   in fields of hemp
    recumbent
Like a Henry Moore.
Where bloated, Belgian brokers
    never tamper.

(*Umbra* II, 36)

Reed ironically places Lumumba's corpse as a sculptural figure in a landscape, attesting to aestheticization's distancing, depoliticizing effect. The final lines challenge the 'common sense' assumption of good faith on the part of colonial powers, ironically suggesting their opposite: that Lumumba has been murdered, directly or indirectly, as a result of Belgian 'tamper[ing]'. Referring to Lumumba only by his first name, Reed performs both an ironical condescension – Lumumba, a world leader, is patronisingly reduced to an (over-)familiar term of address – and extends an intimate solidarity to the slain leader, whom he would later describe as having 'a poet's eyes' (Reed 2000B, 105). The poem's pithy ironies, accomplished through careful negotiations of tone, rely on politics as the elsewhere of poetry: the poem ironically performs the aestheticization it decries, while also suggesting the pitfalls of uncritical hero worship and reliance on figures of martyrdom. Reed works through implication and through leaving telling spaces such as the tab created by moving the word 'recumbent' from the first line – where it would fit more naturally in both visual and grammatical terms – to the second. As the poem's most notable typographic feature, this gap immediately draws attention to itself, rendering the opening two words as a statement in their own right which emphasizes Lumumba's being, his present existence ('Patrice is'). This is then belied by the unstated fact of his death: the somewhat arcane word 'recumbent' suggests both a person and an effigy lying down. The irony is further amplified by the fact that Lumumba's corpse was actually dismembered and dissolved in acid to prevent it from becoming a martyr's monument (De Witte, 141–2). Reed claims Lumumba as a figure of living inspiration: neither depoliticized, so that he resembles a piece of modernist sculpture by Henry

Moore, nor totally erased, his corpse literally destroyed in order to ensure his disappearance from history. Though the deceptive understatement through which all this is accomplished is some way from common understandings of the radical black poetry of the 1960s, its political critique is no less vital.

Rights and riots: Lorenzo Thomas's 'A Tale of Two Cities'

Reed's poem did not appear until *Umbra*'s second issue. In the first issue, produced earlier that year, we find a poem by Lorenzo Thomas which more directly addresses the 1961 UN Protest. Thomas's poem appears to have been written earlier still, given its epigraph from a 1960 *New York Times* article and its address to the protest. The poem was again one of Thomas's first published poems, and, like Reed's, it has never been reprinted. But its complex moves between solidarity and scepticism deftly negotiate the spaces of American cultural politics and anti-colonial resistance abroad, providing a model for the kind of globally aware poetry that the Umbra writers at their best were capable of producing: leftist, politically astute, yet far from simplistically tub-thumping or, as the magazine's Foreword puts it, 'axe-grind[ing]'.

Although Thomas was involved with the Monroe Defence Committee along with other On Guard members, he was too young to be involved in On Guard itself (Thomas 1983, 5–6). Nonetheless, we might expect the poem to be a statement of support for the protest. Instead, it is a far more complex reflection on media receptions of struggles against imperialism, which is not above criticizing the methods adopted by his On Guard comrades. The poem reads in full:

A TALE OF TWO CITIES
    'They were like wild animals', said M.
    Djoumessi – New York Times, 25 Febru 1960

   O the wild dancers, the New York
beer-drinkers, running amok at the UN shouting,
   'You've crucified our saintly Lumumba ... '

   And what about the people's other saints
In Bklyn, do storefront churches worship
     a storefront God?
And elsewhere are there rites? Rights, riots?
How does the mask fit elsewhere on this fraud
    that we call life?

> The Times says nights in Cameroun are terrible.
> Young intellects, old madmen, philosophers and
> poets, machete the non-believers of their
> > political voudoun.
> Who are their saints, what are their rituals?
> > Who sings their hymns, Geo. Beverly Shay or
> > > Clara Ward or good ol' Charlie Mingus?
>
> > My friend, their ritual is death and their
> hymns are marching songs and the groans of their
> > victims.
> Gen. Moumié gange cinq million Soldat. Yaounde,
> > Bassa, Grassfield!
>
> > The screams of victims. Mr. Mingus.
> > > Yaounde, yaounde, yaounde.

(*Umbra* I, 36–7)

The short first stanza presents the UN protest in apparently satirical terms, ironically apostrophizing the protesters as 'wild dancers' and 'New York/beer-drinkers' who 'run [...] amok at the UN' (36). The protestors' sanctification of Lumumba leads to a recurring series of questions which apparently ventriloquize the voice of a white observer who wishes to know the 'saints' and 'rituals' of an ensemble which includes New York intellectuals, jazz musicians and the anti-colonial rebels of the *Union des Populations du Cameroun* (UPC), united through a racist spectre of violence which concretizes in the references to a massacre supposedly perpetrated by the UPC. This is far from a straightforward presentation of On Guard. Given the way the poem subsequently develops, however, we see that, like Reed, Thomas's focus is as much on critiquing the media *reception* of anti-colonial politics as it is on once more protesting Lumumba's death.

Thomas's title sees Dickens's two cities – revolutionary-era Paris and London – become the Cameroonian capital Yaounde and New York. Over greater distances and more obscured geopolitical connections, Thomas draws connections between the murders of Lumumba and Cameroonian rebel leader General Félix-Roland Moumié. Whatever his precise political reading of the Revolution, Dickens's text was invoked in relation to reactionary fears of mob violence in France crossing the channel to England (Hobsbawm, 5). In Thomas's poem, this translates into the fear of Cameroonian rebel violence as a means of justifying neo-imperial manoeuvring for control over colonial territories (or, for that matter, the mass arrests of the UN protestors). In transplanting Dickens's novel to the political situation of the 1960s, Thomas adds a layer of literary-critical irony, presenting a sophisticated and timely consideration of debates surrounding nationalism, racism and revolutionary violence.

The poem's epigraph is taken from a *New York Times* article by war correspondent Homer Bigart, luridly entitled 'Hashish-Mad Rebels Kill 74 in Cameroon' (Bigart, 1). Thomas is likely to have come across Bigart's article as part of a collage of press cuttings related to the use of alcohol and hashish in Tuli Kupferberg's little magazine *Birth* (Kupferberg, 54). Yet while Kupferberg cites the article predominantly for comic effect, as part of a satire on hysterical reactions to intoxicants within straight American society, Thomas (re-)politicizes it within an explicitly racialized context. Deploying the same tropes used in the *Times'* reporting on the Congo – in which the Belgians were portrayed as good men who had brought order and whose departure had triggered a 'relapse' into child-like savagery by the 'natives' – Bigart portrays Cameroonian guerrilla fighters as suffering 'a mad relapse into barbarism' (Hickner, 186–96; Bigart, 1). Bigart's article concerns the reported murder of seventy-four people, mostly women and children, guarded by French African soldiers, by teenaged guerrilla fighters from the non-aligned Marxist UPC in Dschang, Cameroon, in late February 1960. Both the article and Thomas's poem quote a chant, sung to the tune of 'John Brown's Body', which pays tribute to the UPC's exiled leader, General Félix-Roland Moumié. Moumié would be poisoned by the French secret service in November 1960 in an uncanny echo of Lumumba's execution, most likely undertaken with CIA involvement (Tande, 60–4).

Thomas refers directly to Bigart's article in the following lines, halfway through the poem:

The Times says nights in Cameroun are terrible.
Young intellects, old madmen, philosophers and
poets, machete the non-believers of their
political voudoun.

(*Umbra* I: 36)

The ironically understated tone of 'The Times says nights in Cameroon are terrible' suggests that the *Times* at once engages in the most lurid of racist stereotypes ('a mad relapse into barbarism') and reduces the political complications of violence, civil war and anti-colonial struggle to something that can be dismissed as a mere unpleasantness, to be balked at in mild horror and then ignored. Exactly whose 'political voudon' is at stake is unclear. On the one hand, Thomas could refer to the apparent massacre of their enemies by the UPC fighters: Bigart claims that, before the massacre, the rebels had participated in 'juju rites, where they were branded with five cuts to the chest to make them impervious to bullets' (Bigart, 1). But on the other, he turns them back on the *Times*, referring to the 'hatchet job' of Bigart's reporting.

Bigart's article relies on his supposed 'neutrality' and 'objectivity' as a *Times* reporter, his use of the passive voice rendering subjective judgements as unquestionable fact.

> The Bamileke people who inhabit this area are regarded as the most civilized of Cameroon tribes. Yet early last Friday, Bamileke youths were slaughtering [their] own tribesmen, a mad relapse into barbarism. (1)

Bigart does not outline who sets the standards of 'most civilized', nor what 'civilized' itself might mean. By refusing the active voice, Thomas exposes the discursive framings around such contentious events. Bigart's account omits to mention that the Bamileke's struggles responded to a decades-long campaign of murder and torture by French forces both before and after Cameroon's nominal 'independence' in 1960, under the *Union Camerounais* government of Ahmadou Ahidjo (who acceded to his role without elections). Ahidjo had risen through the ranks of the previous French colonial administration and continued to be supported by Gaullist armed forces, drafting a new constitution based on De Gaulle's 1958 Presidentialist constitution ('2 mars 1960'). Ahidjo signed Franco-Camourenaise 'cooperation agreements' which served to keep Cameroun as, effectively, a French garrison state, dominated by a police intelligence service which 'was to all extents and purposes a mere outpost of the French intelligence service' (Anyangwe, 8–12). The UPC's struggles opposed post-independence measures designed to protect colonial interests, which, cloaked in the language of 'civilization' and 'progress', stigmatized national liberation struggles as 'savage', 'tribal' or 'barbaric'. Indeed, Ahidjo's government, in collusion with the French, was essentially attempting to wipe out the Bamileke, a process which would continue throughout the decade.

Thomas ends the poem by quoting the chant the rebels are said to have sung to the tune of 'John Brown's Body': 'Gen. Moumié gange cinq million Soldat. Yaounde, / Bassa, Grassfield!' (37). This chant registered resistance by the Bamilike in the 'Grassfield' region and the Bassa people in the southwest, alongside the name of the Cameroonian capital, Yaounde; the Bamilike resistance was both regionally specific, and in that sense 'tribal', and conducted in solidarity with others. In its original form, 'John Brown's Body' memorializes the militant fight against slavery, and its use by the UPC forms a deliberate parallel to an American context. Brown, the prototypical 'race traitor', was still a symbol of militant resistance to slavery and one of the few white historical figures whom advocates of Black Power would openly praise (Hayden, Harper; Du Bois 1909; Quarless; Ronda; Oren 2006). The use of Brown by Africans further translates such figurations, aligning struggles against African colonialism with those against American domestic slavery. Thomas's poem amplifies the threatening connection felt between Brown and America; if African soldiers can use Brown as a heroic exemplar, what of African-Americans? As Bruce A. Ronda notes: 'For readers of Brown [such as Frederick Douglass and W.E.B. Du Bois], the Old Man sometimes takes on the appearance of a Jacobin during the Reign of Terror, willing to inflict fear and violence against the remaining enemies of the French Revolution in the name of the larger social good' (Ronda, xix–xx). Recalling the spectre of the Revolution behind Thomas's title, such rhetoric might be used by either defenders or detractors – just as *vodoun* might be portrayed either as a 'mad relapse into barbarism' or – as in Ishmael Reed's later 'Neo-HooDoo' aesthetic – as a valuable tool of resistance and cultural adaptation. Thomas's poem treads ambiguously through this maze. John Brown, the French Revolution and the Cameroonian rebels are caught in a mesh of historical overdetermination, posed simultaneously as forces of Enlightenment modernity and as the regressive polar opposite to such forces.

The poem's third stanza opens with an apparent moment of direct address which provides not a moment of clarity but of further confusion.

> My friend, their ritual is death and their
> hymns are marching songs and the groans of their
> victims.

The 'ritual is death' appears to refer to the UPC but could also once more describe Bigart's own rituals of racist othering. Bigart's description of 'juju rites' deploys the spectre of savage violence unleashed once the 'restraining' influence of colonial powers has been removed, tacitly endorsing the use of equally violent measures to combat them. In the spirit of Tuli Kupferberg's collage, Thomas extends this characterization to an incoherent and wide-ranging parade of others felt to threaten the American way of life: jazz musicians, Civil Rights activists, rioters and the UN protestors. Bigart's description of the rebels as 'hashish-mad' leads Thomas to the spectre of the American 'drug fiend': the fear that 'New York/beer-drinkers' or hash-smokers might become politically organized is, Thomas suggests, a serious threat to the established order. Thomas ironically extends the stereotypes of 'hashish-mad rebels' to African-American urban life, with its 'rites', 'rights', 'riots', store-front churches and music. The telling pun which elides 'rites', 'rights' and 'riots' suggests that, for some, the fear of Civil Rights activists is inseparable from the conglomeration of 'hashish-mad' African 'rebels', preachers, protestors, jazz musicians and beatniks.

While the immediate inspiration for Thomas's appropriation of Bigart may, via Kupferberg's collage, have been hashish, in the poem itself, such connections occur principally through music. Charles Mingus first appears as 'good ol' Charlie Mingus'. Yet Mingus – the incendiary musician, composer and sometime poet – rejected such racist interpellation in such fiercely anti-colonial works as 'Haitian Fight Song' and the establishment of an independent recording label and jazz festival with Max Roach, challenging white promoters' control over recording and performance. (In this regard, see Calvin Hernton's unforgettable coinage 'Mingus Tse Tung' (Hernton 1976, 64).) Mingus's work frequently made use of furious, parodic ventriloquy – quotations of 'Dixie' or 'Shortnin' Bread', passages spoken in imagined African languages and denouncements of racist politicians or inattentive audiences. Thomas initially places Mingus's modern-day 'hymns' alongside those of the white gospel singer George Beverly Shay (or Shea), a participant in Billy Graham's evangelical crusades, and black gospel singer Clara Ward (as well as the UPC's version of 'John Brown's body'). By the poem's end, he has become 'Mr. Mingus', a figure, ostensibly, of dignity and respect. However, this transformation is not necessarily complete. In a 1962 review of the album *Mingus in Wonderland*, Baraka would criticize Mingus's 'tendency to editorialise', claiming that political content should emerge from the form of the music rather than being superimposed on it and that Mingus 'saying Africa will rise even risks the faint damned image of minstrelsy' (Mingus 1959; Baraka 1962B, 103–4). 'Mr. Mingus" attempts to present himself as a political spokesman might thus be seen as misguided – particularly when we consider the juxtaposition of his name with 'the screams of victims' (37). Yet Mingus himself was aware of the perils of a token Afrocentrism – his piece 'Passions of a Man', recorded the same year as the Lumumba protest, features vocalisms delivered in what appears to be a fake African language interspersed with cries of 'Mau Mau', 'America' and 'Freedom' (Mingus 1962). This is not to say that Mingus precludes the possibility of genuine engagement with non-American cultures on the part of domestic black radicals. Indeed, it is precisely the instability of gestures such as those found on 'Passions of a Man' or in Thomas's poem that enables them to retain a militancy adaptable to events, tactically flexible and open to the complexities of violence as a tool in anti-imperialist struggle (see also Thomas 1966, 62).

Like the telling space in Reed's 'Patrice', Thomas leaves open a space for the political possibility offered by Third World liberation struggles, the music of Mingus – and even the incoherently politicized 'beer-drinkers' of Brooklyn and the Lower East Side – as a revolutionary force, however incoherent and disparate. As Eben Wood argues:

> The 'third way' posed by Thomas's poem accepts neither mass media complicity in narratives of Cold War polarization that implicitly endorse the great American way, nor magical 'rites' by which the totems of neocolonial nationalism are simply repeated by a violence that is both real and false at the same moment. (Wood, 300)

Thomas is wary of appropriations of various kinds, while still deploying them as a symbolic affront to conformist imperial narratives. Though 'Tale' is far from a straightforward 'protest poem', its parallels between African-American radicalism and anti-imperialist struggles tellingly reframe geopolitical connections otherwise subsumed into media narratives of racism and anti-Communist hysteria.

'Cry Freedom': Askia Touré

The presence of these poems by Reed and Thomas in *Umbra*'s first and second issues links to the extra-literary political activism exemplified by the participation of Umbra members in On Guard and the 1961 UN protest and serves as one of many concrete illustrations of the group's politicized poetics. Diagnostically negotiating an ironically posed course between the 'descriptions' that pass for the 'common sense' of white supremacy, as well as the problem of liberation movements reduplicating the very forms they struggle against, particularly through forms of political violence, these poems are exemplary instances of what Umbra's group project could and did accomplish. I now to turn to an uncollected poem by Askia Touré arising from the protest, 'Cry Freedom', published in *Liberator* in May 1963 (Touré 1963, 9–11). Like Thomas and Reed, Touré sarcastically comments on the media reception of the 'riots' and rejects aesthetic and political stereotyping. His poem, however, is more of a rousing call to arms than theirs, and the militant, internationalist focus of his work would come to be a significant influence on Baraka's writing and the development of the BAM aesthetic. The context of public performance to Touré's work is vital. Umbra's dramatic, collective readings were a key part of their ethos, not least among them Calvin Hernton's declamations, influenced by his training as an actor, and David Henderson's use of song, influenced by his early career as a musician. Touré's work was likewise politically militant, conscious of performance and heavily influenced by African-American music. As Lorenzo Thomas writes, 'his style of presentation [...] was never "dramatic reading", but very nearly song' (*EM*, 130). Indeed, along with its political content, this song-like presentation was a fundamental influence on Baraka. As he later noted:

> Poets like Larry Neal and Askia Touré were, in my mind, masters of the new black poetry. [...] Askia had the song-like cast to his words, as if the poetry actually was meant to be sung. I heard him once up at the Baby Grand when we first got into Harlem and that singing sound influenced what I was to do with poetry from then on. To me, Larry and Askia were the state of the art, where it was, at that moment. (*Autobiography*, 236–7)

Born Rolland Snellings in 1938 in North Carolina, Touré, like Calvin Hernton, lived with his grandmother (in La Grange, Georgia) until he was six years old, a landscape which played a key role in his early poetic imagery before joining his family in Ohio. He participated in a successful sit-in at Roosevelt High School, where he also began singing doo-wop in local nightclubs, this early musical career drawing links to David Henderson's early experience with Harlem vocal groups. However, upon graduating in 1956, he left music behind and, like Baraka, joined the Air Force, initiating a government investigation of racism at Wordsmith Air Force Base in Michigan. After his discharge in 1959, he moved to New York to study visual arts and saw himself as 'reborn on Brooklyn's teeming streets' through his participation with On Guard, Umbra and *Liberator*, for which he became a staff member, writing a series of extremely influential Black Nationalist articles (Touré 1963, 11; Tinson, 140). The biography printed underneath 'Cry Freedom' in *Liberator* notes:

> Rolland Snellings, painter-poet, was born in North Carolina, raised in Ohio, and reborn on Brooklyn's teeming streets. During 1960–61 he attended art school briefly, paying starvation dues and listening to Malcolm X. Spent 1962–63 on Manhattan's lower east side, ANECCA Art Exhibitions, Poetry Workshop, UMBRA Magazine: Striding along. (Touré 1963, 11)

As well as On Guard, Umbra and *Liberator*, Touré was active in the Revolutionary Action Movement (RAM), a leftist-internationalist organization which turned towards Maoism and advocated armed revolution in America; he served on the editorial board of the group's 'literary arm' *Black America* from 1963 to 1965. It was in the incendiary essays published in *Liberator* that Touré had his greatest impact: works such as 'Afro-American Youth and The Bandung World' and 'Keep on

Pushin': Rhythm and Blues as a Weapon' (1965) strongly influenced Baraka's own writing and set out a theory of revolutionary internationalism which emphasized the importance of African-American aesthetic practice in the liberation struggle. He also came to increasing prominence as a poet: in 1965, *Liberator* named him 'Poet of the Year' (Baraka was named 'Playwright of the Year'). Touré also served on the staff for *Black Dialogue* and as editor for the *Journal of Black Poetry*; with Larry Neal, he co-founded the journal *Afro World* in 1965 and the same year participated in Baraka's BART/S and organized the Harlem Uptown Youth Conference. Indeed, Ishmael Reed credits Touré with a significance equal to that of Baraka in BART/S, calling him its 'philosopher': 'if anybody is father of the Black Arts movement in New York it was Askia Touré' (Reed 2014B). Touré was also active in San Francisco and the South, particularly Mississippi and Atlanta, where, as he notes, he 'helped to lead SNCC from Civil Rights to Black Power' (Touré 2004). In 1966, he co-authored the SNCC's 'Black Power Position Paper' with William Ware and Donald Stone. He would go on to teach alongside Baraka and Sonia Sanchez in San Francisco in 1967 as part of the first Africana Studies programme in America, as well as working on the editorial board of *Soulbook*. Converting to Islam and renaming himself around 1968 (*BF*, 688; Touré, 'Jihad!', *Black World*, 1969, 10–17), Touré has continued to be active as a poet, activist and BAM historian, authoring notable works such as the epic *Dawnsong* (1999), which draw on African history and mythology as part of a fiercely anti-colonial praxis.

In the 1960s, Touré's Marxist-influenced, Third Worldist Black Nationalism was a key component of the Umbra aesthetic, linking the 'Movement' activism of the South with a keen sense of the growing militancy of urban radicalism of Malcolm X, in particular, and the necessity of linking African-American struggles against domestic racism to worldwide anti-imperialism in Vietnam, China and Cuba. In his poetry and his essays, this is figured through incantatory repetition, the use of apocalyptic, biblically inflected language and an insistent reference to non-Western history and to contemporaneous political struggles. Decades later, Lorenzo Thomas provided a cogent characterization of his work and its importance to the other Umbra poets.

> Touré is not, by any stretch of the imagination, a street poet, and he has never written in the contemporary vernacular […] His poetry and other writings develop from a global, and indeed, cosmic perspective. […] In the early days of the Umbra Workshop, he was deeply aware of the need to liberate African peoples everywhere. At a time when most of us were more concerned with what was passing in Alabama and with the contested rights of black people to participate in American democracy, Touré had on his wall for ready reference

a full-sized map of Africa (on which many nations that are now independent appeared as European colonial states). In the context of the Umbra group, Touré was an opener of directions and new fields of thought. (*EM*, 127–9)

It is a report on a street reading of the poem 'Cry Freedom' by Touré which opens Art Berger's 1963 article on Umbra for Communist journal *Masses and Mainstream*, the first major piece to appear on the workshop.

> On the corner of 126th Street and Seventh Avenue, more than 500 persons massed about a chunky, young Afro-American who declaimed in a reedy voice, electric [...] This was living poetry to a living audience, on the streets of the Harlem ghetto. *Verse armed to the teeth with dynamite*; lines that burned like a fuse to the bitter end, blowing degradation sky-high. The poet was Rolland Snellings of the Umbra Society, a new movement of Negro poets. The occasion was a rally on behalf of Mrs Willie Mae Mallory, freedom fighter, who is resisting being returned to Monroe, N.C. to face trumped up charges of kidnapping. (Berger 1963, 3)

Anticipating his influence on Baraka and participation in the BART/S experiment, Touré emerges as a talismanic figure not only for his 'electric' reading but for his presentation of politically charged poetry within an activist context. Mae Mallory, who had a background in Communist groups and had organized a highly visible protest against New York's school system in 1957, had participated in the On Guard protests in 1961, where she marched with Baraka and Calvin Hicks. As she recalled, when a security guard grabbed her, 'I cracked his head with my shoe heel. Then I wrapped my fist in the necktie of another guard' (Tyson, 237). An early advocate of armed self-defence, she had travelled to Monroe County the same year to visit Robert F. Williams and organize armed resistance against Ku Klux Klan (KKK) terror. She and Williams were falsely charged with kidnapping a white couple, leading Williams to flee to Cuba and to Mallory's imprisonment, and On Guard was active in the fight to prevent her extradition to Monroe County to face the kidnapping charges (Calvin Hicks was executive director of the Monroe Defense Committee). Touré, himself a member of groups which advocated armed revolution, was no stranger to such contexts, and his work both mobilized and was mobilized by then. The most overtly political of the Umbra poets, certainly at this stage, Touré's work, and its intersection with On Guard and with Mallory's cause, usefully illuminate intersections between radical activism and radical aesthetics that predate the far better-known work of the Black Arts and Black Power Movements several years later.

In 'Cry Freedom', literary and political radicalism are placed on an equal plane. A long poem in four sections, it was published in *Liberator* the summer before Umbra's first issue appeared, alongside visual art by Umbra members: Tom Feelings's drawing depicting a protest and a photograph of Touré by LeRoy McLucas. The poem's incantatory rejection of Ellisonian invisibility and its emphasis on linking conditions in the African-American ghetto to imperialism worldwide (for instance, Italian Fascism in Ethiopia (10)) hark back both to the earlier anti-imperialism of artists and activists such as Claude McKay and to the biblical tradition of prophecy – all this through specific reference to the On Guard protest of 1961. The opening dedication is to 'the black Nationalists, Matthew Meade and Mustapha Bahir', who had participated in the Lumumba protests (Tinson, 192), and, harking back to Thomas's own *détournement* of the *New York Times,* ironically juxtaposes the *Times* report on the protests with a statement of 'race' achievement belied by the continuing sufferings of African-Americans under the depredations of white supremacy.

> 'They were led by the mysterious man in Arab headdress.' (The *New York Times* on the UN Riots, February 1961)
>
> 'A century of "Negro" progress and freedom' (A 'Negro' publication). (Touré 1963, 9)

A note on the next page (presumably by Touré) explains further:

> Matthew Meade, young nationalist freedom-fighter and scholar, is typical of the breed of educated nationalist now leading colonial peoples to nationhood. He is one of the new generation of Afro-American militants (known to the 'black conservatives' as 'Africanists'), who are forging a new day for black people in colonialist North America.
>
> Mustapha Bahir, Harlem street speaker and U.N. demonstrator, who was recently accused of murdering a businessman in Harlem. This affair seemed to delight certain elements within the black community who made the most of it. (10)

In line with his sarcastic ventriloquizing of biased media reportage by both the white establishment and the black middle class, Touré rejects the labels placed on young radicals, artistic and political alike – 'Angry Generation, Lonely Generation, Black Renaissance, / New Negro, Black Nationalist, etc., etc.' – which 'classify me, hypnotise me, ostracize me; / Will me away from your sight' (10). The poem is in multiple parts and juxtaposes italicized, song-like repetitions with statements of solidarity and survival. Linking the UN protests to a rejection of black literary spokesmen – both Ellison, whose invisible man is repeatedly repudiated in the first section, and James Baldwin (who 'doesn't write of me. He has other hang-ups') – the poem is an anti-Ellisonian statement of identity and visibility and of solidarity with Meade and Bahir. Reflecting on the often-hostile media coverage which stigmatizes black radicals, Touré turns this into a statement of togetherness and purpose. The poem addresses the twin dilemmas of Ellisonian invisibility and stigmatized visibility – the 'classif[ications]' which

> will me away from your sight
> Hide me from the watchin' world; the 3/5 colored
> Watchin' world. (10)

But Touré insists that he addresses another audience:

> They see and hear; they care.
> They see and hear, they care.
> The 3/5 colored watchin' world. (10)

The final section repeatedly invokes Meade, 'my friend of down and out Brooklyn [...] Angry, American, western black man', repeatedly affirming '*Matthew, I walk with you*', 'Lion. Brother of my ebon heart' (10–11). The ties of friendship – ones themselves forged through shared involvement in political action – transpose onto the ties binding the speaker to the African-American people struggling against racism and, more broadly, to the international struggle against imperialism represented by 'the 3/5 colored watchin' world'. Insisting that the United States is a colonial power, and thus anticipating the theory of 'domestic' or 'internal' colonialism later adopted by Baraka and the BPP (Baraka 1971B, 65; Howe, 87–101), Touré rejects the reactionary gaze of the *Times* for that of other liberation movements who might look to the actions of African-Americans, just as African-Americans might look to them, 'From Cairo to Conakry, to Capetown, / to Chicago' (11). The individual refrain of the first section – 'I'm not an invisible man' (10) – now turns to a collective one, addressed to Meade:

> *We are not invisible men and Lord,*
> *if they don't free our people:*
> The heavens will open up and
> the western earth will tremble till
> the glass-house cities crumble to dust. (11)

The singular, non-invisible voice of the first section is now extended to the 'we' which includes not only Matthew but also 'my people' who are the poem's ultimate addressees. The poem concludes with an apocalyptic invocation typical of Touré's style (an aspect particularly influential on Baraka's nationalist work): liberation is figured through 'Holy Fire', the destruction of cities and the collapse of civilizations in language reminiscent of biblical plagues and prophecies against empire. All this is figured through music: not only through the repeated invocations of spirituals ('we shall overcome', 'let my people go', 'walk together chillun' (10–11)) but through numerous references to contemporaneous black musicians, who are united with activists, politicians and the biblical last trumpet in a defiant and even 'universal' ensemble, 'Pumpin rhythm; / Singing, dancing, improvisation of the last days of Christ' (10).

Matthew,
We'll sing the song of Fire
With Cecil and Ronnie,
Max and Abbie,
Miriam Makeba,
Walter and Nannie,
Jerry and Rita,
And Malcolm X [...]

Elijah shouts – from the mountaintops:
Let My People Go!

Matthew,
I walk with you
to the last trumpet call [...]

Sing the song of Fire!
Beat the tamborines! [sic]
Sing the Song of Death!
Ease the pain:

Cry Freedom!

(11)

Joined by Max Roach, Abbey Lincoln, Miriam Makeba and others, the poet here is singer, with italics indicating song, whether of Touré's own invention or quotations from spirituals and Civil Rights anthems. Opposing the disguised particularity by which white imperialism lays claim to universality, Touré insists:

My song, like
Rain, is universal.
Listen while I blow my horn.

(10)

As he would reiterate in essays throughout the 1960s, it is through music, above all, that Touré's call to international liberation is accomplished. In the 1965 essay 'Afro-American Youth and the Bandung World', Touré presents Third World liberation movements in terms of African-American music via an opening reference to Marx and Engels's *Communist Manifesto* and to Martha and the Vandellas' 1964 'riot-song' 'Dancing in the Streets'. Primarily a political essay reporting on urban insurrection and global anti-imperialism, the text also reads as something like a prose poem, which, like Touré's verse, plays with references to Marx, the Bible, spirituals and jazz through incantatory repetition.

> The spectre of a storm is haunting the Western World. [...] The Great Storm, the coming Black Revolution, is rolling in like a tornado; roaring from the east; shaking the moorings of the earth as it passes through countries ruled by oppressive regimes; [...] Yes, all over this sullen planet, the multi-colored 'hordes' of undernourished millions are on the move like never before in human history. They are moving to the rhythms of a New Song, a New Sound; dancing in the streets to a Universal Dream that haunts their wretched nights [...] From the steaming jungles of Viet Nam to the drought-ridden plains of India: Dancing in the Streets! From the great African savannahs to the peasant-ridden mountains of Guatemala: Dancing in the streets! Yes, the world's peoples are on the move – gathering forces for the Catharsis of History: the final War, the biblical Armageddon!

(Touré 1965, 4)

'There's no hiding place in a horn': A word on music

Reed's, Touré's and Thomas's poems were the most immediate reactions to the death of Lumumba and its relation to the political activism of Umbra members. By way of conclusion, I will briefly discuss poems by the elder Umbra members Raymond Patterson and Ray Durem as ways to further contextualize the deployment of African-American music alongside the internationalist politics exemplified by Umbra and On Guard. Music could be used both as spur to protest and as a way to mourn continuing injustice: notably, the fact that Lumumba's murder was not acknowledged, and the Congolese independence movement – as with the American liberation movements of the 1960s of which On Guard were early precursors – would be defeated and betrayed.

However ironized its citations of gospel, hymns and saints, Thomas's poem does, indeed, as Daniel Kane notes, borrow from 'African-American blues and church discourse' (Kane, 83). The line shouted by 'the New York/ beer-drinkers', 'You've crucified our saintly Lumumba' may echo the title of a leaflet handed out in Harlem, reported in Robert L. Teague's March 1961 *New York Times* column on the rise of a nascent Black Power movement, which mentions the UN protest in its opening sentences: 'They've lynched our saviour, Lumumba, in the old fashion Southern style' (Teague, 1). Likewise, in 'Patrice', Reed's first-name address to Lumumba both critiques the disrespect with which he was treated by world leaders and affects mournful intimacy with a lost martyr. Rhetoric such as that found in the Harlem leaflet, by which Lumumba is figured as martyr, Christ figure, saint and ordinary man, thus feeds from the language of street protest and activism into the poetry produced by members of Umbra. While Thomas, Reed, Touré and, as we'll see, Durem, figure Lumumba and Third World politics through the more aggressive and experimental forms of bop and free jazz, Raymond Patterson's 'Lumumba Blues' is written in a more conventional blues form. The poem explicitly turns towards the forms of African-American music not simply as reference but as a formal mode by which to figure a grief at once political and personal. One of the older members of Umbra, Patterson had been a member of the Harlem Writers Guild alongside Sarah E. Wright and Rosa Guy, and his reading with Calvin Hernton in 1957, and the organizing of a reading series featuring future Umbra poets in Harlem in 1960, formed an important base for what would crystallize as Umbra in the summer of 1962 (Oren 1984, 168, 181 n.2). That his 'Lumumba Blues' was written nearly two decades after the activities of Umbra and On Guard indicates the extent to which these events continued to reverberate long after their initial moment. Indeed, the poem's late date of composition only serves to exacerbate its status as a poem of lament in which, as with the elegies for Malcolm X and John Coltrane that would become characteristic of Black Arts writing, the belatedness felt when responding to the murder of political leaders and the tension between feelings of despair and appeals towards continuation of struggle are cemented by the formal structure.

Patterson's poem is, like much of his work, written in blues form: a structure in which repetition and lament are closely entwined. As Reed had addressed Lumumba by his first name in a gesture of intimacy, so Patterson presents the Congolese leader as a victim, 'a poor black boy', who 'didn't want much, just like you and me'. The poem recalls the trope of Lumumba as lynch victim present in the Harlem street leaflet and again found in Touré's *From the Pyramids to the Projects* (Touré 1990).

> Poor ole Lumumba
> Thought Freedom had a friend.
> Poor Lumumba,
> He thought Freedom had a friend.
> Well they blinded both his eyes
> And lynched him in the end.
>
> Lord, Lumumba! See what they did to you!
> Poor black boy, I see what they did to you.
> I can't help feeling they done that to me, too.
>
> Freedom! Lumumba,
> I hear you calling still.
> Freedom! Oh, Freedom!
> I hear you calling still.
> I won't forget,
> Don't think I ever will.
>
> (Patterson 1989, 36)

Patterson here focuses on those elements of mourning exemplified by the blues. At the same time, as the poem moves from the past to the present tense, in which 'I hear you calling still', the poem retains a hopeful attitude towards 'Freedom', based on the refusal to 'forget', which tempers its tones of lament. In an era when the anti-colonial revolts of the 1960s were frequently in danger of co-option or outright defeat, Patterson suggests that Lumumba's suffering, with which the speaker viscerally identifies, forms the basis for international, pan-African solidarity, motivating them to continue the struggle against the forces which led to his murder. As he writes, 'Take folks more than a little to forget that crime' (36).

In his poem 'Hipping the Hip', published posthumously in *Umbra*'s third issue, Ray Durem exhibits a more starkly militant stance. The poem does not mention Lumumba but likewise links anti-colonial politics to African-American cultural forms. Durem's adaptation of 'hip' discourse is, as in much of his work, satirically two pronged: he mocks the (predominantly white) Mailer-esque 'white negro' hipsters who exploit Afro-American culture (also a target of 'The Inverted Square', satirically dedicated to Lawrence Ferlinghetti and published in the same issue, and David Henderson's 'The Ofay and the Nigger', published in the first issue). At the same time, he adopts the 'cool pose' and hip language of jazz musicians as a subversive force.

HIPPING THE HIP

Juice
is no use,
and 'H'
don't pay!

I guess revolution
is the only way

Blues – is a tear
Bop – a fear
of reality.
There's no hiding place in a horn

Chinese may be lame
but they ain't tame

Mau Mau only got a five-tone scale
but when it comes to Freedom, Jim –
they wail!

dig?

(*Umbra Anthology*, 59)

Durem links the Kenyan anti-colonialist Mau Mau guerrilla fighters, Maoist China and African-American blues and bebop. These parallels between music and political insurrection do not subordinate the one to the other, and Durem, as Thomas, plays with the tokenism of attributing too great a political agency to certain cultural forms. While the 'hip' white audience whom Durem addresses find their forms of rebellion in 'H'(eroin), alcohol, the blues and jazz, they understand neither the culture from which musical forms such as the blues and jazz emerge, nor the spirit of international solidarity in which they are produced. The five-tone scale of pentatonic African music serves as a metaphor for the Mau Mau's political agency and castigates the stigmatization of Africa as a 'backwards' nation predominant in racist caricatures of the Mau Mau as brutal savages (of the kind that recur in the descriptions of the Camerounaise quoted in Thomas's poem). For Durem, music as metaphor points out both the discrepancies of a commitment solely to an aesthetic (or worse, lifestyle) radicalism and the internationalist links between domestic and Third World liberation movements (Kelley, 65–6). Both Durem and Thomas seek to weaponize stereotype and cultural appropriation, turning them back on their creators, maintaining an ironized distance which does not preclude genuine political belief. We must also not forget that many jazz musicians at the time *were* involved in political activism: Archie Shepp was a member of both Umbra and On Guard, while Max Roach and Abbey Lincoln were involved with the 1961 UN protest and produced fiery denunciations of international and domestic racism on albums such as *We Insist! Freedom Now* (1961). Whatever the representational traps these poems self-consciously negotiate, 'when it comes to freedom', such music – along with the poems – continues to 'wail'.

Conclusion

As Konstantina Karageorgos notes, the activities around the 'July Sojourn' in Cuba and Fidel Castro's visit to Harlem in 1960 and the Lumumba Protest in 1961 manifested a neglected current of black internationalism, often with ties to Communist organizations or, at least, non-aligned Marxist affiliation – as attested in particular by the involvement of Calvin Hicks, Rosa Guy and Sarah E. Wright – which reliance on nationalist-inflected, anti-Marxist accounts by Baraka and Cruse can relegate to the background (Karageorgos, 129–30). Nonetheless, the activism around Cuba and the Congo in which Baraka, Wright and Hicks were centrally involved continued beyond the demise of On Guard. In January 1965, Baraka edited the 'black revolutionary newspaper' *In/Formation* under the auspices of Totem Press (the newspaper is listed as a 'pre-publication copy' and appears never have fully made it to press). Firmly internationalist in orientation, the editorial proclaims:

> IN/FORMATION will be distributed internationally. It will cover the world, in order to spread specific word of the American black man's plight, but also to bring home hard to our own people the similarity of their oppression with the other peoples in Africa, Asia, and Latin America. (*In/Formation*, 2)

As Lorenzo Thomas notes, *In/Formation* was a group postdating the Organization of Young Men and On Guard and predating BART/S. Formed in summer 1964 'for the purposes of publishing an investigative community newspaper for the

Village' and responding in particular to tensions arising from the Harlem Riots, the short-lived group once again involved the participation of a number of Umbra members (*EM*, 142–3). From its title – which echoes the military vocabulary of On Guard (as Sarah E. Wright put it, 'this is time to rally all of us *on time* to get in the march for freedom – together!') – to its internationalist focus, the organization was clearly modelled on the activity around On Guard (Wood, 163). Notably, the newspaper, of which Calvin Hicks is listed as a member of staff alongside Baraka, A.B. Spellman, Leroy McLucas and the Patterson brothers, contains an article by Spellman, 'Uncle Charlie in the Congo', which retreads the details surrounding Lumumba's death and follows through to subsequent developments (*In/Formation*, 3, 7–8).

Both *In/Formation* and the poems by Umbra members discussed above form part of a growing trend of Third World Internationalism that would increasingly become central to the BAM and the Black Power Movement, which continued to cite Lumumba as hero and martyr. He appears, for instance, in the pantheon of victims in Baraka's manifesto 'The Revolutionary Theatre', on the Wall of Respect painted by the Visual Arts Workshop of the Organization of Black American Culture (OBAC) in Chicago, and in later poems by Umbra members Archie Shepp ('Poem for Malcolm/Mama Rose') and Rashidah Ismaili ('Bajji'), as well as in poems by Ted Joans, Jayne Cortez and others (Ismaili, 33–4; Ira Dworkin). Both African-American Communist Nelson Peery and Black Panther Bobby Seale named their sons after him; on the tenth anniversary of his 1960 Independence Day speech, the Black Panther newspaper argued: 'By liberating North America and in the reality of intercommunalism we therefore liberate the Congo and Lumumba's death will at last be avenged. His dream will be reality.' Yet the involvement of British and American intelligence agencies was never acknowledged, and the Congo remained mired in civil war. More locally, in New York, On Guard and Umbra's leftist internationalism would transition to the separatist rhetoric espoused by Baraka and Ron Karenga, a politics Baraka himself would later characterize as 'narrow nationalism' (*Autobiography*, 298). For all the internationalist possibility offered by Ray Durem's poem, it was a text by Durem that caused Umbra's ultimate split, and Durem himself died virtually unknown in 1963, following decades in geographical isolation in Mexico under constant FBI surveillance. Rejecting the white chauvinism of the Communist Party, after having fought in the International Brigades, Durem's proto-nationalism never found a broader movement within which to house itself.

Likewise, in many ways, the ultimate tragedy of this moment is that Umbra never achieved sufficient prominence to affect the course of black radical aesthetics in an open or acknowledged way, even if their influence spread widely in unacknowledged ways. Baraka would not (re-)discover the potentials of a left-wing, internationalist politics until the mid-1970s by which point the momentum for a mass movement was severely hampered by the ravages of COINTELPRO, police brutality, political assassination and the emergence of post-Fordism. In downplaying the role of the Umbra writers, whose activities had already manifested such a politics, and in seeing the moment of the early 1960s solely as one of bohemian confusion (in line with Baraka's and Harold Cruse's accounts), we also lose the sense of this moment of possibility. Work such as James Smethurst's comprehensive account of the BAM has begun to suggest that the historical recovery of such moments allows for revisions of the standard account, moving beyond a focus on individuals and broad trends and giving more emphasis to collective struggle. But the work is only just beginning.

2

'Poems That Kill': Amiri Baraka's Magic Words

On Guard's transition into Umbra during the early 1960s marked an early stage of possibility. I now turn to Amiri Baraka, suggesting ways in which Baraka's much better-known work of the mid-to-late 1960s grapples with related issues of political tactics, (self-)representation and the use of violence. Emerging from the climate created through Umbra and On Guard, Baraka's poems transition into the militant demands of a new, Black Power consciousness. Though these poems share a similarly sceptical, critical function to those of the Umbra poets, they also seek more comprehensively to blur the lines between word and world, poem and weapon, aesthetic intervention and political action.

Beginning in 1963, when Baraka was on the brink of national success with the Obie Award–winning play *Dutchman*, moving through to 1965, the year of his move away from the East Village, the founding of BART/S, and his turn towards nationalism, and ending with his trial for weapons possession following the 1967 Newark Rebellion, I offer readings of three poems which chart a stage in Baraka's development at a time of intense turmoil. The first is 'Black Dada Nihilismus' (1963), whose presentation of acts of violence ensures that it remains one of his most contentious works. The second is 'Black Art' (1965) in which the context of the BART/S in Harlem offers a new sense of political and aesthetic possibility. The third is 'Black People!' (1967), whose deployment in Baraka's trial saw it become an icon of the dictum, put forward in a 1968 broadside protesting Baraka's arrest, that 'Poetry is Revolution' (Van Newkirk). Baraka's poetry of the mid-1960s, in particular, 'Black Dada Nihilismus', has often been read as a polemical screed. However, I argue that such work is far more complex and knowing in its broad referential range. Re-examining these poems in depth allows us to see just how fully Baraka critically engages with the American poetic tradition via such figures as Joyce Kilmer, Archibald MacLeish, William Carlos Williams and Jack Spicer, as well as with Hermeticism, magic and histories of imperial violence. Emphasizing the poems' references to both international and local politics – Lumumba, the FLN, and the Harlem and Newark Rebellions – shows us to see that they did not emerge from a vacuum. Often referencing the same political conflicts as the Umbra poets, Baraka's concerns emerge as neither singular nor unprecedented, charting the attempt to move from isolation into a viable collective voice to which Umbra was already committed.

'Black Dada Nihilismus' (1963): 'A cult of death'

Initially published in *Evergreen Review* in early 1963, and reprinted in *The Dead Lecturer* the following year, 'Black Dada Nihilismus' remains one of Baraka's most notorious poems (Baraka 1963B; *TDL*, 61–4). Prefiguring his move from the East Village, the poem has come to exemplify a rhetoric of violence highly influential in the development of Black Arts writing. Baraka's biographer Jerry Gafio Watts sees the poem as 'moral perversion' disguised as 'revolutionary credibility', while Edward Margolies describes it as 'a destruction of syntax, order, and sense [...] an expression of hostility [...] rage [and] contempt' raised to the level of a 'monomaniacal obsession' in which 'fragments of fantasy, feeling, and ideas [are] tossed together in a whirlpool of hysteria' (Watts, 530–1, n.22; Margolies, 194–5). Watts's and Margolies's assessments are sweepingly judgemental and crude: they are profound misreadings of the poem. The multifaceted and ambiguous address of 'Black Dada' and its densely referential, circular structure cover the entire span of Western imperial history, challenging existing stereotypes and political strategies. But the poem remains contentious. Is Baraka really, as Werner Sollors has claimed, 'in love with racial violence as a means to exorcize the middleclass Negro's cultural complicity with oppression' (92)? Does he present the 'nihilist joy' of a 'bloody Weltgeist'? Or is the poem instead more akin to Sean Bonney's characterization, as a Du Boisian 'sorrow song', which figures anti-imperialist revolution as still trapped within the forms which have generated it, and from which it seeks to break out (Bonney, 101)?

Baraka's relatively infrequent readings of the poem are far from what Sollors calls a 'screaming incitement' (Sollors, 92). At the Asilomar Negro Writers Conference – a five-day conference held by the University of California at Berkeley in Asilomar State Park in August 1964 – Baraka read 'Black Dada' as part of a set with Gwendolyn Brooks. Coordinated by Herbert Hill, the (white) labour secretary of the NAACP, and a former American Socialist Workers Party (SWP) member, the conference took place in luxurious surroundings, a far cry from the urban environments in which Umbra's work had flourished or, indeed, from Baraka's own involvement in East Village poetry scenes. As Hoyt W. Fuller noted in his conference report for *Ebony* later that year:

> The conference [...] had been advertised for months before it finally convened on the grounds of California's rustic Asilomar State Park August 5, and some 200 writers, teachers, social workers, students, housewives, artists and intellectuals took up residence – at $100 a head – in the two dozen or so redwood lodges to spend five rather hectic days meeting, listening to, and arguing with the galaxy of Negro writers – and each other – among the ponderosa pines and cypresses there beside the mild Pacific. (Fuller 1964, 130)

Fuller further notes that, of the 200 attendees at the conference, the majority were white (127). While Fuller's piece wryly ironizes the racial dynamics of the conference, dwelling in something like the style of a travel brochure on 'the more certain pleasures of night clubs in Monterey, scenic drives around the fabulous peninsula or private parties in the lodges', in the pages of *Ebony*, it was itself juxtaposed with unintended irony with advertisements for wigs and hair straighteners (131). Within this context – in which James Baldwin and Ralph Ellison, along with Baraka, Arna Bontemps, Gwendolyn Brooks, Nat Hentoff and others, were the advertised 'faculty members' – Baraka's participation caused some controversy, attesting to his growing public profile (indeed, the interview with Louis Armstrong which immediately follows Fuller's report in the pages of Ebony shows Armstrong reading Baraka's *The Dead Lecturer*). As Fuller notes:

> LeRoi Jones, the waspish poet-playwright, struck fire with the audience. His major address dealt with 'Philistinism and the Negro Writer', but his asides on the sterility of the Negro middle class drew blood. (132)

Baraka's conscious radicalism was a polarizing force: his paper was challenged by what Fuller calls 'a coterie of California-born young intellectuals who, incredibly enough, publicly suffered from the Negro middle class identity syndrome', while Baraka was surrounded by a 'clique of younger Californians, un-affectionately dubbed the "Mau-Mau" by its denigrators', which appears to have included Berkeley social worker and SNCC activist Myrtle Glascoe and *San Francisco Sun* reporter Bettye Jean Hughes (132, 134). Despite this, Baraka's reading of 'Black Dada' appears to have had less impact than one might expect from the poem's reputation: indeed, Fuller notes of Baraka's reading with Gwendolyn Brooks that both authors were 'alert to the tension in the audience created by strong partisan feelings about their different styles, and displaying a kind of respectful deference rare among poets' (134).

Introducing the poem at his Asilomar reading, Baraka reads out the title, pausing to gloss each word with understated irony:

> which, uh, I think you know what black means. [*Laughter*] I think you know what dada means, whether, daddy, or, say a movement in France, uh, dedicated to restoring fresh looks at the world. And nihilismus is simply a Latinisation, or making nihilism into a Latinic phrase. (Baraka 1964B)

Addressing a predominantly white audience at a conference, sponsored by the University of California, which still adopted the usage 'Negro', Baraka's 'I think you know what black means' plays on a terminological instability acknowledged by the audience's laughter. The poem stands in awkward relation to the titular spirit of 'black dada' – a spirit fused from the contested notion of 'blackness', the idea of forbears, the European artistic avant-garde and the philosophical-political notion of Nihilism. As we shall see, the poem pre-emptively ironizes its own claims to transgressive agency. Baraka's ironic 'gloss' suggests that 'what black means' is both cripplingly under- and overdetermined, caught between racist signifiers of primitive violence and the lack of alternative vocabularies for self-definition. In 1960, Baraka had refused the roles into which black writers were forced:

> I'm fully conscious all the time that I am an American Negro because it's part of my life. But I know also that if I want to say, 'I see a bus full of people,' I don't have to say, 'I am a Negro seeing a bus full of people.' (*Conversations*, 6–7)

Four years later, however, he directly refuted this statement, insisting: 'I don't think I am seeing a bus full of people. I think I am a *Negro* seeing a bus full of people' (Sollors, 74; Eberstadt). Likewise, in 'Philistinism and the Negro Writer', the paper delivered at the Asilomar Conference which, as Fuller put it, 'drew blood', he argued:

> The first thing the Negro writer has to say is, 'Well, I am a Negro', which is a great, dramatic thing [...] If I point out a bird, a black man has pointed out that bird, and it is the weight of that experience in me and the way I get it from where it is to you that says whether or not I am a writer. (Baraka 1966D, 55–6)

Yet the poem itself refuses any stable 'black' persona. A three-page poem in two parts, 'Black Dada Nihilismus' begins with a full stop.

>   Against what light
> is false what breath
> sucked, for deadness.
>
> (*TDL*, 61)

This opposition to light implicitly rejects the metaphorical claims of Enlightenment philosophy. Refusing Eurocentric notions of progress, which exclude black life from the West's ensemble, the opening full stop – a marker of an absent preceding sentence, which cannot be sounded – loops back from the unpunctuated concluding line, establishing the poem's circularity and its oscillation between noise and silence, black and white, light and dark. Having rejected both the false light of Enlightenment and that of Christianity (*TDL*, 61), Baraka critiques those who seek to assimilate with the dominant American culture, erasing the visible signs of their race: 'the ugly silent deaths of Jews under // the surgeon's knife' (*TDL*, 61–2). Deploying what Sean Bonney calls 'remarkably callous' parallels between plastic surgery and surgical experiments under the Nazis, Baraka likens the indifference of middle-class Jews in pre-Holocaust Germany, 'who believed that it was only the poor Jews who would suffer', to the Gandhian-Christian non-violence espoused by the black middle class ('the umbrella'd jesus'), presenting both as acts of self-mutilation (Bonney, 96; Goffman, 100–4; *H*, 149–50; 1966D, 60–1).

Against such processes, Black Dada forms a Hermetic cult.

B.D.N., for the secret men, Hermes, the

blacker art. Thievery (ahh, they return
those secret gold killers. Inquisitors
of the cocktail hour […]

(*TDL*, 62)

Détourning the opening phrase of Fascist sympathizer Ezra Pound's 'The Return', these 'secret gold killers' are at once the Conquistadors who killed Aztec leader Moctezuma, the murderers of Patrice Lumumba in the Congo, the forces of the Spanish inquisition and New York socialites whose debates elide racial violence. Prefiguring the calls to Black Dada in the second section, the poem invokes 'the blacker art' of Hermes Trismegistus:

[…] Trismegistus, have

them, in their transmutation, from stone
to bleeding pearl, from lead to burning
Looting […]

(*TDL*, 62)

A syncretic combination of the Greek god Hermes and the Egyptian god Thoth who would become the patron of alchemy and astrology, Baraka later claimed Hermes Trismegistus as an 'Occult Teacher of Black People' (Baraka 1969D). Here, Hermes's transmutation reverses the traditional alchemical progression from 'Nigedro' (blackness, putrefaction, decomposition) to 'albedo' (whiteness), parodying the washing away of impurities as 'murder, the cleansed purpose' and presenting the highest stage of transmutation as 'burning/looting' (61–2). These lines refer not only to acts of imperialist violence but also to black urban insurrection and to the reversal of value enacted by black rioters to which we will return in the closing analysis of 'Black People!'. 'Burning/looting' is turned back on the West through cultic, alchemical means, which simultaneously reveal the cultic basis of Western imperial power. It is this which allows the speaker, at the close of the first section, to 'find the West // a grey hideous space' (*TDL*, 62).

Emerging in a series of tightly packed three-line stanzas, the poem's second section begins with a gesture of disavowal.

> From Sartre, a white man, it gave
> the last breath. And we beg him die,
> before he is killed.
>
> (*TDL*, 63)

Sartre's introduction to Frantz Fanon's *The Wretched of the Earth* had argued that, given the extreme brutality of French colonial conduct in Algeria, white Europeans 'must face that unexpected revelation, the strip-tease of our humanism', revealed as 'nothing but an ideology of lies, a perfect justification for pillage' (Fanon 1963, 24–5). In 'Black Dada', Sartre's own 'last breath' is the last gasp of the West's 'grey hideous space'. He serves as a representative of the West whose death he predicts: the poem's solidarity does not extend to even the most militant of its white allies. But members of the Black Dada cult possess only a limited capacity for violence:

> [...] Plastique, we
>
> do not have, only thin heroic blades.
> The razor. [...]
>
> (*TDL*, 63)

Baraka draws a contrast between the 'plastique' (plastic explosives) deployed by the French OAS (*Organisation Armée Secrée*) – a far right, anti-independence terrorist group – and the weaponry available to their opponents (Bonney, 97).

These lines also echo Sartre's ventriloquization of Fanon in his introduction to *The Wretched of the Earth*: 'Let us start fighting; and if we've no other arms, the waiting knife's enough' (Fanon 1963, 12–13, 63–6). Via Fanon's and Sartre's writing on Third World struggles, Baraka draws out the problems of insurrectionary strategy discussed in earlier letters to Ed Dorn (Pisano, 100, 108–9, 115–16). The assassins lack both adequate weaponry to conduct armed struggle and a public voice: as with Thomas's 'A Tale of Two Cities', they are denied a presence equal to that of colonial forces on the world media stage.

Despite their violence, elided with that of the human sacrifices performed by Aztec priests ('why you carry knives? Or brutaled lumps of / heart?'), these murderers lack the revolutionary capacity of the Algerian FLN. Instead, they remain integrated with American society.

> [...] Why you stay, where they can
> reach? Why you sit, or stand, or walk
> in this place, a window on a dark
>
> warehouse. Where the minds packed in
> straw. New homes, these towers, for those
> lacking money or art [...]

(*TDL*, 63)

These lines simultaneously allude to public housing projects for the poor – 'those / lacking money or art' – and to the 'brain factory' or 'ivory tower' of the academy, 'where the minds packed in / straw'. Baraka had himself studied at the Historically Black Howard University and frequently denounced what he saw as the delusion of middle-class success that such institutions fostered, calling Howard 'a monument to the missionary mentality'; here, he once more critiques the assimilation of the African-American middle class via the false notion of social ascent (Newfield, 12; Baraka 1966D, 51–2; Hare). In response, Black Dada's 'cult of death' emerges from under the earth, via another allusion to Fanon, to take revenge on white America.

> [...] A cult of death,
>
> need of the simple striking arm under
> the streetlamp. The cutters, from under
> their rented earth [...]

(*TDL*, 63)

This chthonic emergence explodes into an invocation to Black Dada which forms the poem's most infamous passage.

> [...] Come up, black dada

nihilismus. Rape the white girls. Rape
their fathers. Cut the mothers' throats.
Black dada nihilismus, choke my friends [...]

(*TDL*, 63)

Largely due to these lines, the poem is often seen to embody what Ajuan Maria Mance calls 'a new aesthetic of masculine anger and might' – not least through its citation in Eldridge Cleaver's 1968 *Soul on Ice* (Cleaver 1968, 26; Mance, 211). This sexualized rhetoric of violence would recur in many BAM poems and is typical of the misogynist targeting of white women found in Baraka's work of the period (*TDL*, 48–53; *BF*, 576). Though these lines react to the racist myth of the black rapist – a myth used to justify the brutal lynching of numerous black men during the nineteenth and twentieth centuries (Davis, 172–201) – their inhabitation of this stereotype is deeply problematic. As Alice Walker suggested in 1977, many read the poem as

> advice to young black male insurrectionaries (women were not told what to do with *their* rebelliousness). [...] It was clear that [Baraka] meant [these lines] literally. (Walker, 92)

Yet, for all Baraka's misogyny, these lines serve not as an instruction manual for young male revolutionaries but as a despairing mimicry of racial and sexual stereotype. The call to Black Dada is divided across two stanzas, introducing an element of prosodic hesitancy at the very moment of apparent certainty (Kim, 347). Emphasizing the deliberately artificial construction 'nihilismus', Baraka undercuts and aestheticizes the force of murder and rage it designates. By characterizing the nihilistic rage that leads to rape and murder in terms of a European avant-garde art movement, and rendering the word 'nihilism' in 'Latinic' form, Baraka suggests that this violence is already mediated through white stereotypes of the violent, rapacious black male which come to personify a whole philosophical concept.

In a symposium published in *Negro Digest* in September 1964, Baraka responds to the statement 'your audience, I would imagine, is white', with 'it would have to be' (Baraka 1964E, 20). 'Black Dada' first appeared through the associated enterprises of the *Evergreen Review* and Grove Press, whose publications were mainly received by a white, middle-class audience (Glass, 120–1). Considering which audiences actually received and read the poem's invocation is crucial to its meaning. The poem is painfully aware of this dilemma, its self-aware performance of 'what black means' linking it to the poems by Reed and Thomas analysed in the first chapter, which chart the difficulties not only of practical resistance to imperialism but within the sphere of representation in which such conflicts are framed.

In this regard, 'Black Dada' usefully compares to another poem by Thomas, written the following year, which more archly deploys the stereotype of the black male rapist in relation to anti-colonial revolution. As well as *Umbra* and *Liberator*, Thomas often published in New York School venues such as Ted Berrigan's *C*, venues in which, as he would later note, 'reference to the social and political situation of black people in the United States' might attain a different emphasis (Thomas 1983, 6). Thomas's 'The Unnatural Life' was published in the first issue of *Lines*, a magazine edited by Aram Saroyan which featured white poets such as Berrigan, Fielding Dawson, Ted Greenwald and Tony Towle, and would have been read by a primarily white audience (Thomas 1964, n.p.; *TB*, 17). While Baraka responds, to some extent, by aiming to shock a white readership, Thomas more explicitly ironizes the rape/murder scenario found in 'Black Dada' within the context of a black revolution. The poem's second stanza begins: 'And the idea of revolution is also depicted' (*TB*, 17). The 'depiction' of this revolution is deliberately placed in the passive voice, removing the subject who does the depicting, as if the idea of revolution were a subject for literary criticism. This 'idea' is framed through written signifiers: the NOI's newspaper, *Muhammad Speaks*, and the work of the Négritude writers, via an epigraph from Aimé Césaire and a reference to Leopold Senghor which ironically echoes the enthusiastic presentation of such work by New York School poets such as Frank O'Hara.[1]

> I have been so busy of late, translating
> 'Two or Three Chants' by Leopold Senghor and
> Thinking about the coming revolution.
>
> (*TB*, 17)

However, the speaker soon turns from the activities of translation, reading and thinking to fantasies of murderous violence, linked to the notion espoused in the 'Supreme Alphabet' of the Five Percenters, a group who had formed in Harlem in 1964 after splitting from the NOI, that 'everything is going to be everything'.

The cashier returns and pays for his life
Because everything is going to be everything.
My copy of Muhammad Speaks covers the table and the wind, and
The door hanging open, frightened because I am here
That I might forget these young delusions of love, afraid
As I emerge from my fashionable jacket my brain turns
Black and hateful Like a beast, your color rising in my nose
And you are raped and murdered in the usual manner.

(Thomas 1964; *TB*, 17)

Like Baraka, Thomas's 'idea of revolution' invokes the stereotype of the black rapist, emphasizing that this paranoid white fantasy of black revenge has become the 'usual manner' of depictions of blackness and of black revolution. Unlike Baraka, Thomas directly addresses a second-person auditor, playing up the racial divide between (black) speaker and (white) reader. The absence of a collective pronoun in Thomas's poem renders the speaker's 'revolution' isolated and individualized: in the words of the poem's epigraph, from Aimé Césaire: 'What I am is a man alone / imprisoned in white' (17). Referencing the contentious issue of interracial relations between black men and white women – an issue which has been cited as one of the reasons for the breakdown of On Guard, and as causing tensions within Umbra itself (Oren 1984, 178–80; Ismaili, 586; Touré 1964, 14–15; *Umbra* II, 18) – 'young delusions of love' suggests both the Christian vocabulary of non-violence opposed by the NOI and sexual relations. Thomas plays on the racist notion that, once the speaker 'emerge[s] from my fashionable jacket', they will 'turn black and hateful'. In this, they are provoked by the threat of emergent Black Nationalism as seen in the references to the Five Percenters and to *Muhammad Speaks*.

These references to nationalism, as with the elision of the conflicts in Cameroon, the Congo and New York in 'A Tale of Two Cities', are complex ways of (re)figuring stereotypical white mediations of black militancy, which stigmatize any such militancy as violent atavism, invoking the myth of the black rapist used to justify Klan violence and the lynching of thousands of African-American men. Though Thomas's response is more ironic and less despairing than Baraka's – the poem ending with an expression of parodically genteel exasperation: 'I should never have moved into your neighborhood!' (*TB*, 18) – both poems respond to the representational dilemmas facing figurations of black militancy as atavistic pathology.

In both 'The Unnatural Life' and 'Black Dada Nihilismus', revolutionary violence can only be expressed through the minstrel stereotype of black men as rapists and murderers. These are complex, context-dependent performative gestures which resist a stable subject position. There is certainly despair here, but there is also a biting, satirical humour. Thomas would later suggest the influence on Baraka of Robert Desnos's radio show based on the murderous sociopath Fantômas, as well as the third part of Kenneth Koch's 'Fresh Air' (1955), which appeared alongside work by Baraka in *The New American Poetry* and which gleefully and comically imagines the elaborate murders of academic poets by 'the Strangler' (Thomas 2008, 112–15).[2]

> Summer in the trees! 'It is time to strangle several bad poets.'
> The yellow hobbyhorse rocks to and fro, and from the chimney
> Drops the Strangler! The white and pink roses are slightly agitated by the
>   struggle,
> But afterwards beside the dead 'poet' they cuddle up comfortably against their
>   vase. They are safer now, no one will compare them to the sea.
>
> Here on the railroad train, one more time, is the Strangler.
> He is going to get that one there, who is on his way to a poetry reading.
> Agh! Biff! A body falls to the moving floor.
>
> (Koch, 232)

There are further predecessors such as Kenneth Rexroth's 'Thou Shalt Not Kill' (1953). Thomas's comment is made in relation to the later 'Black Art' but applies more easily to 'Black Dada', which first appeared when Baraka was still very much a part of the New York poetry scene, alongside Koch. While Black Dada is partly an impersonation of an impersonation, a minstrel stereotype turned back on its creators, considering the influence of Koch opens up another dimension. The poem reads somewhat differently if it is also based on the figure of a white murderer of whites which had already assumed semi-jocular connotations within the poetry circles of which Baraka was a part. Indeed, viewed from this angle, Koch's poem in fact presents 'the Strangler' as *more* heroic than Baraka's murderers. While the tone of both poems is very different, it seems strange to read 'Black Dada Nihilismus' as a straightforward endorsement of violence when such considerations never even occur to readers of 'Fresh Air'.

Baraka's poem can be seen as rewriting and extending Koch's. Whereas Koch refers to literary figures of satire, Baraka refers to the victims of imperialism and to his former allies: 'Black dada nihilismus, choke my friends / in their bedrooms with their drinks spilling' (*TDL*, 63). The figures being attacked are not only academic poets but 'my friends' who define themselves *against* academic poets. Baraka's increasing frustration with the lack of political commitment among white New York poetry circles, and his registration of the irony that Koch himself was now on the way to becoming an academic, saw him write in a letter to Ed Dorn, 'That cat's flipped right into the Phd mambo. That Dr. Koch shit has completely aborted his finer instincts I wd say', and, later 'FUCK KENNETH KOCH' (Pisano, 129, 158). The increasing distance between Koch and Baraka is further indicated by the fact the group Black Mask 'assassinated' Koch with blanks in protest at Baraka's conviction following the 1967 Newark Rebellion (Kane, 171–3). Koch's poem creates a kind of comedic collectivity – itself dependent on the context of poetry communities in which it could be understood as a pertinent comic statement – through the imagined destruction of another collective to which it is in opposition (that of academic poets). Nearly ten years later, Baraka seems to undermine the possibility of *any* determinate and viable collective. His imperial enemies are at once more dangerous, and his poetic murder of them more anguished in its use of stereotype.

Koch's murders are rendered through playful, cartoon onomatopoeia: 'Agh! Biff! A body falls to the moving floor' (Koch, 232). These lines manifest a playful pleasure in sound, incorporating that which is 'non-poetic' into the poem as part of its assassination of pretentious literati. Though just as self-aware, the use of sound in 'Black Dada' is far less playful. Following the call to 'choke my friends', the poem describes the sound of its own preceding invocation in lines which finally break from the previous three-line stanza form.

> Black scream
> and chant, scream,
> and dull, un
> earthly
>
> hollering [...]

(*TDL*, 63–4)

Baraka's earlier work presents the condition of inarticulacy as one of crippling powerlessness, of enforced or acquiescent silencing associated with the Middle Passage, with a solipsistic Modernist pose inadequate to political reality, and with self-absorption, fantasy and mute submission to historical injustice

(*TDL*, 11, 30, 31, 45; *BM*, 44, 62). Yet against such 'ugly silent deaths', this 'black scream' is no simple moment of release. Thoth, the Egyptian ancestor of Black Dada's Hermes, is the god of writing, yet his place within the Black Dada cult does not lead to a written articulation of grievance but to a fresh act of silent or screaming illegibility. The attempt to recover black mythologies is still inarticulate, hesitant and uncertain. The only alternative to silence is the 'black scream' which, serving as the return of the repressed, cannot be articulated as language. And even this initial 'scream / and chant' returns in the following lines as 'scream, / and dull, un/earthly / hollering'. Anticipating precisely the criticism subsequently made against it as 'screaming incitement' (Sollors, 92), the poem describes both the sound of Black Dada itself and its own calls to Black Dada. The possibilities of incantatory, repetitive oral effects subsequently deployed in Baraka's nationalist work (*BM*, 151–2, 155, 189–91; *BF*, 653–6; 1967c) are blunted by the description of Black Dada's 'un/earthly hollering' as 'dull', turning murderous intensity into bathetic boredom. Self-consciously anticipating the limitations of rhetorical calls to violence, Baraka's poem, like Thomas's 'A Tale of Two Cities' and 'The Unnatural Life', is aware of the ways it reinforces already-existent stereotypes of black criminality. Its form tests the limit of the content it has often been taken to carry.

The poem's closing page links the 'the lost / nihil German killers' to 'all our learned art': the violence of Western imperialism which reached an apotheosis in Nazism is inseparable from the twinned history of *all* Western art.

> [...] 'member
> what you said
> money, God, power,
> a moral code, so cruel
> it destroyed Byzantium, Tenochtitlan, Commanch
>   (got it, *Baby!*

(*TDL*, 64)

As with Baraka's sardonic introduction to his reading of the poem at Asilomar – 'you all know what black means' – the vernacular exclamation '(got it, *Baby!*)' parodies the bathetic response of the one who 'gets' what the poem is saying. The knowledge this phrase sarcastically embodies cannot be acted upon. As Baraka earlier wrote in 'The Politics of Rich Painters' (1962): 'It is a cheap game / to patronize the dead, unless their deaths be accountable / to your own understanding' (*TDL*, 33). The poem proceeds with a dedication listing some of those deaths:

For tambo, willie best, dubois, patrice, mantan, the
bronze buckaroos.

      For Jack Johnson, asbestos, tonto, buckwheat,
      billie holiday.

           For tom russ, L'Overture [sic], vesey, beau jack, [...]

(*TDL*, 64)

The following year, Baraka's essay 'The Revolutionary Theatre' called for a 'theatre of victims' (Baraka 1965, 4). Likewise, here, defeated black revolutionaries such as Patrice Lumumba, Denmark Vesey and Nat Turner appear alongside Baraka's grandfather Tom Russ, himself a victim of political violence (Pisano, 60), African-American entertainers such as Billie Holiday, and the minstrel performers Mantan Moreland and Willie Best. The poem acts on behalf of all of those who have fallen victim to the West's 'grey hideous space'.

It ends, as it began, quietly, with an ironized final prayer to the voodoo god Damballah.

(may a lost god damballah, rest or save us
against the murders we intend
against his lost white children
black dada nihilismus.

(*TDL*, 64)

In early 1963, Robert Duncan wrote to Baraka to challenge his characterization of Damballah as a 'lost god', insisting that he is instead a 'world god' (Duncan, 401–2, 577). Baraka replied to Duncan that Damballah was a 'shamed god' (402), and this shame links to the ensemble of victims in the closing dedication. As with the reclamation of Willie Best as 'the renegade behind the mask' in 'A Poem for Willie Best', the minstrel symbol worn by the guerrilla armies in *The Slave* (1964) and the rewriting of the Jack Benny Show in *Home on the Range* (1967) to reclaim the 'shamed god' Damballah is a step towards reclaiming power (*TDL*, 18; *Conversations*, 174; 1968D). Likewise, Baraka will come to argue that, though African beliefs have been stolen by the West, they will return to destroy it in turn. In his totemic poem 'It's Nation Time' (1970), Christ, Buddha, Krishna, Moses, Allah and the voodoo *loa* Shango are reclaimed as 'black', invoked as part of ensemble to 'strike' at white America (*SP*, 199). Yet Black Dada's calls turn only to silence: the answer that never comes to a prayer that cannot be spoken in articulate speech. (Recall here that, in Haitian *vodoun*, Damballah appears as a snake who can only speak with a hiss (Rigaud, 73).)

'Black Dada Nihilismus' calls on Damballah not to *attack* white civilization but to *prevent this* attack: to 'rest or save us / against the murders we intend / against his lost white children' (*TDL*, 64). The entire poem is, in this sense, a failed invocation, whether prayer or magic spell, its forms of utterance still trapped that which they seek to destroy. For Fred Moten, the poem exhibits a 'tragic political despair' as a 'function of the weakness of its relation to ensemble' (Moten, 94). The poem is 'elegiac', rather than celebratory. Its metaphorical ensemble can only speak in screams: at once those of the murderer and the murdered, a 'chant' which parodies the condition of song. Yet the poem does represent a first stage in Baraka's developing revolutionary poetics. The 'secrecy and despair' which his short story 'The Screamers' (1963) claimed could be found in 'the black cults of emotion' of African-American music, or the 'action so secret it creates' described in a poem for the exiled Robert F. Williams soon transforms into a theorization of guerrilla warfare (*Fiction*, 184; *TDL*, 44). As early as 1961, Baraka had reportedly helped to smuggle guns to Williams in Monroe County (Tyson, 205, 344, n.73); by December 1964, he was asserting that 'guerrilla warfare by blacks is inevitable in the North and the South [...] You can't use nuclear weapons against us when we kill a few cops [...] There is no way of saving America [...] Every black is a potential revolutionist' (Newfield, 12). Initiated for the first time in 'Black Dada', terms such as 'Black Art' and 'Black Magic' play on the notion of occult rituals practised by an ensemble of cultic secret societies, assassination gangs, the *lumpenproletariat* and guerrilla warriors. As Baraka writes in 'American Sexual Reference: Black Male' (1965):

> Guerrilla warfare is the newest threat to the White Eyes, and the bomb won't work – only darts, and knives, and indigenous stealth. Guerrilla/Gorilla; and the white man has always spoken of the nonwhite as monkeys, apes, gorillas. (*H*, 245)

Western stereotypes are turned back on those who produced them, from 'gorilla' to 'guerrilla', for 'change is the only constant in the world. Many times a reversal of what already exists' (245). Such linguistic reversals characterize new modes of political activity. For Baraka, the deliberate, critical ambiguity of 'Black Dada' was ultimately a dead end. While the murders it presents are entwined with the white power structure they attack, he would increasingly seek in subsequent work to make a 'Target Study' of the enemy (*BM*, n.p.).

'Black Art' (1965): A politicized objectivism

Over the next few years, Baraka's strategic thinking underwent numerous shifts – from cults, guerrillas or riots to electoral campaigns. Importantly, though, the ambiguous identifications of 'Black Dada' are replaced by an affirmative embrace of blackness, which includes the earlier poem's hatred of white supremacy, but adds to it the element of collective racial solidarity – of love for the black community. This turn manifested not only in the work itself but in the collective contexts in which it was written and presented. Following his move from the East Village, Baraka's work increasingly turned towards a black audience. The original title to 'Black Art', 'The Black Arts', recalls the title of the Black Arts Repertory Theatre/School which Baraka had founded in Harlem in 1965 and for which the poem serves as a kind of manifesto or, as Baraka called it two years later, 'an aesthetic statement of principle' (N.d.A; Baraka 1967B). In the climate of BART/S, 'Black Art' moves away from the ambivalent, assemblages and invocations in 'Black Dada', envisaging a clear role for poetry in relation to an African-American collective. While 'Black Dada' was published by *Evergreen Review* and Grove Press, 'Black Art' first appeared in *Liberator* in January 1966, the month after Baraka had left New York for his birthplace, Newark. It was subsequently reprinted in *Black Fire* and as the title poem to a section of Baraka's 1969 collection, *Black Magic* (Baraka 1966B; *BF*, 302; *BM*, 116–17). *Liberator* was founded in 1961 by Daniel Watts, a participant in the 1961 UN protest addressed in the previous chapter; its first issue was a direct response to Lumumba's death. The magazine, which proclaimed itself 'the voice of the black protest movement' and called for 'the immediate liberation of all colonial peoples', had criticized strategies of non-violent protest from early on, publishing work by Umbra members Askia Touré, N.H. Pritchard, Calvin Hernton and Lorenzo Thomas, alongside Malcolm X, Harold Cruse and Larry Neal (Tinson, 16). Baraka served on the editorial board from July 1965 to December 1966 (Dace, 93), and 'Black Art' appears in an issue featuring a front-cover photograph of Baraka and an essay on his work by Larry Neal (Neal 1966). *Liberator*'s presentation of cultural work encouraged poetry to be read as part of a movement of coherent anti-colonial, non-violent opposition. 'Black Art' is firmly situated among ongoing debates about pan-Africanism, domestic policy and the role of politicized art in struggle. Informed by Baraka's experience of collective organizing at BART/S, the poem, later described by Larry Neal as 'a central assertion in both the Black Arts Movement and the philosophy of Black Power' (Neal 1968, 31), calls for aesthetic and political attack.

In 'Betancourt', written after his formative visit to Castro's Cuba in 1959, Baraka had asked 'I want to know what a poem is' (*TDL*, 41). The answer then was: 'A / turning away ... / from what / it was / had moved us' and 'A madness' (41). In 'Black Art', 'poems' are said to be, variously, 'bullshit', 'teeth', 'trees', 'lemons', 'black ladies dying', 'poems / like fists', 'dagger poems', 'Assassin poems, Poems that shoot / guns', 'Poems that wrestle cops into alleys', 'Black people' and the 'Black World' itself (*BM*, 116–17). This accumulating list of definitions falls into distinct groupings that mirror the argument of the poem, transformed from the ambiguous images of the opening section – poems as inanimate objects ('teeth or trees or lemons') – to the more inflammatory racial and political rhetoric of the central section – 'poems' perform as 'assassins' who 'shoot guns', 'wrestle cops into alleys', and 'set [...] fire and death to / whities ass' – and finally to collective affirmation – poetry (now in the singular) as a 'black poem' equivalent to 'a / Black World', spoken by 'All Black People'. 'Black Art' calls for a movement from political passivity to the revolutionary violence which will allow self-determination and in which poetry will participate. While, for Werner Sollors, '"Black Art" implies that poetry must die so that the poem can kill,' Baraka never suggests that poems will become entirely redundant (Sollors, 199). Rather, the use of the term 'poem' as a self-reflexive refrain serves to expand existing senses of what a 'poem' might be.

'Black Art' develops a trope from Baraka's recent jazz criticism, which had figured the 'new music' of John Coltrane and Sonny Rollins in terms of metaphorical 'assassination' and 'killing' (1962B, 1967A, 55, 1999, 228). The metaphor here is taken further, however, with assassination targeting, not jazz critics or 'the old music' but political enemies. The term is still metaphor, but it pushes at the limits of metaphor both within and without the space of the poem. 'Black Art' is a formalist work – but the forms it takes are in equal parts literary and sociopolitical. Rather than *collapsing* distinctions between poetry and material action, as Sollors argues, it mediates between them. The poem begins with a sentence that references and engages with at least five influential definitions of poetry from the American tradition.

> Poems are bullshit unless they are
> teeth or trees or lemons piled
> on a step. (*BM*, 116)

These lines *détourne* and critically respond to, variously: William Carlos Williams's *Paterson* ('no ideas but in things'), Joyce Kilmer's 'Trees' ('I think that I shall never see / A poem lovely as a tree'), Archibald MacLeish's 'Ars Poetica' ('A poem should not mean / But be'), Marianne Moore's 'Poetry' ('I, too, dislike it') and Jack Spicer's *After Lorca*, published alongside Baraka in *The New American Poetry* ('I would like to make poems out of real objects. The lemon to be a lemon that the reader cut or squeeze or taste – a real lemon like a newspaper in a collage is a real newspaper') (Williams 1986A, 262–3, 1986B, 55; Kilmer; MacLeish, 127; Thomas 2008, 114; Moore; Spicer, 133).

Baraka's initial collection of 'real objects' is harder to place within a realm of readily available political or artistic signification than the later 'assassin poems, poems that shoot guns'. The connection between 'teeth' and 'trees' is apparently arbitrary, linked solely by sound, the plosive alliteration of the two words leading into the gentler assonance of 'lemons' and 'step'. The objects which a poem must 'be' in order not to be 'bullshit' emerge through sound and the way this drives forward the poetic line rather than for their 'being' or signification. In that sense, despite the provocative opening phrase – 'Poems are bullshit' – the gap between poem as linguistic mediation and poem as object, or action, is initially reinforced, rather than challenged. Trees could be cut down to make paper for the printing of poems, and teeth could bite on lemons (or, as happens later in the poem, be knocked out by 'steel knuckles'), while the lemons themselves, far from being eaten or used, are merely piled upon a step, equivalent to Spicer's 'real things' which 'become garbage' (Spicer, 133). As a collection of objects, teeth, trees and lemons are neither sources of information – like Spicer's newspaper – nor of cutting, squeezing and tasting – like his lemons. Yet this is not merely a resigned statement of the inability of the poem to be or to act on the real object. In his letter addressed to the deceased Federico Garcia Lorca, himself a victim of Fascist violence, Spicer envisages of a punning 'correspondence' between language and the real – one which extends after the poet has died or the object decayed. Baraka seeks a more active mode, of resurrection, rather than preservation.[3]

In the next sentence, 'poems' become dying humans:

Or black ladies dying
of men leaving nickel hearts
beating them down. (*BM*, 116)

If poems relate to things in the world, Baraka asks, why might such 'things' not be suffering humans, as much as 'trees or lemons'? The grotesque distortion of 'nickel hearts' – hearts made of small change – renders both life and death economically determined, a point capped by the pun on 'heartbeat', 'nickel hearts / beating [...] down' dying women. Touching on a frequent target of this period, the exploitation of black prostitutes by white pimps (*BM*, 169–71), these lines reproduce the paternalistic attitude exemplified in such poems as 'Beautiful Black Women' (*BM*, 148–9), whereby women must be 'rescued' from the clutches of white men by black men. Nonetheless, the passionate criticism of sexual exploitation in 'Black Art' is too easily overlooked in readings of the poem which focus only on its most extreme elements (see also *BM*, 169–71).

Gradually, the poem moves out of its initial condition of inertia and suffering:

> [...] Fuck poems
> and they are useful, wd they shoot
> come at you, love what you are,
> breathe like wrestlers, or shudder
> strangely after pissing. (*BM*, 116)

'Fuck poems' appears as a statement of frustrated dismissal. But the next lines imply that this 'fucking' is also a violent refiguration, 'fucking up' or 'fucking over' poetry in order to make it 'useful'. Neither should the literal meaning be overlooked. As indicated by the progression from 'shoot / come' to 'shoot / guns' fourteen lines later, the poem adopts a rhetoric of masculinist liberation from 'emasculated' sexual frustration. Suggesting a sexual logic behind the poem's political violence, this repetition reproduces the problematic depiction of black male sexuality in 'American Sexual Reference: Black Male' (1965). 'Passive' sexuality is replaced by 'masculine' self-assertion in contrast to the desexualized poetry Baraka had earlier attacked ('My friend, the lyric poet, / who has never had an orgasm' (*TDL*, 67)). Yet the sexuality on display is initially a deferred, frustrated attempt at fulfilment. At this stage of the poem, humanity can only manifest itself in the 'shudder[ing]' of bodies, which, having 'shot come', 'breathe like wrestlers', implying a negative vision of sexuality as contest, rather than loving act. The 'love' sought at the poem's end – where that word is repeated three times in the space of three lines – is here distorted by the competition and sexual dissatisfaction fostered by the exploitative, racialized economy of prostitution which parodies genuine, mutual exchange.

It is at this point that the collective pronoun enters for the first time:

> We want live
> words of the hip world live flesh &
> coursing blood. (116)

Informed by 'blood' as racial inheritance, 'we' realize the necessity for poems to metaphorically come alive and revitalize the living. At the poem's end, these become poems of love in which 'black people' *are* 'poems & poets & / all the loveliness here in the world'. But they can only reach such 'loveliness' by spilling the blood of other racial groups.

> [...] we want 'poems that kill.'
> Assassin poems, Poems that shoot
> guns. Poems that wrestle cops into alleys
> and take their weapons leaving them dead
> with tongues pulled out and sent to Ireland. Knockoff
> poems for dope selling wops or slick halfwhite
> politicians Airplane poems, rrrrrrrrrrrrrrr
> rrrrrrrrrrrrrr ... tuhtuhtuhtuhtuhtuhtuhtuhtuh
> ... rrrrrrrrrrrrrrr ... Setting fire and death to
> whities ass [...] (116)

This section of the poem reflects the misogyny, anti-Semitism and homophobia frequently noted in Baraka's nationalist work: the poem targets 'owner-jews', 'girdlemamma mulatto bitches', 'cops [...] with tongues pulled out and sent to Ireland', 'dope selling wops', 'slick halfwhite/politicians', 'the Liberal/Spokesman for the jews', 'a negroleader [...] kneeling between the sheriff's thighs', 'a jewlady' and 'beasts in green berets'. Such slurs severely blunt its analysis. Yet the poem's targets are carefully chosen. Through his experience with On Guard and BART/S, Baraka's close attention to local politics suffuses even his most apparently generalized statements. As Lorenzo Thomas notes, readers of 'Black Art' invariably overlook its references to Harlem politics. The 'negroleader pinned to / a bar stool in Sardi's eyeballs melting / in hot flame' is attending a well-known restaurant located in Manhattan's Theatre district, while the lines 'We want poems / like fists beating niggers out of Jocks' refer to 'a tavern on Harlem's Lenox Avenue [which] was, in the 1950s and 1960s, a favourite hangout for politicians connected to the city's Democratic Party machine', located just round the corner from the BART/S (Thomas 2008, 113). As Thomas puts it: 'The reference – as those who heard [Baraka] read the poem on that street corner instantly understood – functions as idiomatic "signifying" ... "talkin' about" pretentious community leaders.'

> Even though 'Black Art' used overdramatized and violent images, it should be clear that the poem effectively limits itself to a call for 'cleaning up' the Harlem community [...] The immediacy and localisation of Baraka's references and images, matched with the stridency of his voice, clearly demand immediate improvement of the actual human environment – not merely through antipoverty agencies, but through the agency of an increasingly effective poetics, by which Baraka means 'consciousness'. (114–15)

There is humour here too. Once more echoing Kenneth Koch, the violence in 'Black Art' is often cartoonish, drawing on tropes familiar from what Thomas calls the 'mass-cult Americana' of comic books and B-movies (114). This is not to say that the calls to violence are not sincerely meant. The last of Baraka's list of targets introduces the international context of Vietnam to what are predominantly domestic references: 'Poem scream poison gas on beasts in green berets.' Here, the Agent Orange used on Vietnamese civilians is turned back on those who use it. The internationalism manifested in Umbra's early work, present as part of a ghostly, distorted collectivity that could only be hinted at in 'Black Dada', becomes more proactive here. In linking urban riots to anti-imperialism, Baraka builds on connections already drawn by Umbra members, in particular, Askia Touré, and, like Touré, 'Black Art' gives them a totemic, galvanizing power (Touré 1964).

Baraka's litany concludes: 'Clean out the word for virtue and love'. Paradoxically, through acts of killing, 'black poems' have become expressions of love.

> [...] Let Black people understand
> that they are the lovers and the sons
> of lovers and warriors and sons
> of warriors Are poems & poets &
> all the loveliness here in the world (117)

This call to black community is shorter and less forceful than its attack on other communities: as David L. Smith notes, forty-one out of the poem's fifty-five lines are dedicated to attack, rather than to affirmation (Smith, 241). Yet the addition of love to Baraka's ensemble suggests that he was increasingly able to envisage viable models of black collective life beyond despairing nihilism. Furthermore, the changed links between local and international contexts, emerging from victimhood to agency, render the poem's acts of violence more rooted within a potential revolutionary movement. Under the influence of Baba Oserjeman's Harlem-based Yoruba Temple, Baraka saw the BART/S as an early experiment in a nationalist reclamation of territory, calling for Harlem to become an independent black nation (*Home*, 277–8). As he later recalled:

> When we first arrived in Harlem, Oserjeman's group was very political. They dressed as traditional West Africans from Nigeria, but upheld the right of black self-determination, declaring that Africans in Harlem must control it. We gave many rallies at which Oserjeman or some other speaker from the Yoruba Temple spoke.
>
> (*Autobiography*, 215)

In an unpublished prose text entitled 'Black Rules', he writes:

> *Harlem is a Black Nation.* We must have economic and political control. The jews, the Italians, must go. They must turn over 'their' properties to Black People. We must have full sovereignty as a people [...] White people must not be allowed into Harlem without permission from *The Black Judges.*
>
> (N.d.D)

Unlike the 'Back to Africa' ideology espoused by the Garveyite movement, which still had a significant presence in Harlem, Baraka's nationalism was firmly focused on American soil. Given this, 'Black Art' must thus be seen a political intervention more precise and specific in its scope than 'Black Dada Nihilismus'. The persistent anti-Semitism of both the poem and the prose text attests to the incoherence of some of these ideas, which Baraka himself would later critique. Yet his changed conceptions of the relations between poetry and political action would set the ground for the most notable intersection in his work between poetry and civil unrest thus far and one of the key moments in the Black Arts Movement as a whole.

'Black People!' (1966): Magic and the law

Through the success of the Obie Award–winning *Dutchman* in 1964, Baraka was already a figure of nationwide notoriety by the time he wrote 'Black Art'. But it was his arrest and beating by the police during the July 1967 Newark Riots and his subsequent trial for alleged weapons possession that marked him out as a figure of real political significance. As Komozi Woodard writes: 'The 1967 Newark Rebellion catapulted Amiri Baraka into the political arena' (84). By 1970, Baraka would be described in an FBI memorandum as 'the person who will probably emerge as the leader of the Pan-African movement in the United States [...] regarded as the "Black Messiah"' (Maxwell, 117). It is in this context that 'Black People!' plays a crucial role. While 'Black Art' *called for* acts of violence, 'Black People!' *participated* in actual social unrest.

Written in 1966, the poem first appeared in the December 1967 issue of *Evergreen Review* (Baraka 1967E; Lask, 51). Opening a feature on Black Power, it was printed on a double-page spread of new work by Baraka, followed by an interview concerning his work in Newark in which he discusses his arrest during the riots. The poem's initial publication immediately establishes a contextual link to the recent events in Newark, one cemented by the poem's use as evidence in Baraka's

January 1968 sentencing. Because of this, as Werner Sollors notes, 'Black People' 'is likely to be [Baraka's] most widely known work. It was printed in innumerable newspapers and journals; not, however, in the poetry sections, but on front pages' (Sollors, 200–1). Baraka understood this: the poem symbolically closes his 1969 collection *Black Magic*. Before close-reading the poem and ending the chapter on its deployment in Baraka's trial, I will clarify its contextual background.

By late 1965, BART/S faced near-total collapse. Funding from the government HARYOU (Harlem Youth Opportunities Unlimited) anti-poverty programme has been terminated, following anxieties that BART/S endorsed an 'anti-white' agenda, and internal conflicts between different factions in the organization subsequently led to a firefight in which Larry Neal was wounded in the leg. As Askia Touré recalls:

> Later, reactionary Islamic extremists pulled a coup at the BARTS: word on the street was that they physically attacked Amiri. They trapped me and several local activists inside the Theatre, pulled guns, and announced that they were going to assassinate myself – 'and that n—-r, Larry Neal.' Amiri's friend Bro. Charlie and two of Malcolm's bodyguards saved my life as we backed out of the BARTS. The next day, a bomb was thrown into my apartment, which I shared w/two young RAM activists ... we were long gone, though. [...] Larry Neal, the brilliant young poet and scholar, *was shot down in the street.*

(Touré 2004)

BART/S was raided by the police in March 1966 and shut down soon after (*Autobiography*, 329–30). Baraka, however, had already left the city, returning to his birthplace, Newark, New Jersey, in December 1965. Swiftly attempting to implement new versions of the BART/S endeavour, he organized a Black Arts festival and established the Spirit House, a venue he would describe as the 'only community theatre' in the city (*Autobiography*, 230; *Conversations*, 28). Departing to teach in San Francisco for the spring semester of 1967, where he was involved with the Black Arts Alliance – activity that attracted the attention of HUAC (HUAC 1968, 2167–2169) – by the summer of that year he had once more returned to Newark. On July 13, the beating of a black taxi driver by two white police officers sparked six days of rioting in the city (Dockray, 3–4). These riots – or, as Baraka called them, this 'rebellion' – were crucial for his developing sense of revolutionary possibility, and it was in their wake that his poetry received one of its most notable entries into public life. On the first night of the riots, Baraka, along with actor Barry Wynn and accountant Charles McCray, drove around in his station wagon picking up those who had been injured on the streets – those, that is, caught outside in the police sniper fire that more often hit innocent civilians than the supposed black gunmen endangering the 'law-abiding' and 'respectable'. Still out at night, and thus breaking the police curfew, the van was surrounded by police who proceeded to beat Baraka with the barrels of their guns. According to Baraka's autobiographical account, only the intervention of bystanders and citizens shouting and raining down objects on the police from the safety of their windows saved his life (*Autobiography*, 261–2; Schneck, 16–18). Baraka's arrest instantly became a *cause celèbre*: Jean-Paul Sartre, whom 'Black Dada' has begged to die, called the police station at which Baraka was being held to demand information (Baraka 2007), and photographs of his bandaged head spread across newspapers nation- and worldwide. He was subsequently brought to trial on the charge of weapons possession in November of that year.

'Black People!' was not published until after the riots, though it was written before them in 1966 (Lask, 51). However, in an unusual move, the notoriously racist judge, Leon W. Kapp, allowed the poem to be introduced as evidence, reading out an excerpt in court as part of his final summation to the (all-white) jury on 4 January 1968 (Kent 1967, 3). In large part due to this prejudicial speech, Baraka was sentenced to up to three years in prison, a sentence which provoked public support from the American Civil Liberties Union and saw Allen Ginsberg's Committee on Poetry produce a statement of support, signed by many of his old poetry colleagues from New York, including John Ashbery, Charles Olson, Diane di Prima and John Wieners (Waggoner 1968; Hudson, 31; Committee on Poetry 1968).

It was, increasingly, in readings, both in Newark community centres and across the country, that Baraka's poetry had its greatest impact. Baraka's increasing embeddedness in a community is vividly captured in a report given by Lorenzo Thomas on a reading of 'Black People!' given by Baraka shortly after his return to Newark. Visiting Newark with Ishmael Reed, who ran the weekly political newspaper *Advance* there before his move to Berkeley, the pair came across

> a union hall or community centre sort of place where Amiri Baraka was reading feverish political poems to a few cheerful working-class black folk [...] mommas, sisters, little brothers, and wives. Cousins nieces nephews [...] He was shouting and singing his poems [...] Dig it. Christmas Eve in cracker-laced Newark, in the deeps of the Bottom. Baraka come talking that talk [...], reciting his crazy new poems. 'No Money down, no money never?' The people were saying 'yeah, uh huh' laughing and bopping their heads. Like in church. In this undecked hall. I was amazed at what the poems were doing. Baraka was *home*.

(*EM*, 147–50)

Reed and Thomas both feature in Baraka's short story 'Answers in Progress', a 'premonition' of the July riots, written in April 1967 and published in *Umbra*'s third issue (*Umbra Anthology*, 39; *Conversations*, 101). The text imagines the city following a successful black revolution; its communal atmosphere in which political organizing, the music of Sun Ra and an encounter with visiting extra-terrestrials combine with domestic happiness, reflecting Baraka's new-found sense of community. As Thomas notes, rather than 'fle[eing] home to lick his wounds' after the much-publicized failure of the BART/S, Baraka's 'rhetoric escalated and carefully particularized his social and political concerns' (*EM*, 150). Texts like 'Black People' and 'Answers in Progress' emerged from the context of Spirit House on Stirling Street, which aimed to apply the collective ethos of BART/S and Umbra without the 'tensions and conflicts' that had destroyed them (Baraka 1969A, 177; Sanchez 1970, 66). As Thomas writes, 'the entire programme was designed as an exercise in organisation to achieve clearly defined goals' (155).

Paying attention to the linguistic specificity of the poem helps us to further set it within its Newark context, and within the new form of Baraka's poetics, based on direct address to a community within which he was increasingly embedded. Beginning by satirically mimicking ghetto advertising, by its end, the poem is a revolutionary call to arms. The poem opens with a conversational address to the 'black people' named in its title, asking: 'What about that bad short you saw last week / on Frelinghuysen?' Baraka draws his auditors in through further questions, giving a sense of the multiple consumer goods available all over the city:

> [...], or those stoves and refrigerators, record players
> in Sears, Bambergers, Klein's, Hahnes', Chase, and the smaller joosh
> enterprises? What about that bad jewelry, on Washington Street, and
> those couple of shops on Springfield? [...]

(*BM*, 225)

As in 'Black Art', the poem's broad collective address couples with geographically specific references. These stores were often the site of demonstrations by African-American women protesting the prices of essential goods for which they struggled to pay and, during the July rebellion, were frequently looted (Mumford, 154–60). Such references might be missed by those unfamiliar with conditions in the city: the poem splits its readers based on the knowledge they already have, along intensely politicized grounds.

Baraka asserts:

> [...] You know how to get it, you can get it, no money down, no money never [...]

(*BM*, 225)

Henry C. Lacey reads these lines as 'a parody, an inverted "sales pitch", spoken in the idiom of the black ghetto dweller':

> The poem is perhaps best understood as counterstatement to the well-known 'rip-off' advertisements of the radio stations aimed at the black communities across the country, advertisements infamous for doping the poor into purchases of shoddy goods and interminable payments. (119)

Ironically reappropriating the notion of consumer 'purchasing power', the phrase 'no money down' – echoing advertisements for payment on instalment plans – becomes 'no money never', taking the utopian promise of the absence of money at its word. Further riffing on 'money', Baraka writes:

> [...] money dont grow on trees, no way, only whitey's got it, makes it with a machine, to control you.

(*BM*, 225)

While the fact that 'only whitey's got it' emphasizes Newark's racial division of wealth, Baraka once more reverses the 'common sense' of idiomatic phrasing, moving from buying, to looting, to killing.

> you cant steal nothing from a white man, he already stole it he owes you anything you want, even his life [...]

This argument is encapsulated in the poem's most famous lines.

> [...] All the stores will open if you will say the magic words. The magic words are: Up against the wall mother fucker this is a stick up! Or: Smash the window at night (these are magic actions)

These 'magic words' gave rise to a slogan appropriated by the radical left, the student movement and the BPP during the late 1960s. While the widespread dissemination of these magic words as a militant slogan drew from Baraka's poem, Baraka himself appropriated them from a phrase initially uttered by

Newark cops to African-Americans in their custody (Perlstein, 238). The poem completely transforms the term's political valence, reclaiming white policemen's sarcastic reclamation of 'motherfucker' – a word associated with black vernacular speech. In the introduction to his 1971 dictionary *Black Slang*, poet Clarence Major, who appears in *Umbra* and in *Black Fire*, argues that, while such white imitations are '(for kicks and to slander) the slave's speech', black slang sees 'those imitated […] turn […] around and imitate […] the imitators imitating them' (Major 1971, 11). Deploying 'the local magic beneath spoken words' (14), through parodic changes, reversals and disguises, based on local reference, it performs transformative work on normative language from 'beneath' the surface of its ostensible meaning.

Major defines the word 'motherfucker', in part, as 'profane form of address; a white man' (Major 1994, 310). In Baraka's poem, the word takes on a specific inflection: to be a 'motherfucker' is to be white; to be white is to be a 'motherfucker'. For Kimberly Benston, 'motherfucker' serves in Baraka's work in general,

> both as a vehicle of archaic power, evoking the irreducible violence of rupture, distance, loss, and restitutive transgression, and as a vessel of symbolic import, carrying the complex burden of ideological critique, reproachful admonition, and oracular fury […] ululating from the culture's subversive margins a long-breathed blues-tinged wail of prophetic outrage and utopic expectation.
>
> (Benston 2000, 189)

At the Asilomar Conference in 1964, Baraka himself argued – in more understated fashion – that

> A man who tries to tell me that I cannot have a character in my play say 'motherfucker' to describe something that my character sees is trying to deny the validity of a certain kind of experience and to deny the expression of that word as honest. He is quite clearly trying to deny a whole world of feeling because he does not know what the word means or how it is used.
>
> (1966D, 57)

Baraka's 'motherfucker' wrests back power, figuring magic as the audible and nameable present, within the frame of a dialogic relation established between the speaker and 'black people'. The magic here is firmly social. Saying 'up against the wall mother / fucker' is a linguistic action that produces political change: a performative utterance that does not reproduce social norms – as in J.L. Austin's example of the marriage contract – but challenges them (Austin, 5). As Lytle Shaw argues:

> For [...] transformation to occur, a condition of possibility is required not so much in the external context – the site – as inside the subjects who will effect the change – the addressee. Magic thus names the shift in consciousness, the instantaneous charge, by which acts that seem to the pre-revolutionary subject simply impossible suddenly become possible; magic explodes the common sense of liberalism, allowing the unthinkable to be thought.
>
> (Shaw 2008, online)

This knowledge is already there – 'you know how to get it' (*BM*, 225) – but requires the linguistic questioning, suggestion, permission and injunction which the poem puts in place to be acted upon. Progressing from the stealing of goods to the stealing of lives, black looters wrest back economic and political control, parodying the consumer ethos which previously reinforced it. Linking Newark to the nationwide and even global struggle against white supremacy, Baraka writes:

> [...] Our brothers
> are moving all over, smashing at jellywhite faces.

'All over' implicitly designates not only Newark itself – 'all over the city' – but 'all over the world'. If 'our brothers' are acting, then 'we must' also 'make our own / World': the poem insists that 'we' and 'our brothers' are drawn together, erasing separation.

> [...] We must make our own
> World, man, our own world, and we can not do this unless the white man
> is dead. Let's get together and kill him, my man, let's get to gather the fruit
> of the sun, let's make a world we want black children to grow and learn in
> do not let your children when they grow look you in your face and curse you by
> pitying your tomish ways.

These imperatives turn the *potential* for action into necessity. The speaker gives permission for his addressees to act on what they already know and then insists on the *necessity* that they do so, moving from parody to strategy to a utopian imaginary in which 'want' and 'need' are fulfilled by more than simply the expropriation of the commodity form.

There are serious political stakes in the poem's performative strategies, which proved a central factor in Baraka's sentencing for weapons possession in January 1968. As part of his closing summary to the jury, Judge Leon Kapp read out the poem, omitting 'obscenities' and replacing them with the word 'blank' (Hudson, 29). Baraka justifiably objected to what he called Kapp's 'demented reading' (*Autobiography*, 272), sarcastically suggesting that Kapp's condemnation was simply a matter of literary taste: 'You mean, you didn't like the poem, in other words' (Hudson, 30). Yet Baraka's courtroom correction of the judge – 'When he read the poem, he left out the profanity, and as he read I supplied it' – suggests that its full force lies in precisely that obscenity (*Autobiography*, 271). The poem's 'magic' exists not only for the 'black people' it aims to inspire but the enemy it aims to overthrow. Kapp's 'demented reading' does not misunderstand the poem, as Baraka claimed. Rather, Kapp is *a close-reader* of the poem, countering its performative 'magic words' with the performative authority of his own courtroom pronouncements. The sarcastic headline to the *New York Times* report on Baraka's conviction – 'the magic word was "prison"' – unintentionally captures the very real forces, instated and justified through the language of the police, government and law courts, which the poem seeks to challenge ('The Magic Word', 6).

For Tom Hayden, the Newark Rebellion was a time when 'people who under ordinary conditions respected law because they were forced to do so now felt free to act upon the law as they thought it should be' (quoted in Shaw 2013, 91). When Judge Kapp sentenced him to be 'confined to the New Jersey State Prison', Baraka replied:

> Sir, black people will judge me, Brother Kapp. Don't worry about that. You represent the will of a crumbling structure and I am a free black man. (Porambo, 5)

Baraka parodies the judge, rather than actually hoping to instate a change of attitude. But his proclamation is also a speech act which undermines legal authority, instead insisting on 'the law as [he] thought it should be'. Rather than asserting immunity from 'judgement', Baraka claims that the standards of 'black people' differ from those of a racist legal structure. Whereas Kapp's sentence is singular – albeit passed down based on the verdict of (an all-white) jury and with the full force and sanction of that power structure (Kent 1967, 3) – Baraka emphasizes judgement in the plural. Both Baraka's poem and his courtroom riposte to Kapp aim to reconfigure the entire legal, moral and poetic structure of white supremacist American discourse. In the following chapter, I address poems of urban insurrection by David Henderson which emerge from similar moments of political possibility. Writing of New York in the context of the 1964 Harlem Riots, Henderson's work further delineates the dilemmas of spatial control, advertising and media, commerce, and the role of black music as tool of collective possibility.

3

'Space of a Nation': David Henderson Writes the City

The poetry of David Henderson: An introduction

Born in 1942, David Henderson was one of the youngest Umbra poets: he was just twenty years old when the magazine's first issue printed three of his poems. Yet he was already a most influential figure: coming to Umbra from Henri Percikow's workshop, where he had met Lorenzo Thomas, he developed a close friendship with Calvin Hernton, editing the magazine's first two issues with Hernton and Tom Dent (Henderson 1970, 18, 1980; Hernton 1976, 17, 65, 103, 1993, 583). Henderson's poetry of the 1960s focused on the experience of New York – where, unlike many of the other Umbra poets, he had lived all his life – often filtered through the urban musical forms of jazz and rhythm and blues. The oral delivery of his poems was an important influence on Baraka's Black Arts aesthetic, and his poem 'Keep on Pushing' (1964) is prominently cited in Baraka's 1966 essay 'Poetry and Karma' and Larry Neal's afterword to *Black Fire*, where the poem was reprinted (Baraka 1971B, 25; *BF*, 655). Henderson's keen sense of New York's multi-ethnic culture would lead him to develop what he called a 'third eye/world' aesthetic to his work with the Nuyorican Poets Café and to his editorship of the final issue of *Umbra, Latin/Soul* (Dent 1980B, 111). As well as *Umbra*, Henderson published in countercultural contexts such as *Evergreen Review, Fuck You* and Hettie Jones's anthology *Poems Now*, and Black Arts–oriented venues such as *Negro Digest, Freedomways* and Baraka's *Black Fire*. Like Lorenzo Thomas, his publication record spans black and white publications, but his poetry always retains a firmly African-American focus. As he noted in 1972: 'I grew up in Harlem as a black nationalist. In the Umbra workshop on the Lower East Side in the early Sixties, we established a basic ideal of black consciousness' (Middlebrook, 40).

As well as poetic activity with Umbra, and at the St Mark's Poetry Project, Henderson worked in schools with the Teachers and Writers Collaborative – where he crossed paths with Muriel Rukeyser and the young June Jordan – and was active as a labour organizer (Lopate, 39, 76–81). His first pamphlet, *Felix of the Silent Forest*, was published by The Poets Press with an introduction by Baraka in 1967; the same year, he spent time in New Orleans, where he participated in poetry readings organized through the Free Southern Theater (FST) (Dent 1969, xv, 164–6). In the late 1960s, Henderson moved to California, also the base of his friend Ishmael Reed. Here, he continued his involvement in radical education projects, working with the University Without Walls, a community-based alternative college for people of colour, advising the Oakland Unified School District and Berkeley Public Schools and teaching at UC Berkeley and San Diego. Henderson's first full-length collection, *De Mayor of Harlem*, appeared in 1970. Collecting work written over a seven-year period, the book's division into three sections reflects the trans-geographical connections on which his work insists, from New York – 'De Mayor of Harlem' (1962–66) – New Orleans – 'The Louisiana Weekly' (poems written in summer 1967, during his time with the FST (Dent 1969, xv, 164–6)) – and back to New York once more – 'Fork of the West River and Beyond' (1966–69).

Following Umbra's split in 1964, Henderson assumed soul editorship of the group's magazine and was responsible for publishing three further issues. These issues extend the Umbra project alongside newly emergent Black Arts writers, responding to contemporaneous political events and reflecting Henderson's developing cross-cultural aesthetic. Indeed, as a publication, the *Umbra Anthology* of 1967/1968 serves in some ways as a more fully developed manifestation of the group's aesthetic than the earlier issues with higher production values and a diverse selection of writings. Partially derived from the issue shelved after the split, it places Umbra writers such as Hernton, Thomas and Ray Durem alongside younger writers such as Yusuf Rahman and Julia Fields; it presents Baraka's 'Answers in Progress' alongside Henderson's own 'De Mayor of Harlem', dedicated Baraka in the wake of the 1967 Newark rebellion, and maintains the links to older writers established in the second issue's 'Richard Wright Mnemonicon', featuring work by the recently deceased Langston Hughes and by the iconoclastic, San Francisco–based Beat poet Bob Kaufman, credited with earlier inventing the word 'Beatnik', and then undergoing a ten-year vow of silence following the assassination of John F. Kennedy. (Henderson would later produce a radio show on Kaufman.) In 1970, Henderson edited a fourth issue from Berkeley entitled *Blackworks from the Black Galaxy*. Here, material from the original Umbra writers appears once more alongside younger writers like Tom Weatherly and older 'griots' like Hart LeRoi Bibbs, whose *Diet Book for Junkies* was printed as an illustrated supplement. The final, *Latin/Soul* issue from 1974, co-edited with Barbara Christian and Victor Hernandez Cruz, exemplifies Henderson's new attitude to the 'third eye/world'. (Fine work has been done on these connections in Crawford, 107–36.) Since then, Henderson has published two further books of poetry: *The Low East* (1980), once more concerning New York, while California forms the setting to his most recent book, *Neo-California* (1998). His abiding interest in music saw him author the first biography of Jimi Hendrix in 1978 and to record with Sun Ra, Ornette Coleman and David Murray. He continues to be active in New York poetry scenes.

As his editorial projects, involvement in alternative education projects and activity as a labour organizer all suggest, Henderson's work sits at intersections between the Old and New Left, social work and a growing sense of multicultural poetics, primarily based in New York, but with a diasporic sense that extends not only across America but across the world. This chapter focuses on Henderson's figuration of New York in the early and mid-1960s, particularly in relation to music, the 1964 Harlem Riots, and the complex intersections between the spaces of Harlem and the Lower East Side. As Baraka writes in his preface to *Felix of the Silent Forest* (1967): 'These are local epics with the breadth that the emotional consciousness of a culture can make' (Henderson 1967, n.p.). Baraka's phrase 'local epics' is particularly suggestive, capturing the ways in which Henderson's poems traverse the territory not only of New York but of global politics and the diasporic survivals of 'atavistic', African-derived cultures. Henderson sees New York as the nation in microcosm: he knows that US foreign policy, economic conditions in the 'ghetto' and the contested terrain of African-American culture are fundamentally linked. His poetry is a sustained study of what he called 'the enigmas of our Neon Diaspora': the repeated dispersals, from West Africa to America, from the American South to the North, from Harlem to the LES, that concretize in the experience of the modern city (*BF*, 232).

'Harlem to Lower East Side'

In a 1972 interview with Dianne Middlebrook, Henderson notes:

> In *Felix [of the Silent Forest]* I wrote mainly about Harlem, but I wondered, 'Am I in the wrong slum?' In *De Mayor [of Harlem]* the question is resolved: Harlem to Lower East Side – space of a nation. I make my poems out of two worlds: black

nationalist Harlem and the multicultural Lower East Side – the East Village, a mixed bohemia. (Middlebrook, 39)

Henderson suggests here an important dilemma facing many of the Umbra poets. Though he grew up in Harlem, Henderson was drawn to the LES and to the collective atmosphere of Umbra, the area's diversity contributing to his developing multicultural aesthetic. Nonetheless, Harlem still held a strong pull not only due to its literary past but as a still-thriving centre of black culture and politics – from Fidel Castro's visit to the Hotel Theresa, to Lewis Michaux's nationalist bookstore and Malcolm X's street-corner speeches. Baraka would famously turn to Harlem as 'home' following Malcolm's death in 1965, establishing the BART/S (*H*, 107, 266, 277–8; *BM*, 108). As he notes, even before this, 'downtown' African-American artists frequently went 'uptown' to Harlem: 'working in Harlem politically, that became the badge of our sincerity' (Smethurst 2014, 13). The twin pulls of Harlem and the LES had earlier manifested in the organizational structure of On Guard, which met on the LES but had offices on Harlem's 125th street, a politicized area where Castro had stayed and Malcolm often spoke (Dent 2018, 442). As Tom Dent notes: 'I think the decision to have the office in Harlem and not on the Lower East side was a result of the fact that, very consciously, the group wanted to be Uptown' (443). Yet, as we saw in the first chapter, On Guard, with its primarily activist focus, failed to offer the Umbra writers the opportunities for creative work they desired. As Dent notes:

> In terms of fellow artists, the Lower East Side offered opportunities and friendships and connections that did not exist in Harlem for whatever reason. During the time of the Harlem Renaissance, they might have, but by 1960 they did not. (448)

Paradoxically, it was only on the LES – an area which, while extremely multicultural, had a minimal black presence – that Umbra could come together as a group, meeting in Dent's downtown flat and reading in LES coffee houses and bars (Dent 2018, 244–53). For his part, Langston Hughes, one of the most totemic writers of the Harlem Renaissance and a mentor to many members of Umbra, wrote:

> Now in the sixties, LeRoi Jones, Welton Smith, Calvin Hernton, David Henderson, and numerous young black writers do their balling and brawling downtown in Greenwich Village – integrated. But in the twenties we had so much fun and like Harlem so well that we did not think about taking the long subway ride to the Village, where the artists and writers gathered. We let them come uptown to us. (Hughes 1966, 18)

The uptown-downtown split was particularly vexed for Henderson, given that he had moved *from* Harlem to the LES. Henderson was keenly aware of the compromised class status of the new LES bohemians, whose activities paved the way for the gentrification accomplished by a later generation of middle-class whites (Ismaili, 588). His early poem 'The Ofay and the Nigger', published in *Umbra*'s first issue, is a satirical presentation of the appropriation of African-American culture by the liberal middle class.

> The ofay
> and
> The nigger
> say
> Quote and unquote
> Because they must obey
> PARLANCE
>   – the god of interracial love,
> understanding and Northern mongrelization.

(*Umbra* I, 41–2)

In 'Downtown-Boy Uptown', the opening poem of *Felix of the Silent Forest*, Henderson describes himself as:

> Downtown-boy uptown
> Affecting complicity of a Ghetto
> and a sub-renascent culture [...]
> I stand in my low east window looking down.
> am I in the wrong slum?

(*FOTSF*, n.p.)

Henderson writes as a native New Yorker but always with a keen sense of alienation. As he writes in 'Downtown-Boy Uptown', 'I changed my speed and form for lack of a better tongue.' In the satirical 'So We Went to Harlem', Henderson presents himself as 'David the pimping Rinehart', referencing Ralph Ellison's ambiguous, shape-shifting character, able to assume any disguise and with an ambivalent hold over the ghetto. Here, he ironically rhapsodizes Harlem as:

> HARLEM! The exotic land of the Midnight Air
> And nefarious mediocrity. HARLEM! Where brown men
> And women dance all day and sing all night.

(*FOTSF*, n.p.)

Yet even in Henderson's more ambiguous poems about 'affecting complicity of a Ghetto' (*FOTSF*, n.p.), a sense of the racialized and class dynamics of urban space is always present: the UN Protests of 1961, the World's Fair and Harlem Riots of 1964, and the murder of Malcolm X at the Audubon Ballroom in 1965. His ears are always tuned to the ground – to the radios, street gossip and political speeches – of African-American communities. Henderson and Thomas offer a much more intensely politicized and racialized vision of New York than that of the contemporaneous New York School, with whose writers they maintained contact (Smethurst 2005, 136–7). Like the work of associates such as Frank O'Hara and Ted Berrigan, their poetry frequently ventriloquizes vernacular speech and catalogues urban space through *flâneur*-like figures traversing the multicultural spaces of the city (Thomas 1979, 24–8). But their ironized registration of New York as a space of urban degradation, linked to the violence of global politics, means that theirs can never straightforwardly be a poetry of celebration: for Henderson, the influence of Langston Hughes's later work, particularly the collection *Ask Your Mama* (1961), links to an older tradition of black radical leftism, vernacular and the importance of jazz and blues to forge a poetry that is at once New York–centric and internationalist in its scope (Hughes 1961).

Through the self-framing suggested by the titles to his first collections, Henderson presents his complex position in negotiating the New York environment. In *De Mayor of Harlem* (1970), Henderson adopts the honorary, folkloric position which had been bestowed upon the dancer and actor Bill 'Bojangles' Robinson and emcee and DJ Willie Bryant. Laying claim to this title is in some sense a boast, but its ironies echo those inherent in the position itself, which belies the *lack* of political control faced by African-Americans in a predominantly African-American neighbourhood. In his entry on Henderson for the *Dictionary of Literary Biography*, Terry Joseph Cole argues that this position has been 'politically powerless, existing, to Henderson, as another false idol created to sop the attention of black Harlemites, a placebo who serves as a symbol of institutional American's benign neglect' (Cole, 75). Henderson's use appears more multifaceted – the titular poem, in its original printing in the *Umbra Anthology* described as a 'night letter to Newark/for LeRoi (1967)', presents the abjection of a neighbourhood 'where multitudes vomit pass out / witness death by many stabbings', yet insistently urges: 'talk to me talk to me / tell me like it is' (*DMOH*, 13–15). The mayor here seems less of a 'false idol' than an analogy for Henderson himself, a clear-eyed chronicler of urban deprivation within a charged political situation. But Henderson is ever aware of the complicities and corruptions fostered within Harlem. 'They Look This Way and Walk That Way

As Tribal As They Can Be under the Law' is a caustic portrayal of 'sherman the barbecue man / former famous mayor of harlem', whose opportunistic exploitation of the influence of Islam on the black community – 'no pork chops on the menu' – is offset by the framed photographs on his walls of Rockefeller and Truman (Henderson 1970, 42).

Meanwhile, the title poem to *Felix of the Silent Forest* is dedicated to cartoon character Felix the cat ('Noveltytoons, USA'). For Lorenzo Thomas, the appearance of Felix may constitute 'Henderson's only nostalgic reference to the media [...] all of his other attention to such things seems for the purpose of irony' (Thomas 1978, 71). But Felix is again an ambiguous figure. Punning on the notion of the 'hepcat', Felix is a ghetto *flâneur*, careful to 'vary' his 'gait' and to 'change [his] speed and form'.

> Felix walks the City
> sometimes fast sometimes slow
> like a dying man wanting everything he sees.
>
> (*FOTSF*, n.p.)

Having internalized the logic of the city's perpetual consumption,

> Often
> Felix walks the City hungry in every sense
> of every gastric salivating phenomenon.

Yet he is also a figure of loneliness.

> Felix sits in any bar 3 or 4 for a dollar
> wondering if
> anyone he loves
> wonders where he is

A lonelier and more hesitant figure than 'David the Pimping Rinehart' in 'So We Went to Harlem', Felix's status as observer merges with that of 'De Mayor' and of Henderson himself. Here, context is everything. In poems like 'Yin Years' (1965), Henderson unites this persona with a sense of collective, anti-imperialist possibility found in the Harlem and Watts Riots and in the struggles of Cuba and Vietnam. The mobility embodied by the 'Mayor', Felix and Rinehart is an underground strength, a mode of disguise associated with the artistic and political underground, which, like that of Ellison's subterranean invisible man, can also serve as a form of perverse power.

Henderson ultimately departs from Felix's own seduction into consumerism and the traps of invisibility that, as we've seen, had been so forcefully rejected in Touré's 'Cry Freedom'. As he puts it in the same poem:

> No longer have we cause to stay away
> for not diving in
> > it is the age of epaulet & picket line
> > vertigo and alliance.

(*FOTSF*, n.p.)

As noted on the dust jacket to *De Mayor of Harlem*, Henderson had worked as a union organizer and picket-line boss. In 'Felix', these lines also serve not only to indicate political commitment but to the equivalent found in Henderson's poetic approach, insistently 'diving in' to the world of commerce, police brutality, artistic experimentation and political activism found in New York.

Henderson's early work frequently charts the street rituals and the culture of Harlem. This engagement is sometimes despairing. In 'bopping', Henderson extends the etymology noted by Langston Hughes for bebop as the sound of 'police beating Negroes' heads' with truncheons (Hughes 1949, 6). For Henderson, 'bopping' is a masculine ritual of both camaraderie and intramural violence:

> [...] the eternal wars
> among ourselves   our gangs:
> > the Crowns   Chaplins   Sportsmen
> Boston Baldies   Young Sinners   Enchanters   Duschon Lords.

(*FOTSF*, n.p.)

Henderson writes:

> we bopped to give cause to the causes
> that died before they got to us [...]

> We bopped when about to fight
> and we bopped when happy [...]

> From street duels
> until
> wedlock or the cops
> shot us down
> bopping [...]

(*FOTSF*, n.p.)

At the same time, there is pride and dignity in this ritual swagger, just as Hughes's bebop musicians channel the rage and hurt of racial violence into a vital form of African-American modernism. In other poems, Henderson notes the commodification of African-American rhythm and blues and dance rituals but sees in them real collective possibility. Henderson himself had performed in a vocal group called the Starsteppers, an experience documented in the poem 'Boston Road Blues', and would sometimes sing the song refrains that pepper works such as 'Keep on Pushing' (*BF*, 233–8). In 'Neon Diaspora', Henderson writes of vocal group The Drifters, comparing their performance at the Hotel Theresa to Castro's visit in 1960:

> The Drifters are in Harlem
> The Drifters are at the Theresa
> Staring over the soot-stained ghetto
> Just as Castro did in '60.
>
> (*BF*, 230)

Henderson presents the urban songs of 'these fine slickheaded ghetto boys' as anthems for Civil Rights struggles in the 'Black Belt South': Atlanta, Birmingham, Jackson, Los Angeles, Jacksonville, Chicago and Illinois.

> These fine slickheaded ghetto boys have wheeled
> their agony through streets of iron, beast, blood
> and fire singing *their* songs of freedom to the blackbelted
> bucks of our America.
>
> (*BF*, 230)

Though they play to 'the aristocracy [...] the fully employed, steady working hands of Harlem', 'the/privileged, the responsible', manifesting 'the enigmas of our Neon Diaspora' (*BF*, 230–1), their music at its core contains what Henderson calls an

> Elemental sexuality (that has been our only hope for so long)
> I love those black bastards with all the heart I dare.
>
> (*BF*, 232)

'Keep on Pushing'

This reclamation of music, often associated with the thriving black performance culture of Harlem, is central to Henderson's work. 'Keep on Pushing (Harlem Riots/Summer 1964)' is perhaps the most sustained example and the one most immediately tied to a political context. The poem first appeared in radical leftist newspaper the *National Guardian* in 1965 and was included in Baraka and Larry Neal's anthology *Black Fire* in 1968. A major statement, the poem's success suggests the importance of Umbra writers to the emergence of the Black Arts aesthetic. Neal's afterword to *Black Fire* notes the poem, 'where [Henderson] gets a chance to sing' alongside work by Touré, Hernton and Reed as evidence of 'a new synthesis; a new sense of literature as a *living reality*' which partakes of the 'collective ritual' found in black music, 'but ritual directed at the destruction of useless, dead ideas' (*BF*, 655). Likewise, Baraka recalls:

> 'Keep on Pushing', which poet David Henderson made into a great poem, was one of our themes [...] Rhythm and blues took on a new meaning. Those artists, too, were reflecting the rising tide of the people's struggles [...] [and] had signalled earlier, downtown, that the shit was on the rise. (*Autobiography*, 210)

A long work in six sections, the poem is a narrative of movement through Harlem during the July riots. The poem is titled after the hit song by Curtis Mayfield and the Impressions, and fragments of the song recur throughout, serving as a contrast to the police brutality occurring during the riots, Harlem gossip and reported speech which comes from street corners and radios: the smooth talk of radio DJs, racist university professors condemning black unrest and the ghetto's daily whirl of commerce. (In this sense, Henderson's four-page 'documentary' serves as equivalent to Umbra member Raymond Patterson's 'Riot Rimes U.S.A.', a series of eighty-five pithy poems with the quality of sardonic maxims, reports and lyrics written from multiple angles, perspectives and voices (Patterson 1969, 99–185).)

In the lead-up to the riots, Harlem was a hotbed of unrest: poor housing conditions and continuing police brutality were challenged by activist movements, often involving CORE. A major rent strike had taken place the previous year; in April 1964, a school boycott saw 12 per cent of children stay away in protest at school conditions; and, the same month, protestors blocked trains and highways for the 1964 World's Fair taking place at Flushing Meadows Park, Queens (Halsted, 1–5). Describing itself as a 'universal and international' exposition, and lasting for an entire year, the fair's theme was 'Peace through Understanding'. Containing pavilions representing large numbers of manufacturers, its display of American culture and technology and promotion of a consumer ethos was 'a study in corporate excess', glaringly contrasting the heavy police presence, crime rate and economic deprivation of Harlem, only amplified by the presence in the fair itself of a controversial minstrel show (Gan, online). The fair's framing of America in a global context – 'Man's Achievement on a Shrinking Globe in an Expanding Universe' – serves as an ironic registration of white America's status as a world power earlier challenged by the anti-imperialist internationalism of On Guard. Henderson's work of this period, with its balance between the multiculturalism of the LES and the Black Nationalist orientation of Harlem, serves precisely the opposite function to the corporate globalism of the fair, which he ironically registers as a 'death festival' (Henderson 1966, 100).

It was from this background that the riots erupted on 16th July after the police murder of fifteen-year-old James Powell. The riots lasted for six days, involving protests, the looting of stores and heavy police deployment, leading to frequent brutality against unarmed civilians; during this time, Harlem was effectively 'occupied territory' (Halsted, 3). Henderson's poem notes the presence of police on every block, ready to beat and arrest any young African-Americans showing signs of discontent, militancy or disturbance. As he drily notes:

> Police Commissioner Murphy can
> muster five hundred cops in five minutes.
> He can summon extra
> tear gas bombs, guns, ammunition
> within a single call
> to a certain general alarm.

(*BF*, 239)

Nonetheless:

> a shot   a cry   a rumor
> can muster five hundred Negroes
> from idle and strategic street corners
>   bars   stoops   hallways   windows
> Keep on pushing.

(*BF*, 239)

These lines attest to both the lack of viable institutions for the city's dropouts and the collective potential that still exists in Harlem, exploding into the politicized actions of the riots, signalled by the first appearance of the titular Impressions song. Given that the 'five hundred cops' are far more heavily armed and easily mobilized than the 'five hundred Negroes', the odds are stacked against the rioters.

> I see police eight per square block
> crude mathematics
> eight to one
> eight for one
> I see the store owners and keepers—all white
> and I see the white police force
> The white police in the white helmets
> and the white proprietors in their white shirts
>
> (*BF*, 239–40)

Ironically appearing to the forces of American 'democracy' supposedly represented by imperial interventions in Korea and Cuba, Henderson asks:

> Am I in the 1940's?
> Am I in Asia? Batista's Havana?
> where is Uncle Sam's Army? The Allied Forces
> when are we going to have the plebescite [*sic*]?
>
> (240)

The poem's political radicalism is here registered in the allusion to nationalism: the notion that black Americans constituted a 'nation within a nation', first formulated by Martin R. Delany, and later taken up by black radicals such as Harry Haywood and Stokely Carmichael and, later, by Baraka, and registered, as we saw in the first chapter, in Askia Touré's 'Cry Freedom' (Haywood 1978, 124; Carmichael and Hamilton; Baraka 1971B, 65).[1] Through comparing the events in Harlem to American imperial intervention in Asia and Cuba, Henderson suggests that the police in Harlem essentially function as an occupying army. Further, he anticipates the calls made by the Republic of New Afrika (RNA) and in the BPP's ten-point programme for a UN-sponsored plebiscite on the issue of an independent black nation (Kelley, 95, 127–8; Woodard, 73). Henderson will go on to sketch out the geographies of resistance through the figure of music. While cultural forms in themselves cannot fight the police, they do feed into political action, becoming indelibly associated with the spirit of the 'long hot summer' (Touré 1964, 13). At once 'idle and strategic', Harlem, as an intensely politicized space already characterized by the activism of CORE, rent strikes, education boycotts and the street-corner speeches of Malcolm X, will not take Powell's murder lying down (*BF*, 239). This is what Henderson calls 'Harlem's 2nd law of Thermodynamics' in which Harlem's residents respond to police violence, 'Helmet to barehead / nightsticks bullets to barehead' (*BF*, 241). Even if the odds are such that this reaction cannot be 'equal', it is at least 'opposite'.

Henderson documents the ironies by which black labourers are forced to participate in the aftermath of violence initiated by the police, repairing the properties which represent their continuing exploitation.

> I see Negro handymen put to work because of the riots
> boarding up smashed storefronts [...]
> The pine boards are the nearest Lenox Avenue will ever have
> to trees.
>
> (*BF*, 240)

This image recurs the following year in 'They Are Killing All the Young Men', juxtaposed with that of cleaners wiping up the blood of the murdered Malcolm X at the Audubon Ballroom.

> The thin Times today tells
> of three black scrubwomen
> put to work
> on the blood
>   (just as the handymen of Harlem were put to work
>   after the riots – patching up)
> 3 scrubwomen
> Scrubbing up blood – their blood.
>
> (Henderson 1965a, n.p.)

Such labour is connected to advertisements for white-owned business noted in the fourth section of 'Keep on Pushing'.

> I see plump pale butchers pose with their signs:
>   'Hog Maws 4 pounds for 1 dollar'
> 'Pigs ears 7 pounds for 1 dollar'
> 'Neck Bones Chitterlings 6 pounds for 1'
> Nightclubs, liquor stores bars 3, 4 & 5 to one block
> 3 & 4 shots for one dollar
> I see police eight to one.
>
> (*BF*, 241)

As Henderson later writes, 'THE POLICE PROTECT THE STORES' (*DMOH*, 68). This increase in police presence amplifies the daily exploitation of the black community. As Thomas notes, Henderson is critical of the practices of both white proprietors and black businessman whose embrace of the gospel of self-reliance leads to collusion with the interests of the white power structure, such as 'sherman the barbecue man', whose parlour is adorned with photos of Rockefeller and Truman (Henderson 1970, 42). In this climate, shops 'owned by absentee white folks, fronted by exploited and irascible black help' are infected by the 'awful madness' of 'commercialism', which 'affects the innocently menial scrubwomen and marginally employed handmen' (*EM*, 125). For Thomas:

> the psychic effect of all this might be identified in another country as colonialism. The socio-economic background of these poems is horrible. Money can't change you, but money on its meanest levels corrupts care [...] Simply put, the debased spirit of acquisitiveness encouraged by capitalist commercial society produces monstrous results wherever it interfaces with ordinary human concepts of feeling and care. (*EM*, 125–6)

These advertisements, suggesting the mediated nature of representations within the 'ghetto', are paralleled in the fifth section, which ironically comments on Harlem as a place of music and dance, noting the white appropriation of such culture, which is simultaneously denigrated and fetishized.

> At night Harlem sings and dances
> and as Jimmy Breslin of the Herald Tribune says
> they also pour their whiskey on one another's heads.
> They dog and slop in the bars.
>
> (*BF*, 241)

Both echoing and parodying this discourse, Henderson calls on Harlem's inhabitants to

>   Come out of your windows
> dancehalls, bars and grills, Monkey Dog in the streets
> like Martha and the Vandellas
> Dog for *NBC* [...]
> Dog for Adlai Stevenson
> and shimmy a bit
> for 'the boys upstate'.
>
> (242)

Referencing Martha and Vandellas' totemic riot anthem 'Dancing in the Streets', Henderson is aware of damaging effects of racial stereotype, performed 'for' the media and political establishment. But the return of the Impressions' refrain, set off from the rest of the stanza by its right-aligned indentation, allows it to metaphorically 'push' through to another audience:

'cause you got soul
Everybody knows ...
Keep on Pushin'.

(242)

In its sixth section, the poem tunes into WWRL, 'the radio station that serves / the Negro community', where 'the colourful unison announcers / declare themselves "The most soulful station in the nation"' (242). The 'rhythm and blues vehicle' is interrupted by 'the lecture series on democracy' in which Professor Robert Scalapino announces that 'violence only hurts (and he emphasizes hurts) / the cause of freedom and dignity', urging 'the troubled / restless residents of Harlem and Bedford-Stuyvesant to stay / in their homes, mark an end to the tragic and senseless / violence', before 'a rousing mixed chorus ends with / "And the home of the brave"' (243). Recalling the poem's earlier address to what Scalapino calls 'the fruits of democracy', Henderson implicitly asks, '*Whose* home is this?' But just as WWRL can be used by the forces of the white establishment (as Henderson caustically notes of Scalapino, 'eight to one he's white, representing management'), the return of WWRL's regular R&B programming following the sounding of the anthem aligns music and riot, illustrating the futility of Scalapino's appeals.

The rhythm and blues returns
a flaming bottle bursts on Seventh Avenue
and shimmies fire across the white divider line.

(243)

Nonetheless, the sound of the Impressions over the radio has to compete with a parade of commercial distraction and media pacification, from Professor Scalapino to radio personalities ambivalently personified in WWRL DJ Douglas 'Jocko' Henderson, who advertises alcohol and aspirin and urges the rioters to stay calm.

    Then Jocko scenes radio WWRL
late at night he hustles wine: Italian Swiss Colony Port
sherry and muscatel. Gypsy Rose and Hombre 'The man's

> Adult western drink',
> But by day and evening
> His raiment for Harlem's head is different
> Zealous Jocko coos forward
> his tongue baroque-sinister
> snakes like fire 'Headache?   — Take Aspirin'
>   'Tension?
>   ….take *Compoz*!'

(*BF*, 244)

The cost of such cheap alcohol is vividly rendered in 'Yin Years', the 'racist sugar / of imported fruit drinks' creating 'broken bottle limbs' in 'a high kind of poison & logical euthanasia' (Henderson 1966, 102, 111). The remedies that Jocko suggests are, it seems, little better than the truncheons which beat the 'bareheads' of Harlem residents.

In Baraka's own riot poem, 'Black People!', radios themselves are made 'beautiful' because they carry black music which reflects and encourages urban insurrection and the expropriation of property.

> [...] Dance up and down the streets, turn all
> the music up, run through the streets with music, beautiful radios on
> Market Street, they are brought here especially for you.

(*BM*, 225)

Yet, as Henderson more insistently foregrounds, what radios play is mediated through the control of programming and scheduling and, indeed, the record industry control of black music itself. Nonetheless, in the later poem 'Jocko for Music and Dance', Henderson writes of Jocko with great affection:

> sometimes Jocko is the only person I know
> the only person from my past who offers memory
>   without propaganda
>
> let me speak of tribal ritual & dance
> let me declare Jocko my atavistic purveyor of tribal tunes
>   and gossip –
>
>   the medicine man who strings the tendons of memory incarnate.

(*DMOH*, 58)

Jean-Phillipe Marcoux identifies Jocko as a 'cultural hero who moonlights as trickster' (Marcoux, 167–8): recalling Henderson's borrowing of the title 'Mayor of Harlem' from Willie Bryant, another prominent radio personality of the 1950s and 1960s, Jocko becomes part of Henderson's pantheon of cultural figures who, however ambivalently, speak to a sense of black, working-class community and a vitalizing cultural tradition. Jocko, known for his use of rhyming and hip catchphrases, was extremely popular among African-American audiences in Philadelphia and New York (Barlow, 143). In the 1950s, his show *Rocket Ship* had deployed a vernacular version of the Afro-Futurist vocabulary associated with Sun Ra, referenced at the end of Henderson's poem (*DMOH*, 58). Going into business, he fostered R&B showcases at Harlem's Apollo Theatre, entering the stage on a model rocket ship and promoting the new energies of artists such as James Brown (Barlow, 141, 144). Jocko was also politically active, marching on demonstrations in Philadelphia and New York City and interviewing Martin Luther King and Jesse Jackson on his show, interviews credited by some as contributing to King's and Jackson's increasing nationwide prominence (Barlow, 210). Yet, while the music, rhyme and catchphrases found on black radio often served to fan the flames of riot – most notably when Nathaniel 'The Magnificent' Montague's 'Burn, Baby, Burn!' became associated with the 1965 Watts Riots, costing him his job – radio DJs such as Jocko just as often served a pacifying function (Barlow, 213–18; Vincent, 159–61). During the summer of 1964, as Jocko recalls, he had the role of pacifying the rioters: 'I was there in New York when they had the riots […] I was on the scene with my quiet machine tryin' to keep 'em quiet' (quoted in Barlow, 213). Henderson's poem captures this ambivalence. The attempted pacification of the rioters by 'zealous Jocko', 'his tongue baroque sinister', plays into the ghetto commercialism that exists in conjunction with repressive forces. Yet it is Jocko who plays the rhythm and blues anthems that, in the poem, ultimately come to symbolize the collective resistance embodied in the riots.

As Touré insists in his incantatory use of the Impressions in 'Keep on Pushin': Rhythm and Blues as Weapon' and Martha and the Vandellas in 'Afro-American Youth and the Bandung World' (both 1965), and as Baraka reiterated in 'The Changing Same' (1966), such songs served as coded calls to arms, marketed as innocuous entertainment, but contextually reappropriated as the soundtrack to rioters' attempted reclamation of ghetto space (Touré 1965A, 1965B; Baraka 1967A). In his afterword to *Black Fire*, Larry Neal suggested that the strength of poems such as Henderson's lay precisely in its appeal to music (*BF*, 666). It is fitting, then, that the poem leaves the final words to the Impressions.

Keep on a' pushin'
Someway somehow
I know we can make it
with just a little bit of soul.

(BF, 244)

For Baraka, while this song provides 'a core of legitimate social feeling', that feeling remains 'mainly metaphorical and allegorical' (1967A, 238). What Henderson's poem does is to place the 'metaphorical and allegorical' lyrics of such works inside a context that is concrete and particular. While 'we' in the original song only require 'a little bit of soul', in Henderson's poem, this concept is transformed into the collective spirit that united Harlem's inhabitants against the forces of private slumlords, ghetto exploitation and the armed response of the American State.

'Yin Years'

'Keep on Pushing' emphasizes the economic critiques and nationalist focus on culture that characterize Henderson's work on Harlem. I'll turn now to his poem 'Yin Years', written the following year from the background of the Harlem Riots and the subsequent Watts Rebellion. Here, Henderson locates himself downtown, away from the spaces of Harlem as black community. But this work is no less keenly aware of the political stakes on every street corner, every loft, every subway train and every skyscraper in New York. 'Yin Years' first appeared as a seven-section poem in the anthology *Poems Now* (1966), edited by Baraka's former wife Hettie Jones. Though subsequently reprinted in *Felix of the Silent Forest* (1967) and *De Mayor of Harlem* (1970), these versions cut four of the original sections, and my analysis here focuses on the original, longer version (Henderson 1966, 100–9). Dated 'Bowery, New York/summer 1965', the poem addresses the downtown experience, informed by the uptown Harlem Riots of the preceding summer, overlaying confrontations between the massed forces of the police and the African-American 'natives' of New York with the deployment of American armed forces against the Vietcong. As Thomas notes, Henderson's work, though nationalist-inflected, does not 'recourse to overt politics of exhortation' (*EM*, 126). 'Roam[ing] low' in the Bowery's streets (Henderson 1966, 109), Henderson appears, in contrast to Baraka's and Touré's contemporaneous work, as a figure able to disguise himself and to report on the city's conditions from the sidelines: like Rinehart, Felix or the Mayor of Harlem, watching, waiting and observing.

Yet Henderson also theorizes a collective struggle between the forces of the state and private business interests and the counterculture, ghetto dwellers and anti-imperialists in Vietnam. This poetic ensemble suggests the new forces accessed through the political activity of On Guard and the BART/S. Indeed, the developing presence of an African-American collective voice – whether through Umbra in poetry or in R&B and 'the new music' – which might be said to constitute a second New York Black Renaissance to follow that of the 1920s, fostered in, but not limited to, the spaces of Harlem and the Lower East Side (Szwed, 194–6).

The poem opens with an ironic reference to the previous year's World's Fair: 'New York City is a death festival' (Henderson 1966, 100). Placing himself on the roof of his loft apartment, he surveys the spaces of downtown Manhattan, noting the sharp contrasts of wealth from district to district.

> Looking downtown
> from bowery roofs
> the location marks
> the balance of this city
> to which all structures
> of the city hall boys fan
> /East by North.
>
> (100)

Though very much a poem of specific locations, 'Yin Years' also links dizzyingly between these, often in incantatory lists: 'These are years of yin / from Korea to Vietnam / Yalta to Geneva' (Henderson 1966, 109). In a pun on the poetic line, the limit reached in conditions of political despair, and the New York subway, the second section ends by describing the state of the nation:

> the beginning of the line
>   the end of the line/America
>   the den of beggars & thieves
> *it furthers one to have somewhere to go.*
>
> (Henderson 1966, 104)

This 'line' is ironically juxtaposed with a quotation from Hexagram 24 of the *I Ching* in Richard Wilhelm's translation: 'THE JUDGMENT//DURATION. Success. No blame./ Perseverance furthers. / It furthers one to have somewhere to go.' As the title indicates, 'Yin Years' taps into the countercultural embrace of non-Western cultures: the 'end of the line', beyond America, is the 'beginning' of a symbolic turn towards the East. The poem participates in the increasing adoption of alternative spiritual systems, music and dress that characterized the BAM just as much as it characterized the more prominent white counterculture: an embrace, later in the poem associated with the Vietcong and resistance to US imperialism, which anticipates Henderson's later concept of the 'third eye/world'. Cultural connections between America, Asia and Africa are set against the spaces of New York finance capital, the ironically figured 'magnificence of the Woolworth building' juxtaposed with the 'holocaust' or 'urban renewal' (100). Henderson's link is based on puns: the 'East' is a culturally rejuvenating force with a spiritual dimension, represented by both the *I Ching* and the Vietcong. But it also puns on the East Village: these are not just spaces of one nation. As the poem continues, Henderson presents the police who congregate 'by Bowery', ironically described as 'angry family men / visionaries of rare steak' (104). This leads to a dramatic encounter, harking back to the Harlem Riots and the Watts Riots of August 1965, as well as to American intervention in Vietnam.

>   —blue veined blonds
>   versus people of the fields
>   Smith & Wesson fire arms
>   versus bamboo shards & marijuana [...]
>   too many rushing natives howling
>   strange rage
>   Vietnam Los Angeles Santo Domingo Harlem ...
>   The British of the 18th century
>   lined-up against the Colonials
>   in platoon order
>   to employ maximum firepower
>   ... yet the farmers of the fields
>   prevailed.
>
> (105)

Henderson also deploys this comparison in 'They Are Killing All the Young Men', the same year:

> Inasmuch as the New York cops beat out Secretary of War
> MacNamara and the occupational force of Vietnam
> With the use of poison nerve gas (Harlem riots, summer of 1964)
> that does not count as it pertains to Foreign Policy.
>
> (*FOTSF*, n.p.)

There are suggestive parallels between such lines and the account of the Watts Rebellion given in Nelson Peery's autobiography *Black Radical*. As Peery notes, there were quite material links between the events in Watts and Vietnam. 'More Americans died fighting in Watts Saturday night than in Vietnam that day': eighteen people were killed, and thousands beaten and arrested (Peery, 225). Peery reports a black teenager, released after being beaten by the police, saying: 'We goin' back. They ain't seen the last of us. We're gonna Vietcong their ass tonight' (216). An army division on its way to Vietnam was turned around mid-ocean in order to deal with the urban insurrection in Watts; in response, the Liberation Army of North Vietnam sent a message of solidarity and thanks to the people of Watts (221). As Peery puts it: 'In Watts the Vietnam war came home. All the talk of freedom and self-determination finally hit a target' (227).

In 'Yin Years', Henderson's identification between the East (Village) and Asia both parodies the response to the nascent counterculture and to ethnic minorities by businessmen from Wall Street, the police and the military and appropriates such discourse for its own ends. The ensemble of 'rushing natives' stand for guerrilla resistance. This resistance is to British imperialists by Americans in the eighteenth century – a link cemented, as Henderson notes, by the Harlem location of a number of key battles in the War of Independence, many of which featured black soldiers (Middlebrook, 39). But it is also resistance to twentieth-century American imperialism by the 'natives' of Harlem and Watts and by those opposing American intervention in the Dominican Republic and Vietnam. Eliding the spaces of country and city, Henderson parallels the 'urban guerrilla concept' developed earlier that year by Robert F. Williams in which the tactics of guerrilla warfare adopted from Che Guevara and Mao Tse-Tung were applied to those of American cities (Williams 1964A, 6). But Henderson also figures guerrilla warfare through the pastoral, opposing the technologized space of the modern city.

> now it is the 20th century
> natives and farmers learn knowledge of machine
> is finite
> knowledge of verdure
> absolute [...]
>   that no technology can approximate [...]
> It is the plastic men of technology
> against the natives of the land

(Henderson 1966, 106–8)

The sufferings of the starving masses who 'by necessity fast' become modes of Eastern asceticism and mystical illumination, rejecting the consumerism and excess of 'the overfilled/overkill peoples' (108) who are 'held together by technology of machine and drugs'. Realizing that 'knowledge of machine / is finite', they instead possess 'knowledge of verdure [...] that no technology can approximate'.

Henderson now turns from urban pastoral visions of anti-imperialism, back towards the narrator, who can slip among all the diverse groups in the Bowery: whether

> the long-haired people of music [...]
> who dress strangely
> and sing America
> with Chinese accentuations

or street drinkers, bums and junkies, 'who appear like hoboes gypsies the insane' (Henderson 1966, 109).

> by Bowery
> my dress is among the bums
> the police cannot tell us apart
> until I open the door to my loft
> and disappear
>   those who make friends
>   those who roam low
>   in the streets
>   reap reward.

(110)

The edited version of the poem ends ambiguously on an apparent vision of uniformity:

> the caste of men
> who by neon fluorescence
> are not unlike one another/
> everyone in America

(*FOTSF*, n.p.)

Henderson appears to suggest that East Village bohemians are just as subject to 'facelessness' and invisibility as the majority of the white American populace.

The longer printing in *Poems Now* extends these lines in a manner that moves – however haltingly – beyond this vision. To be sure, the loft spaces inhabited by LES artists are likened to the reservations to which Native Americans were driven and, once more, to the Ellisonian invisibility of the 'underground'.

> These old loft buildings
> belong to us
> these vacant streets of
> dying men and darkness …
> for we have been shipped by society
> (Indians by reservation)
> told to keep moving
> or to lie in vacant places/unseen
> and like the Negro
> the culture of the caste
> is intact & underground.
>
> (111)

The 'underground' is symbolic of both disguise – that which allows Henderson to 'roam low' and 'lie in vacant places / unseen' and the hellish enclosure of invisibility. Henderson's poem 'Psychedelic Firemen' likewise draws on the figure of the underground man, earlier developed by Ellison and Richard Wright, linking fairground rides, Auschwitz trains and the New York subway as a circling through hell reminiscent of Baraka's *Dutchman* or the slave ship.

> the weirdest
> rollercoaster through manhattan by underground express
> iron cars trains of auschwitz
> jangling metal grit   subway air
>
> MAN DOES NOT BELONG UNDERGROUND.
>
> (*DMOH*, 27)

Here, like Touré in 'Cry Freedom', Henderson vehemently rejects invisibility. For Ralph D. Story, 'he's saying that black folks will express themselves out in the open and refuse – from this point on – to be suppressed or remain silent' (Story, 137). Henderson's poetics convey a sense – in 'Psychedelic Firemen' and 'Keep on Pushing' – of emergence into public visibility, reclaiming spaces through festivity or riot, while – in 'Yin Years' – maintaining a tradition of resistance which is necessarily underground and full of disguises, uniting bohemians, bums and guerrilla fighters. In 'Elvin Jones Gretsch Freak' (1965), Henderson adds to this ensemble the historical memory of the Underground Railroad. Via musical references, from the blues to advanced modern jazz – the performance by the John Coltrane Quartet at the Five Spot that occasions the poem, Duke Ellington's 'Take the "A" Train' and Howlin' Wolf's 'Smokestack Lightnin'' – the subway links to figures of migration and escape.

> "A" train long as a long city block
> the tenements of the underground rails [...]
> fumes of tracks   /smokestacks.

(*FOTSF*, n.p.)

While these train tracks punningly link to notions of order, decorum and 'toeing the line' – 'our city fathers keep us on the right track' – the invocation of the Underground Railroad also suggests a lineage for metaphorically subterranean activity connected to a vital tradition of slave resistance. Likewise, at the end of 'Yin Years', the 'culture of the caste' (108) suggests not just the racial divisions reinforced by those forces which drive black artists underground but a reversal of norms. Akin to the fugitivity of the Underground Railroad, to guerrilla armies and to Baraka's cults, these underground ensembles lie just under the surface, ready to participate when energies such as those of the Harlem Riots flare up once more.

Of course, as with Baraka's cultic forces, that which lies invisible or underground as often represents the forces of the state and of private interests as it does their opponents. 'They Are Killing All the Young Men', written during the same period as 'Yin Years', provides an index of the figures of police spies and the FBI, blamed for the murder of black radicals. The poem is dedicated 'to the memory and the eternal spirit of Malcolm X 1927–1965' and was written in response to his assassination – the event that provoked Baraka's move to Harlem and that formed the basis for poems by many Umbra and BAM poets (one of the best being Raymond Patterson's 'At That Moment' (Patterson, 1969, 31)). The poem was first published, without title, as a supplement to the final issue of Ed Sanders's *Fuck You: A Magazine of the Arts* in June 1965 and subsequently in revised form in *Felix of the Silent Forest* the following year (Henderson 1965A, 28; *FOTSF*, n.p.). It is the final poem in that book, ending on a despairing note.

Henderson once more presents the event through its mass-media filtration: the confused ways in which he hears of the news and subsequent reactions among 'rank and file' street knowledge, and the contrasting apologias of official media outlets, are symptoms of the conditions that killed Malcolm. Recalling the On Guard protests and Lumumba's presence in Baraka's 'The Revolutionary Theatre' and 'Black Dada Nihilismus', Henderson links the death of 'young men' such as Malcolm X and John F. Kennedy to that of Lumumba. A series of rising questions about the lack of FBI protection for Malcolm leads him to exclaim:

> does anyone remember Patrice Lumumba?
> Does anyone remember the circumstances
> of *his* murder?
> Is anyone concerned with the strange deaths
> of bright youngmen
> 			(Kennedy, Malcolm, Lumumba, et al).
>
> (*FOTSF*, n.p.)

At the same time, Henderson draws an important distinction between Kennedy's and Malcolm's deaths, particularly the ways in which they were reported. Contrasting the R&B played after Malcolm's death to the 'strange elevator Muzak' played after Kennedy's, he writes:

> 	Rhythm and Blues is now
> it is the reality of our Time
> has Malcolm X assassinated in New York City
> Dallas of the East.
>
> (*FOTSF*, n.p.)

Cutting between the banal TV programming juxtaposed with the news of X's assassination – 'sports on network TV', 'gay restaurant music', 'the Westminster Dog Show' – Henderson proceeds to that which is erased from such reports.

> Rank and file knowledge has the Black Muslims
> infiltrated by the FBI CIA G-Men Treasury agents
> and the New York City Police Department.
>
> (*FOTSF*, n.p.)

Yet these assassins remain 'faceless' spies, America 'a nation of 007s'. Baraka's own, widely anthologized elegy for Malcolm, 'A Poem for Black Hearts', insistently calls its auditors to action:

> For Great Malcolm a prince of the earth, let nothing in us rest
> until we avenge ourselves for his death, stupid animals

that killed him, let us never breathe a pure breath if
we fail […]

(*BM*, 112)

Henderson instead ends ambiguously on the 'invisible men' who assassinated Malcolm. Against the deaths of 'young men', he seeks another grouping – not only one which acts through the visible actions of riot but one which might turn the 'invisibility' of the police, spies and assassins against them. From Harlem to the Lower East Side, Watts to Vietnam, the Audubon Ballroom to the Five Spot, spontaneity and flexible redefinition lead to a potent collective capacity, but it is also imbricated with continuing histories of erasure, misrepresentation and violence. Despite the moments of potential he frequently finds in riots and in the artistic and political underground, Henderson is always aware of the frailty of the collectives his poems describe. These questions of tactics, representation, the role of violence and the role of black music come to the fore once more in the texts on riots by Calvin Hernton examined in the following chapter.

4

Language, Violence and 'the Collective Mind': Calvin C. Hernton

A central figure in Umbra, Lorenzo Thomas calls Calvin Hernton 'the mentor of the entire group. He showed people directions, and he pointed out what was valuable to pursue. (Thomas 1981B, 28). His work has been much anthologized over the years, and he was one of the more prolific of the Umbra writers early on, publishing two full-length books by 1966 (Hernton 1965B, 1966D). However, he remains an obscure figure, sometimes briefly cited in studies of the BAM but almost never read in critical depth. The current chapter focuses on Hernton's writings of urban insurrection. Beginning with his poetry of New York City – particularly the poem 'Jitterbugging in the Streets', which develops and extends the work of David Henderson with whom he was extremely close (Hernton 1993, 581) – I then move to Hernton's essays on riots – the majority of them written after his move to England in 1965 – focusing in particular on 'Dynamite Growing out of Their Skulls'. Published, like 'Jitterbugging', in Baraka and Larry Neal's anthology *Black Fire* in 1968 – a volume described on the back cover as 'a flaming prophecy of future turmoil' – 'Dynamite' stands out as one of the most explicitly militant texts in a book characterized by explosive rhetoric and is arguably Hernton's most polemical piece of writing. Addressing racial unrest in America, with particular reference to urban rioting in Harlem and Watts, Hernton brings to bear his observations from social work, his experience of state surveillance and police harassment forming a kind of invisible backdrop to his analyses. Hernton's prediction of a coming race war veers between militant endorsements of violence and awareness of the deadlock into which violent action can become locked. Invoking stereotypes of black male rage as both satire and goad, Hernton's essay traverses a wide range of reference – from R.D. Laing to Nietzsche, W.E.B. Du Bois to Gregory Bateson – in a manner that challenges boundaries between the literary, the political, the real and the imaginary: not simply as a means of generic experimentation but as a wrenching testimony to the urgent contradictions faced by African-American radical movements at this time.

Calvin C. Hernton: An introduction

Born in 1932, Calvin Coolidge Hernton was older than many of the Umbra poets. Like Askia Touré, Tom Dent and his close friend Ishmael Reed, he had a Southern upbringing; he was raised by his grandmother in Chattanooga, Tennessee, a formative background explored at length in the following chapter. In the early 1950s, Hernton studied at the historically black Talladega College and at Fisk University, Nashville. Here, as discussed in the introduction, he was briefly surveilled by the FBI on the basis of two early poems: his early experiences of racism and state surveillance proving crucial. Following previous visits, he settled in New York in 1961, working as a social worker in the build-up to the 1964 Harlem Riots; this, along with his earlier Southern experiences, formed the basis of the radical political stance adopted in works such as 'Jitterbugging' and 'Dynamite'. Hernton was an active participant in the LES arts scene from which Umbra emerged, publishing widely in leftist and countercultural journals and magazines, including *Streets, Liberator, Negro Digest, Evergreen Review* and *Peace News*. Accounts of Umbra often focus on his powerful readings: his dramatic performances appeared in Aldo Tambellini's *Black Zero* and on two records – *Destinations: Four Contemporary American Poets* (1964) in which he appears alongside N.H. Pritchard and *New Jazz Poets* (1967) in which his reading of 'Jitterbugging' is featured alongside readings of Henderson, Reed, Art Berger and Joe Johnson.

In early 1965, Hernton, along with other Umbra poets, participated in Baraka's BART/S experiment in Harlem. Following the publication of *Sex and Racism in America* (1965) – a highly controversial sociological study which remains his best-known work – that summer, he took the spontaneous decision to board a ship for England with psychiatrist Joseph Berke (This voyage serves as the basis for his novel *Scarecrow* (1974).) (Hernton 1974, 1–2, 31; Oren 2006, 615). Hernton was involved, through Berke, with R.D. Laing's Kingsley Hall Community Project, and he taught courses for the Anti-University of London. He also participated in events organized by the Caribbean Artists' Movement, a cultural initiative founded by Kamau Brathwaite, John La Rose and Andrew Salkey in 1966, which developed a collective practice deeply informed by, but distinct from, the American BAM with its own ties to a developing scene of diasporic writers and to British Black Power Movement (Walmsley, 152–3, 313–14; Brathwaite 2000, 170). The New York coffee-house scene around Le Metro and Les Deux Mégots, where Umbra had developed a public presence, found its equivalent in the lively reading circuit around London pubs such as The Troubadour in Notting Hill and in academic and art institutions such as the

University of Kent and the ICA (Brutus, 26). In 'An Unexpurgated Communiqué to David Henderson – London 1966', published in *Umbra*'s third issue, Hernton writes, echoing Blake:

> It's astounding how thoroughly policed the skin-forged
>   boundaries are –
> From Notting Hill Gate to Piccadilly Circus
> The West Indians work on the buses
>   *any more fares please.*

(*Umbra Anthology*, 26)

The intersections between Caribbean, British and American Black Power at this time could be incendiary. Most notably, the participation of Kwame Ture (Stokely Carmichael) at the 1967 Dialectics of Liberation conference, largely organized by Joseph Berke, was a hugely galvanizing event for the Caribbean Artists Movement (CAM) and, in the wake of race riots in America, was so inflammatory that he was deported by the British government (Walmsley, 91–3).

Hernton served as a reporter on and representative of the BAM for an English audience, writing articles on Baraka and on race riots for British socialist-pacifist journal *Peace News* (Hernton 1966c, 1966e). As he puts it in his 'Communiqué' (alluding to 'The Witchcraft of LeRoi Jones', his recently published article *Peace News* article):

> I crouch over the ocean injecting ink into the lives
>   of my contemporaries
> Bootlegging feats of sheer witchcraft for crude bread and such –
> Judging and waiting.

(*Umbra Anthology*, 26)

Moving between these scenes – whether the principally white world of anti-psychiatry and the New Left or those around the CAM, British and American Black Power, and the BAM – Hernton could not be pinned to any of them. Based in London and Sweden until 1970, he returned to the United States to take up a position as writer-in-residence at Central State University in Wilberforce, Ohio, before moving to Oberlin College, where he taught until his retirement in 1999. He continued to be active as a writer: his collected poems, *Medicine Man*, appeared from Reed, Cannon and Johnson in 1976; notable other works included *Coming Together* (1971), *Scarecrow* (1974) and *The Sexual Mountain and Black Women Writers* (1987) in which he developed and critiqued some of his earlier writing on intersections between racial and sexual oppression (*MM*; Hernton 1971A, 1974, 1987). Considering himself first and foremost as a poet (Ramey, 118), and initially the most widely published poet in Umbra, Hernton's subsequent neglect may result from his move away from America during the peak period of Black Power: despite his presence in formative BAM endeavours, he has, as with Umbra in general, been virtually written out of the movement.

Though much Umbra writing concerns displacement and alienation, Hernton's exilic status is arguably the most pronounced, whether in the move from South to North, Harlem to the LES or America to England. As he writes in the 'Unexpurgated Communiqué':

> I am in this country illegally [...]
> Oh, I am in this world without a passport to humanity!
> Spaded and shaded.
>
> (*Umbra Anthology*, 27)

Hernton left America at a point of intense racial tension in September 1965: witnessing the Harlem Riots the previous year, he left shortly after the Watts Riots in August. While Baraka and Henderson saw these riots as moments of collective possibility, for Hernton, they were as much as indices of psychological and political alienation, actions born from despair. Hernton writes of the 'Long Hot Summers' of 1964 through to 1968 from afar. The 'Unexpurgated Communiqué' ends in a combination of anguish, despair and defiant resolve:

> Every night I get stoned in the Seven Stars among the wretched
> > of the earth
> > and plot the downfall of empires.
>
> (27)

As the reference to Fanon suggests, Hernton's writing is informed by a tradition of black internationalism, cross-cultural influence and diaspora, seen elsewhere in his poem 'For Ghana, 1957' and his introduction to Janheinz Jahn's *Muntu* (*MM*, 92). Yet this combines with a deep sense of alienation and individual anguish. Hernton's early work, like Henderson's, deals with the 'spaces of a nation' found in New York, between the LES and Harlem. Describing the 'congestion of horrors' and 'venomous ambiance' of the city during the early 1960s, Lorenzo Thomas writes:

> The atmosphere that results is perhaps what Ishmael Reed was talking about when he said of New York that 'it always looks like the final days there.' It looks

like that because New York City began a grim decline just after World War II, a decline that paralleled the disintegration of the global economic and political hegemony the city represents.

(Thomas 1978, 53)

In Hernton's words:

[...] None but
the dead living know the horror of Georgia,
Mississippi and New York.

('Elements of Grammar', *MM*, 88)

'The Gift Outraged'

As Reed notes, the Umbra poets 'were cultural outsiders, who were not native New Yorkers; people who had ambivalent attitudes toward the city where we hoped to make our reputations as artists' (Reed 2012, online). As discussed in the introduction to this book, the Lower East Side, to which these artists gravitated, was a melting pot of different communities, particularly Jewish, Puerto Rican and Eastern European. On the one hand, this provided a stimulating environment, radically different to the high-priced Greenwich Village: the Umbra writers almost universally credit the LES as a space crucial to their development as individuals and as a group (Dent 2018, 451). At the same time, through their involvement with social work, journalism and political activism, the Umbra poets – themselves often forced into a succession of temporary and precarious jobs in order to survive in the city – knew the sufferings of the urban poor first-hand. Furthermore, distinguished by their race, by their bohemian lifestyles and – often, though by no means exclusively – by their education, the Umbra writers were not entirely integrated into the community. As Dent notes, as much as it strengthened the collective bonds within the group itself, this paradox of being outsiders in a community of immigrants who were themselves outsiders could lead to a double sense of alienation (Dent 1980A, 247). Many of the Umbra poets' earlier poems sketch this uneasy balance. This is particularly crucial for Hernton, forming important background for his subsequent writing on urban insurrection.

Dent would later call Hernton's long poem 'The Gift Outraged', 'a marvellous display of his poetic strengths. It is the best piece I have ever seen on the

Lower East Side as I knew it' (Dent 1980, 246). Parodying Robert Frost's 1961 inauguration poem for John F. Kennedy, 'The Gift Outright', Hernton's Surrealist-inflected night wanderings in Tompkins Square Park see him encounter a cast of Holocaust survivors, junkies, winos and bums, reflecting with anguished sympathy on the limits to solidarity with members of the dispossessed.

> [...] where piss-stained benches call forth zombie
> Supplicants pale and dry
> From Buchenwald, Auschwitz, Dachau, Austria
> The Ukraine [...]
>
> they know I am not from wherever
> They once were [...]
>
> Even though I am here [...]
> they know I am not wherever they think they are now –
> Or whoever they fashion themselves to be [...]
> So *this* is Tompkins Square Park?
> What am I doing here?
> Am I in the wrong neighbourhood?
> Why does my heart bleed?
>
> (*MM*, 109)

This final line reads as a despairing joke on 'bleeding heart liberals'; Hernton is characteristically full of self-loathing. Tompkins Square Park, the scene of an 1874 Riot crushed by police, a symbolic location for the labour movement and subsequently a centre for the homeless and dispossessed, is far from simply the 'hip' neighbourhood it might have been for white bohemians and dropouts. Hernton's depiction, for instance, is a far cry from the romanticized depiction of the park given by Bill Amidon in a piece called 'Where Have All the Hipsters Gone?' published in the *Village Voice* in 1972. 'In '63 I could sleep comfortably stoned in Tompkins Square Park on a bench by myself and be awakened around dawn by pure sweet saxophone music. Lately I get nervous there on Sunday afternoons with four friends' (Amidon).

The collective sketched here is one united by dispossession, suffering and mental illness. Such anguish also inflects Hernton's writings on riots. Emerging from his direct experience of state oppression and urban poverty, through social work in Harlem and through living on the Lower East Side, such writings refuse either aesthetic or political distancing.

'Jitterbugging in the Streets'

Hernton's 'Jitterbugging in the Streets' (1965), like Henderson's 'Keep on Pushing', quickly became something a visible work within politicized, countercultural poetry scenes: it originally appeared in New Left magazine *Streets* alongside Baraka's 'Three Movements and a Coda' and work by Sartre and Fanon, was reprinted in a feature on 'Poets of the Insurrections' for *American Dialog*, recorded on the album *New Jazz Poets* for Smithsonian Folkways (both in 1967), and printed alongside 'Dynamite' in *Black Fire* in 1968. Caustically attacking the language used by 'All-Americans' to stigmatize the 1964 Harlem rioters, the poem begins with an ironic parody of the biblical coming of Jesus and of Fourth of July celebrations.

> There will be no holyman crying out this year
> No seer, no trumpeter, no George Fox walking barefoot
>   up and down the hot land
> [...] there will be no Fourth of July this year
> No shouting, no popping of firecrackers, no celebrating,
>   no parade
> But the rage of a hopeless people
> Jitterbugging
>   in the streets.
>
> (*BF*, 205)

Hernton challenges the language of 'common sense' which condemns riots while refusing to do anything about the conditions that produce them.

> You say there are four gates to the ghetto
> Make your own bed hard that is where you have got
> To lay
> You say there is violence in Harlem, niggers run amuck
>   perpetrating crimes against property.
>
> (207)

Hernton's first-person speaker defies such logics with an utterance of his own.

> I say there is no 'violence' in Harlem.
> There is TERROR in Harlem! [...]
> Harlem is the asphalt plantation of America.
>
> (207)

Insisting on the root cause of the riots – not only the murder of ninth-grader James Powell by the police – 'The only Messiah we will know this year is a bullet / In the belly / Of a Harlem youth shot down by a coward crouched / behind an outlaw's badge' (206) – but the entire system that led to his murder, Hernton furiously challenges white America's failure to understand the root cause of the riots.

The poem's title itself comments on racist stigmatizations of black identity by which, as Hernton later argued, black cultural modes are either demeaned or exploited and exoticized (*BF*, 81). In 'Jitterbugging', African-American rioters are condemned for acting on 'instinct' in the same way that they might be praised for their 'natural rhythms'. Their jitterbugging – a dance invented during the 1920s and associated with the Harlem Renaissance and the Jazz Age – is a hideous parody of the physical convulsions undergone in reaction to police violence:

> Jitterbugging
>   in
>   the streets
> To ten thousand rounds of ammunition
> To water hoses, electric prods, phallic sticks,
>   hound dogs, black boots stepping in soft
>   places of the body.
>
> (206)

It is also a reference to Martha and the Vandellas' 1964 'Dancing in the Streets', which serves as an insurrectionary refrain in the contemporaneous work addressed in previous chapters, from Touré's 'Dancing in the Streets: Rhythm and Blues as Weapon' to Baraka's 'Black People!' and Henderson's 'Keep on Pushing'. Baraka, Touré and Henderson insist on the revolutionary messages to be found in such music. Hernton's response is more ambivalent. Describing the riots as a 'genocide', the poem catalogues of violence and suffering in Harlem – from 'the circular plague of the welfare check' to the 'big-bellied agents of downtown landlords […] forcing black girls to get down and do the dog' (208) – ironically juxtaposed with Fourth of July celebrations, TV soap operas and the racist reactions of white Americans to media coverage of the riots – 'venom in the mouth of Christian housewives […] businessmen, civil service/Employees' (206). Like Touré's 'Afro-American Youth and the Bandung World' (1965), the poem references *The Communist Manifesto* – 'There is a spectre haunting America' (207) – suggesting that the riots contain revolutionary potential (Touré 1965A, 4). Yet this barely manifests in the majority of the poem. The one moment of possibility occurs when the speaker encounters a young student whose combination of analysis and militancy sees him take up arms against the police.

> He said he was fifteen years old, and he walked beside us
> there in the littered fields of the ghetto
> He spoke with a dignity of the language that shocked us
> and he said he had a *theory* about what had *perpetrated* the
> Horror that was upon us [...]
> He said he was a business major at George Washington High
> And he picked up a bottle and hurling it above the undulating
> crowd
> Straight into the chalk face of a black helmet!
>
> (*BF*, 208)

But this moment is ended by the exclamation mark. After this interlude, the poem ends on a moment of despair in which 'Niggers will be doing business as usual – / From river to river, / Signboard to Signboard' (208), 'every third child will do the junk-nod in the whore-scented/night' (209), and white America will refuse to 'cry out' against 'the blasting bullet in the belly/of a teenager' which ironically comes to stand in for a Fourth of July celebration (206). The riots ultimately remain an expression of despair, rather than a moment of revolutionary potential: 'the rage of a hopeless people/Jitterbugging/in the streets' (204).

'On Racial Riots in America'

During the mid-1960s, Hernton took his place alongside Baraka as an excoriating commentator on American race politics in a series of increasingly militant essays which appeared as lead stories in *Negro Digest*, *Peace News*, and the 1966 essay collection *White Papers for White Americans* (Hernton 1963, 1964B, 1966C, 1966D). Expressing dissatisfaction with the non-violent leaders of the Civil Rights Movement, the slow progress of white liberals and the religious extremism of the NOI, Hernton turned instead to what he called 'the existential Negroes': the rural poor of the American South and the ghetto dwellers of the urban north, whose growing discontent manifested in the riots that increasingly engulfed American cities. In 'Is There Really a Negro Revolution?' (1964) – first printed in *Negro Digest* in December 1964 and republished in revised form in *White Papers* – Hernton argues for a 'total assault on the culture', borrowing a phrase coined by William Burroughs which formed the motto for Ed Sanders's

Fuck You, the New York little magazine which published the work of Baraka and Henderson among others (Hernton 1964B, 16). For Hernton:

> A revolution – any revolution! – is a ruthless programme of aggression, on the part of the oppressed masses, against the very *foundation* of the powers that oppress [...] Historically, anywhere in the world the only power the masses possess is the power of violence; or the power which is the *threat* of violence! (15–16)

Hernton's essay 'On Racial Riots in America' appeared in *Peace News* following his move to England. Responding to a fresh outbreak of riots in Watts, a year after those of August 1965, Hernton again figures the rioters more as victims than insurrectionists. Noting that the rioters were often starving, and the painful irony by which large numbers of African-Americans fight in America's overseas wars while racial violence continues at home, he compares ghetto police to SS guards and the 'American attitude towards its oppressed to its attitude towards the people in Vietnam' (Hernton 1966C, 3). Ironically appropriating the language of baptism to critique a Christian vocabulary of non-violence, Hernton presents, 'the hell and holy ghost of black people running and falling and screaming and being beaten by cops and washed away by the fierce water hoses' (3). This image, which anticipates Lorenzo Thomas's 'The Bathers' (1970), returns in Hernton's poem 'The Mob' (1967), once more alongside Martha and the Vandellas.

> There is something dreadful
> About our being here this way, undulating
> In the streets,
> Blasted down, flesh scorched by liquid rays
> Of baptismal hose.

(*MM*, 94)

Echoing Malcolm X's infamous comment on the death of Kennedy – 'the chickens have come home to roost' – Hernton presents the 'long hot summers' of the riots as a ticking time bomb.

> Summer sets on the cities
> Like a hen
> On a package with a ticking noise inside –
> New York, Chicago, Birmingham,
> Newark, Atlanta, Watts ...
> The sun is on fire.

(94)

The titular 'mob' is alienated and alone:

> Tottering, we
> Brace ourselves alone
> Against stone [...]
> Rigid before the loneliness in
> The other's skin.
>
> (94)

The solitary suffering of these speakers is only exacerbated by their 'meeting' as part of the titular mob, facing the brutality of police violence on 'the citied streets'.

> When
> If at last we meet
>
> In death-threaded exigence
> It is no accident we scream obscenity –
> All our life is obscenity
> There is nothing accidental about trash.
>
> (94)

Exigence means urgency – a situation that demands immediate action – or, in rhetoric, a situation that prompts someone to write or speak. Yet, though the riots demand rhetoric and action, the only word that responds is an 'obscenity' which reflects, but not change, the violence of current conditions. Such violence extends to the natural world: parodying Hemingway's *The Sun Also Rises*, 'The sun also screams', and the uprising of the 'mob' recedes once more into abjection and separation.

> Forlorn we limp away:
> Head helmets,
> Body bayonets,
> Bloody rags.
>
> (94)

In 'On Racial Riots', Hernton caustically decries the governmental response to Watts: the establishment of a 'Study Committee' presided over by former CIA head John McCone serving only to provide 'more jobs for white advisors, politicians, professors, etc, not to mention the graft, and a few educated uncle toms … great progress!' (Hernton 1966D, 3). Instead, he insists:

> We all know very well what needs to be done. The crux of the matter is that we do not want and are not going to do it short of Armageddon […] The stereotype response [sic] of the power structure in America (forming study commissions, proposing remedies, piecemeal stopgaps, building prison blocks called 'housing projects', and all the rest) amount to nothing more than trying to prolong and maintain the very overall system that, if the basic causes of riots are to be erased, must be utterly destroyed or re-organized. (3)

As in 'Is There Really a Negro Revolution?', Hernton writes of the need for

> the re-organisation of the total American social structure. When I say 're-organization' I mean redistribution of economic, political, and most of all, *military* power in such a fashion that the Negro himself will be in a position to make sure that no-one, public or private, can get away with treating him less than a human being. (3)

The essay ends with a five-point plan for action which includes 'a guaranteed income of $5,000 to every American citizen for the next ten years' and 'dissolution of the FBI, the CIA, and the Department of War'. While this might suggest a precursor to the BPP's Ten-Point Programme, released the following year, Hernton sarcastically concludes in his final paragraph, that, because

> such a 'dream' would revolutionise the total concept and structure of American society […] President Johnson, with the happy blessings of all capitalists and imperialists and other loyal patriotic Americans, God fearers all, would […] be obliged to drop the bomb and end it all. (3)

He protests 'I am not saying this "tongue-in-cheek"' and concludes bleakly: 'since American Negroes do not have a bomb with which to bargain, it seems that they will be left to periodic rioting in the streets for quite some time to come' (3).

'Dynamite Growing out of Their Skulls'

'On Racial Riots' presents a very real dilemma: what to do when facing the entire armed apparatus of the state. Two years later, Hernton's essay 'Dynamite Growing out of Their Skulls' appeared in Baraka and Neal's *Black Fire*. The essay is far more extended and dramatic in its predictions: by this point, Hernton figures rioting less as 'periodic' and more part of a widespread insurrection that could engulf America. While Hernton's earlier essays warned that 'Armageddon' would ensue if white liberals did not do more to help the more militant elements of the Civil Rights Movement (1964B, 22, 1966D, 3), he argues in 'Dynamite' (via Du Bois) that

> violence, only violence, smoldering within the black pits of the psyche, will be at once the tool of liberation as well as the experience which will recreate a sense of manhood and human worth within the souls of black folk. (*BF*, 101)

Baraka himself would later describe the essay as 'violently anti-imperialist' (Baraka 1984B, 318), and Hernton's biographical statement for the book reads as a hyperbolic assertion of his status as a black radical: 'When I left America I was to the left of Martin Luther King. When I return, for I shall, and soon, I will be to the left of Malcolm X and Fanon' (*BF*, 663–4). 'Dynamite' emerged at a time when discourses of armed self-defence were receiving increasing media coverage. The year of the essay's publication, 1968, saw Baraka sentenced to up to three years' imprisonment in January; Eldridge Cleaver's *Soul on Ice* published in February; Martin Luther King assassinated in April, sparking nationwide riots, with Baraka urging for calm (Woodard, 96–7); the murder of Black Panther Bobby Hutton the same month; and widespread media coverage of armed Black Panthers attending Huey P. Newton's trial at the Alameda County Courthouse, Oakland, in July. This was a time of fast-moving strategic shifts: Black Power artists and activists had to respond tactically to the demands of a given situation, rather than rigidly sticking to absolutist calls for immediate armed struggle.

Beginning as a sociological essay, 'Dynamite' draws on Hernton's work with New York City's Welfare Department and ends as a prophecy of violent insurrection described in terms of 'madness' and apocalypse (*BF*, 103). The essay deploys a language of paradox, where African-American urban ghettos 'are the dynamos of oppression, but [...] also the volcanos [*sic*] of liberation' (101), and the 'madness' described at the start of the essay as 'the psychology of the damned' (78) by its end serves as the only means of political transformation and spiritual redemption (102). Hernton begins by insisting that the recent riots have been produced by 300 years of racial oppression, which has wrought immense psychological damage and set off an unstoppable 'boomerang' of African-American violence (78). Decrying the inability of white Americans to understand their perpetuation of the system of oppression, he outlines the denial and exploitation of black cultural forms (81–2), the perpetuation of black stereotypes and their internalization as double consciousness (84). Outlining a number of character types, Hernton first analyses the manifestation of double-consciousness within the 'self-riddled Negro', confused about their position in America (84), before proceeding to attack:

> Middle-class, non-violent, obsessed Negroes who are set up as leaders of the black people. Roy Wilkins, Leon Sullivan, Whitney Young, Absent [Adam] Clayton Powell, Cecil Moore, A. Philip Randolph, James Farmer (Who ever heard of a leader retiring, with benefits!), to name a few of those operating on a wider scale. (93; see also 83–6)

Finally, he comes to the 'existential Negro', a figure recurring from earlier essays (96). Hernton links conditions in the South to the ghettoes of the North (94–5), drawing on his experience as a social investigator for the New York Department of Welfare (95); continues through anecdotes revealing increasing black militancy and frustration with the non-violent Civil Rights Movement (96–8), including a letter from David Henderson on his frustrations working with the government's the War on Poverty programme; and goes on to argue that the 'big city ghettos' are at breaking point (101). Presenting the anecdote which gives the essay its title (101–2), he builds on the image of dynamite in a concluding prophecy of mass insurrection (102–4).

Like Hernton, Tom Dent worked as an investigator for the New York Welfare Department and recalls: 'It was a very painful kind of job [...] The longer you stayed there the more you made yourself immune to suffering and just treated people like a case' (Dent 2018, 449). Hernton's essay is born out of years in the African-American communities of North and South and witnessing first-hand the conditions that give rise to a wave of urban insurrections that many white Americans saw as completely inexplicable. The incendiary concluding passage begins with an anecdote from his time with the Welfare Department (*BF*, 101). Entering a Harlem apartment, Hernton discovers a wall painting by a teenager now in prison, which depicts a 'group of Negroes' being beaten by a combination of 'respectable-looking whites' and policemen, one of whom exclaims 'you niggers love us, don' you'. Remarking on the hair of the victims, which appears to be standing up on their heads with blood on the tip ends, he is corrected by the mother of the artist. '"That's not hair with blood on it," she said, "that's dynamite growing out of their skulls"' (102). This image of dynamite sets the fuse for the explosive final prediction of a nationwide uprising. The essay's conceptual and linguistic framework is united in one image:

> The violence will be spontaneous, without leadership, without control; the fuse will be the chains of depravity running from heart to heart, connecting the subconscious labyrinths of hurt, anger and rage festering in the psyches of these people for centuries, and setting them off like a million live wires unleashed at last from all stations of censorship and better judgement. (103)

Rather than merely illustrating a sociological point through a 'case study', Hernton's language develops and extends the artistic suggestions of the wall painting itself: any pretence at objective, distanced reporting on 'social problems' is abandoned. The concluding prophecy of violent insurrection repays quoting at length.

> The violence will be spontaneous, without leadership, without control [...] Everybody will be a guerrilla – men, women, teenagers, and some children – individual guerrillas urged on by social contagion and the relentless wellsprings of utter insanity. As the collective mind, supraorganic, pitting itself against the mythologized odds of an unsurmountable [sic] monster, this demon will rise, for only demons can destroy demons and thereby become human again. The sense of fear will be wiped from their consciousness, reason will disappear, emotions will evaporate, fear of death will be meaningless, for they have been dead all their lives. Nor will they care about winning, not in any understandable sense of the word, for in and through the act of destroying and killing and dying they shall be winning, a sense of life will be born anew within them. There may be some looting at first, some rapes, and other immoral deeds, but after the first few days their madness shall reach beyond good and evil, deep into the mysteries of Being. Their madness will no longer be attached to any identifiable norm, value or nonvalue – neither money, hate, freedom or revenge. For, having been purged of faith in all human values, in all normal behavior, their madness will be the only god in whom they can put their fidelity without being deceived and betrayed. No doubt, according to the way America will look at them, they will appear as raving Blacks on a rampage of ruin and riot – nothing new, for America has always looked at them this way. But from their side of the [...] equation, phenomenologically, they shall be gods, answerable to no one. (103–4)

I will examine this passage from a number of angles, referring back to the development of Hernton's argument in the earlier part of the essay and focusing on its vocabulary of pathology, the demonic and the 'collective mind', before turning to questions of gender, defeat and political strategy, with regard to the texts' afterlife and to Hernton's novel *Scarecrow*.

'The psychology of the damned'

Hernton's concern with pathology manifests throughout his work: from the poem 'The Patient: Rockland County Sanatorium' (*MM*, 57–8) to the exploration of Laingian concepts of regression in *Scarecrow*. Hernton often self-figures as pathologized due to his uncompromising stand as a politicized African-

American poet: in 'Almost Sunday', he writes, 'If I were your poet, America! […] You would say I was / A mentally deranged Negro gone mad / Under stress of the civilised weight' (100), and likewise excoriates 'a million psychoanalysts' who would stigmatize him as 'monster, demon' in 'Hate Poem' (Hernton 1974A). This agonized, ambiguous language of purgation, martyrdom and redemption is perhaps most apparent in a 1962 author's statement for Paul Breman's anthology *Sixes and Sevens*:

> I write out of a deep, human, psychopathic need for salvation or murder […] Poetry is the innovated strategy and the native idiom of my struggle for self-esteem and self-destruction among Others. (Hernton 1962, 211)

Salvation, murder, self-esteem and self-destruction become equivalents so closely fused that they cannot be separated. Hernton's presentation of the individual poetic voice is always connected to highly politicized questions: the individual cannot be separated from the racialized violence which created them. Moving away from the individual self-framing of such texts, 'Dynamite' nonetheless echoes their vocabulary. In describing the predicted insurrection, Hernton at once reclaims and subsumes the notion of blackness-as-pathology, via Nietzsche, into a 'madness [which] shall reach beyond good and evil, deep into the mysteries of being' (*BF*, 103): a quasi-transcendent language of fulfilment in and for itself.

The essay's vocabulary of madness shifts from its beginning to its end. Hernton's first paragraph opens:

> The ceaseless and unmitigated bigotry, torture, lawlessness and killing that American white men and women have historically inflicted upon black people in this country is now producing a species of black men, women and teenagers who are possessed with the psychology of the damned. Their view of America is the view of those who have been made into monsters […] They are permanent victims of America's madness. They are beginning to feel that they are the *anointed* ones. (78)

Caustically reversing the pathologizing rhetoric which associates blackness with monstrosity, Hernton asserts that the singling out of black people as monsters and victims paradoxically makes them feel 'anointed'. Black people are 'possessed' as if by an alien spirit, this possession serving as a metaphor for the social construction of their apparent 'madness' by white America: they 'have been made into monsters'. Hernton here attempts to trouble the standards by which the discourse of 'madness' is used to stigmatize those seen as a threat to normative values. Even though he argues that black people will become 'more inhuman, more insane' than the treatment meted out to them, his tone is still, at this stage, one of sceptical irony. Prefiguring his later prediction of urban insurrection, he writes: 'White men will be at a complete loss to understand why so many black people have gone mad' (78). The phrase 'why so many black people have gone mad' sarcastically ventriloquizes a white viewpoint, as underscored by the next sentence in which 'the white man' is said to 'understand, see and feel' only 'according to whatever perversities with which he is inflicted' (78). For a group which is already 'perverted' to stigmatize those they oppress as 'mad' calls their judgement into question.

Arguing that, in the face of such characterizations, appeals to non-violence are in themselves near-pathological, Hernton introduces 'the Third Species of contemporary black men, the Existential Negro' by temporarily addressing what seems to be a white, second-person subject:

> Get this, and get it straight: When you meet a black man on the street, you are not looking at *a* Negro of *a* particular generation; no, you are looking at an accumulation, an historical phenomenon, a dialectical synthesis of nearly four centuries enclosed in a single black skin, and – if he is not a middle-class, non-violent Negro, which he is likely not to be – you are looking at dynamite. (96)

Hernton's language turns the racialized denial of subjectivity on its head. By insisting not that white people should acknowledge the 'Negro' as an individual, rather than a generalized other, but that the 'Negro' is *not*, in fact, an individual, he links this enforced lack of individuality to the potential for collective political power. As 'dynamite', this 'black man' is one of the many 'Existential Negroes' who will be set off by 'the fuse [which] will be the chains of depravity running from heart to heart' (103). Still addressing the white subject, Hernton writes that expecting this 'black man' 'to pledge allegiance to a civilization which openly destroys him every day,' an alienation which 'expels him from the integrity of his death' (83), risks 'producing in that man a monster, a demon, that will break loose and kill you even if it means killing himself' (94).

By the essay's end, Hernton has entirely dropped the framing device of the white viewpoint for a prediction which directly describes the rioters as *actually* mad, motivated by 'the relentless wellsprings of utter insanity' (*BF*, 103).

> As the collective mind, supraorganic, pitting itself against the mythologized odds of an unsurmountable [*sic*] monster, this demon will rise, for only demons can destroy demons and thereby become human again. (103)

Though he cites no sources, the term 'collective mind' appears to draw from Émile Durkheim's analysis of shared group assumptions within religion, in contrast to more individualized secular conceptions, and from the Jungian 'collective unconscious' (a term Jung used interchangeably with 'collective mind'). However, the essay rejects both religious and archetypal frameworks, insisting that the collective mind is socially produced by the power structure it seeks to overthrow. This is the opposite of groupthink. 'The collective mind, supraorganic' – itself a metaphor – is said to be a 'demon' which 'will rise', identified with the 'individual guerrillas' who enact the leaderless uprising (103). A singular mind made up of plural subjects, and a mind which is itself 'mad', it moves beyond 'all human values [...] all human behaviour'. As, at the essay's start, Hernton argues that black people in America 'will be more inhuman, more insane, than all the years of terror and violence that will have produced them' (78), so this hybrid 'collective mind' at the essay's end becomes non-human: a 'monster' or 'demon' possessed by a spirit which – like the biblical 'legion' (Mark 5.1–20; Luke 8.26–39) – defies boundaries between one and many, individual and collective subject, and even those of fixed physical form. Hernton's rejection of 'all human values' parodies the already-existent dehumanization of the black subject within a racist power structure. 'America has always looked on them' and 'will look on them' as 'raving Blacks on a rampage of ruin and riot' (104): Hernton's black revolutionaries appear mad to white observers because they reject the normative standards which stigmatize militant reactions to oppression as pathological. Repurposing such language serves here not to confirm racist prejudice but to reclaim agency. The African-American 'collective mind', both created and set off by centuries of accumulated 'hurt, anger and rage', itself becomes a vast stick of dynamite, a demonic conglomeration, a one made up of many, infecting the body politic with a mind of its own.

For Hernton, 'the psychology of the damned' is created through discourse which reinforces contradictory notions of racial essentialism which are then internalized. Early in the essay, he delineates four contradictory 'definitions and roles of the Negro that are propagated and expected by American society' in which, for example, 'black people are violent by nature … BUT, in their attitudes and behavior towards white people, these same black people are by nature childlike, docile, and affable' (84). Instated and enforced through language, such racism is also challenged at the level of language not merely through correction but through parodic inhabitation. If black people are already said to be 'demons', then Hernton will insist on fully inhabiting this stereotype and turning it back on the white power structure. In 'Jitterbugging', Hernton challenged the 'common sense' of reactions to the Harlem Riots; here, he goes a step further. Taking the pathologization of black rioters on its own terms, a metaphorical 'madness' is embraced to refigure riots as insurrectionary moments which aim at the total destruction of a racist power structure. For Hernton, political oppression is also psychological and linguistic oppression. 'Dynamite' manifests the search for what Baraka called a 'new meaning' (584), a new language and a new conception of politics, emerging from and through current artistic and political forms in order to destroy them.

'Manhood' and gender

Writing from Cuba in 1964, Robert F. Williams, whose poetry was published in *Umbra*'s first issue, and who was involved in On Guard before his exile, outlined what he saw as 'The Potential of a Minority Revolution' in America (Williams 1964B, 6). In strikingly similar fashion to Hernton, Williams outlines the blindness of white liberals to understand the urban insurrections increasingly engulfing America, invariably as the results of police violence; decries what he sees as the Gandhian-Christian philosophy of non-violence; claims that conditions are ripe for African-Americans to stage a revolution in the United States; and outlines a detailed list of instructions for guerrilla sabotage. The essay ends:

> The oppressor's heart is hard. The experience of history teaches that he only relents under violent pressure and force. There is very little hope that he will see the handwriting on the wall before it is too late. This year, 1964, is going to be a violent one the storm will reach hurricane proportions by 1965 and the eye of the hurricane will hover over America by 1966. America is a house on fire – FREEDOM NOW! – or let it burn, let it burn. Praise the Lord and pass the ammunition!! (7)

Four years later, and in the wake of similar theorizations by Touré and Max Stanford of the RAM, 'Dynamite' likewise endorses an insurrection that is widespread, unpredictable, spontaneous and unsubordinated to the disciplines of the vanguardist party form (Touré 1964, 13–14; Touré 1965B, 8; Stanford, 11–12; Peery, 213, 226–7). Hernton's rhetoric is at once more widespread and vague than his previous writings: while the 'rage of a hopeless people' is repurposed as mass revolutionary upsurge, even the strategic suggestions present in the five-point programme of 'On Racial Riots' disappear. The problem of strategic implementation forms the brick wall which all these writings eventually come up against. Williams writes:

> Techniques mentioned here are generalized and require a closer study, however, let the cynics take nose that the mighty USA is not as snug and secure as it once was. Yes, a minority war of self-defense can succeed. The Afroamerican can win. (6)

Yet, as Robin D.G. Kelley notes, such strategies were rarely implemented in practice (Kelley, 80–1). Williams remained in exile until 1969 and withdrew from the front lines of Black Power almost as soon as he returned (Tyson, 302–5); the RAM aimed to develop revolutionary cadre in the northern cities which would connect with more militant students in the south but became one of COINTELPRO's first casualties, when leader Max Stanford was charged with a plot to assassinate Roy Wilkins and Whitney Young (Kelley, 90). Likewise, their espousal of a masculinist, highly moralist ethos, based on their conceptions of underground guerrilla units, suggests the gendered problematics that dominated much militant thought at the time (86–7). Hernton too falls prey to these traps, as when he writes, 'the middle-class Negro child is trained to be a sissy' (87), or:

> Only violence [...] will recreate a sense of manhood and human worth within the souls of black folk. (101)

The above suggests two dilemmas for Hernton's essay: first, the problems of translating rhetorical endorsement of widespread insurrection, sparked by the 'Long Hot Summers' of 1964 to 1968, into a political seizure of power; second, the often masculinist framing of insurrectionary strategies, which often reproduced the very discourses otherwise repurposed, parodied and challenged.

As a predominantly male group, Umbra itself was not immune to these gendered problematics. Each issue of the magazine did contain important work by female poets, including, in the first, life-long Civil Rights activist and historian Patricia Brooks. The second prints work by pioneering lesbian author and archivist Ann Allen Shockley, Nann Triggs, Maryanne Raphael and Ree Dragonette: a collaborator of Eric Dolphy, and a close friend of Hernton, Dragonette's 'Buffalo Waits in the Cave of Dragons' begins 'I am God' and inspired Hernton's 'Taurus by After Fire' (*Umbra* II, 46–9; *MM*, 54–6). Notably, Susan Johnn's 'The Weaker Sex, Disgusted' presents the rise of female militancy in the face of racial violence and gender oppression:

> I am only a woman – a dishwashing, supper cooking,
>   baby bearing, sex satisfying machine,
>
> The hell with that – move over brother –
> I'm coming too.
>
> (*Umbra* II, 33)

In the third issue, Alice Walker's poem 'The Hair-Do' sits alongside work by Marilyn Lowen, Anne Fertik, Margareta Olisa and Julia Fields (*Umbra*

Anthology, 9–10, 36, 52–3); and the fourth prints work by younger BAM poets Nikki Giovanni and Jayne Cortez, and a review by Toni Cade Bambara, whose landmark anthology *The Black Woman* was published the same year. The first two issues list, among group members, Florence Squires, Jane Logan (Poindexter), Mildred Hernton, Maryanne Raphael, Ann Guilfoyle and Brenda Walcott. Hernton conducted a mutually productive artistic exchange with Ree Dragonette, and Dent lists as his major influences Walker, Sonia Sanchez, Mari Evans and Sarah Webster Fabio (Hernton 1976, 54–6, 65, 1985; Dent 2018, 261). However, as Rashidah Ismaili notes, female members of Umbra tended to be (predominantly) white partners of the group's majority male core. In her essay 'Slightly Autobiographical' (1993), Ismaili, one of the few black, female members of the group – though her work does not appear in the magazine – provides an incisive analysis of these gender dynamics. Ismaili had come to the group through her close friendship with Umbra artist Tom Feelings (she was also close to Baraka). She recalls the scene:

> On Friday nights Tom Dent would hold meetings of Umbra at his tiny apartment. There would always be a gallon of communal wine, ashtrays filled with cigarettes, and loud voices demanding to be heard over others. After a few hours of discussion of the latest poems and the contents of so-and-so's novel, the girlfriends would start to arrive. I had to leave early because of my son, and I remember having the feeling of being left out. Somehow, it was after I got out on the street that I would notice that all of the women were White.
>
> (Ismaili, 586)

Born in Benin, Ismaili had moved to New York following her marriage in the late 1950s: she notes the difficulties of survival as a single mother, an artist and a doctoral student of African descent.

> Alone, with a small boy, trying to complete grad school and write, I felt very estranged at times from my ebon scribes and painters. They made it clear they were not interested in me because I was Black, African, and too ethnic; i.e., 'not beautiful.' Besides, I did not do drugs or drink. (586)

Paradoxically, the rejection of Ismaili's African identity also paralleled the subordination of black women on the basis of a fantasy of 'African' patriarchal domination.

> These were the '60s, and Black men were coming into their own. Black women had to understand their manly needs, walk ten paces behind, submit to male authority. We were not to question a man's work, even if it were incorrect. We were to dress 'African,' assume the persona of 'The Motherland,' and raise little

> revolutionaries. Most of all, we were to remain unconditionally loyal to the Black man and never, under any circumstance, be seen in intimate association with a White man. This, of course, was in stark contrast to the behavior of almost all of the men I knew – excuse me, brothers – who had not a single 'significant other' but several White women as lovers and wives. Calvin Hernton was to chronicle this dilemma in *Sex and Race* [sic] *in America*, and he was willing to tackle this sensitive issue in serious dialogue. (586)

Ismaili continues:

> African-descended women tried to balance their creative urges with home and the personal demands of their men and families. A few found relative, and some permanent, happiness in the arms of White men. But these sisters paid the price. Some were denounced, others ignored. The pain we inflicted on each other as a negative continuation of racial pathology cost us all dearly. (586)

Ismaili's account is a vital part of Umbra's history: her work is almost completely unknown, and it is to be hoped that further scholarship will be done in this field. The fact that accounts such as hers almost never appear in accounts of Umbra or the BAM is in itself telling. Critiques of sexism within Umbra and the BAM must be tempered by the exclusions such histories can perform. As Askia Touré notes, in focusing on male sexism, accounts of the Black Liberation Movement (BLM) regularly overlook the key work of numerous female artists and activists who waged a continuous battle against sexism with the movement (Touré 2004). The publication of work by female writers and the presence of figures such as Ismaili at the workshops are an important part of the Umbra story. Yet the problematics of gender should not be overlooked. In much BAM writing, the very discourses which seek to overturn oppressive structures partially reproduce those structures under the banner of liberation. In *The Sexual Mountain and Black Women Writers* (1987), Hernton would critique the discourse of 'manhood' within the BAM as a whole (Hernton 1987, 38–42, 38). Yet, while Ismaili credits Hernton for opening an early and sensitive dialogue about complex issues of race and gender, he could also fall into the same traps. 'Dynamite' is not programmatically misogynist in the vein of contemporaneous works such as Baraka's *Madheart* (1966); nonetheless, it adopts the very same vocabulary of 'manhood' he would later go on to criticize. Though his guerrilla army also contains 'women, teenagers, and some children', when Hernton writes that 'only violence [...] will recreate a sense of manhood and human worth within the souls of black folk' (*BF*, 101), 'manhood' and 'human worth' are elided. To be 'human' is, implicitly, to be male.

This argument both reacts to and reproduces the widespread arguments, which, following Daniel Patrick Moynihan's infamous 1965 report *The Negro Family: The Case for National Action*, saw 'race riots' as resulting from the breakdown of the black family, often assuming that 'violence' or 'rage' was a masculine phenomenon. In 1969, for example, Edwin Harwood wrote:

> The Negro youth who hurls a brick or an insult at a white cop is not just reacting in anger to white society, but on another level is discharging aggression towards the father who 'let him down' and females whose hostility towards inadequate men raised doubts about his own sense of masculinity.

(Harwood, 32–3)

The most influential of such analyses was probably William Grier and Price Cobbs's influential *Black Rage* (1968), whose misogyny Hernton would later decry (Grier and Cobbs; Hernton 1987, 87). For Grier and Cobbs, as for Harwood, riots were not political interventions but manifestations of pathologized black masculinity. As bell hooks notes, Grier and Cobbs's training in conservative psychotherapy meant that their aims were directed towards *internal* transformation, mobilized in the interests of individual therapeutic restitution, rather than towards the revolutionary transformation of society as a whole. The 'black rage' of riots might attest to the damaging effects of racism, but the solution was not to be found in such action, which merely manifested pathology.

> [Grier and Cobbs] used their Freudian standpoint to convince readers that rage was merely a sign of powerlessness. They named it pathological, explained it away. They did not urge the larger culture to see black rage as something other than sickness, to see it as a potentially healthy, potentially healing response to oppression and exploitation. (hooks, 12)

Though they rejected analyses such as those of Grier, Cobbs and Harwood, many of the poets in *Black Fire* ended up reproducing their core misogyny. In a 1968 interview, Baraka claimed: 'Our first concern involves being *men*; all the other things play their part in reaching the totality of our manhood' (*Conversations*, 46), and recurring tropes across many of the poems in the anthology – including those by Umbra associates Yusuf Rahman and Hart LeRoi Bibbs – adopt a circular logic by which revolution enables 'manhood', and 'manhood' enables revolution (*BF*, 199, 226–7, 288, 320, 327, 354–5, 364, 373, 380, 436; *Umbra Anthology*, 61). Indeed, in Bibbs's 'Dirge for JA Rogers', 'manhood' becomes the basis for life itself – 'unimpeachable, inviolable and unparalleled immortal' (*BF*, 320).

Reckoning with the legacy of such notions forms a central dilemma of Hernton's 1974 novel *Scarecrow*. In 'Dynamite', the restorative power of violence is predicated on the gendered reclamation of 'manhood'. By contrast, *Scarecrow* presents a self-lacerating exploration of embedded sexual and racial neuroses. Violence is not a moment of possibility which forms a new collective subject; rather, it both prevents the formation of collectives and destroys the individual subject, disallowing any resolution of the entanglements of sex, racism and historical suffering. At the novel's conclusion, Hernton outlines the creation of the American 'New World' through initial acts of resistance to authority by those who were themselves outcasts: '"pilgrims", "settlers", "pioneers", "indentured servants" and other unwanted white trash' (Hernton 1974, 276). Yet the actions of these outcasts reproduced just such exploitation, as they became 'a pack of hysterical aliens who murdered a whole nation, [and] imported, enslaved and stigmatized a once naked black body of people [...], crying "manifest destiny" of the pure white-only race' (276–7). Likewise, 1960s conceptions of the 'new world' of black liberation are seen to have reproduced the oppression against which they arose. The patriarchal model of the 'black nation', predicated on the family unit, with the man at the head and the woman in a submissive, inferior, supporting position (Baraka 1971B, 147–53) seeks to achieve racial liberation while perpetuating gender subjugation. The novel's principal black female character, Maria – a character who, significantly, did not appear until the book's fourth draft (Oren 2006, 616) – voices a feminist critique of such discourses, apparently directed at the 'Nation Time' ideology advocated by Baraka. This break into essayistic prose sees the novel contain its own commentary and one which also comments on Hernton's own flirtation with masculinist Black Power discourse.

> Under the guises of Nationhood, Black Womanhood, Black is Beautiful, Black Familyhood and other such slogans, black men were seeking to put black women on a pedestal where they would be dehumanized and used as crutches to aggrandize the black man's deflated ego or his sense of maleness at the expense of the woman's individuality.
>
> (Hernton 1974, 284)

Attempts to create new modes of collectivity are shown, particularly under the aspect of gender relations, to have partially reproduced those forms of 'white' oppression they defined themselves against: what Baraka would later call 'becom[ing] the enemy in blackface' (*Autobiography*, 323). Maria here appears to voice the coming to consciousness denied to – indeed, reversed by –

Madheart's 'Black Woman', who submits to the slaps of 'Black Man' in the name of 'love' (*BF*, 584).

> At first, when she left her husband and moved up to Harlem, she had thought that Black Consciousness would be her salvation in general, and that Scarecrow would be her proud Black Warrior in particular. Gradually she had come to realise that too many men in the Black Consciousness bag were seeking, under a lot of glorified slogans, to do to black women the same thing that white men had done to white women.
>
> (Hernton 1974, 284)

The violence wrought by the guerrilla army of Hernton's 'Dynamite' includes 'some rapes' which are implicitly justified by the guerrillas' move 'beyond good and evil' (*BF*, 103). In *Scarecrow*, however, the reproduction of unequal gender relations under a new guise is seen as the ultimate stumbling block to individual and collective transformation. As Kobena Mercer has argued, with reference to Fanon: 'My sense is that questions of sexuality have come to mark the interior limits of decolonisation, where the utopian project of liberation has come to grief' (Mercer, 116). Mercer's 'grief' here proves more than a turn of phrase, and it is as much to this sense of mourning and defeat, as well as to moments of possibility – the creation of a liberatory ensemble, often through figurations of political militancy – that Hernton's work addresses itself.

Conclusion

Scarecrow speaks to both the earlier and contemporaneous fractures suffered by black liberation movements, whether aesthetic – the Umbra split and the collapse of BART/S – or political – the opposition between the BPP and US, led by Baraka's ideological mentor, Ron Karenga, and the BPP split between Huey P. Newton and Eldridge Cleaver (Woodard, 116–20). The novel was published in 1974, the year Kalamu Ya Salaam marks as signalling the BAM's decline in which Baraka switched from Black Nationalism to Marxism-Leninism and Newton, like Robert F. Williams before him, fled to Cuba (ya Salaam 1997, 74). For ya Salaam, this decline was due to a combination of 'external and internal disruption': most notably, the state violence which defeated Black Power political organizations. During the late 1960s and into the 1970s, black radical movements faced constant setbacks, whether the assassinations of black leaders with the capacities for uniting diverse groups such as Malcolm X and Fred Hampton, the crippling of the RAM and the fostering of internal tensions within the BPP by COINTELPRO, or the fracturing of a collective political identity and mission into either the co-options of Black Capitalism or the intramural violence of gang warfare (ya Salaam 1997, 74; Sloan; Jones 1998, 337–58, 391–416). As Askia Touré puts it:

> It was U.S. Imperialism's response to the revolutionary BAM/BLM that caused Its 'dissolution': the attacks by the FBI's COINTELPRO on Black radical groups, coupled with the 'recession' and Drug Plagues in the Inner Cities, during the Reagan era which crushed the Movement.

(Touré 2004, online)

In 1971, Hernton had still argued for the 'Revolution' and 'Liberation' which would result in 'the total destruction of America as we have known it in the past and as we largely know it today', during an 'epoch [which] is the negation of the white man's foul history' (Hernton 1971A, 103, 181). Yet such negation failed to arrive: the moments of insurrectionary possibility found in 'Dynamite' and in the writings of Touré, Robert F. Williams and Max Stanford hounded out by state repression and the fracturing of collective resolve. In the next chapter, I turn from Hernton's writings on militant insurgency to those on memory and mourning, focusing on the poem 'Medicine Man': a fraught pilgrimage home to the American South which reckons with the personal and historical traumas that constitute black subjecthood – what David Marriott, in reference to Hernton, calls 'blackness afflicted, mutilated; a fatal way of being alive' (15).

5

'Home Is Never Where You Were Born': Calvin Hernton's 'Medicine Man'

Umbra poets and the South

Writing about the South was a central part of Umbra's aesthetic. The group was formed in New York, and much of their early writing concerns the city. But many of the Umbra writers, most notably Hernton, Dent and Askia Touré, came from the South and returned there subsequently. As Lorenzo Thomas notes:

> In later years, most of these writers would reject the delusion of 'literary New York' and turn toward home – Baraka to Newark, Tom Dent to New Orleans […] taking with them a brand new sense of urgency, black culture, and nationalism. But such cultural and political activism was the fruit of their New York experience.
>
> (*EM*, 121)

Indeed, Dent argues that such movement was central to the Umbra ethos from the start:

> Almost none of us were from New York […] We had come to New York to try to escape our parochial beginnings, our hometowns and neighbourhoods, to find ourselves and each other […] A lot of the community-type friendships that developed were a sharing of where we had come from and what we aspired to do […] Everybody was from somewhere else and that sharing of backgrounds and hopes – that was a beautiful thing.
>
> (Dent 2018, 53, 452)

In the work published during the Umbra period, the twin spaces of South and North are frequently linked. As we saw in the first chapter, Askia Touré's work at this time addressed itself to the forms of urban protest exemplified by On Guard. But *Umbra*'s first issue also contains Touré's 'Floodtide', dedicated to 'the black tenant farmers / of the South' (*Umbra* I, 28–31). As Touré later noted:

> Being from Dayton, Ohio (though Southern-born), I embraced and embodied the folklore and animal tales of the Southern oral tradition, which survived via my grandparents and the writings and language of our local Poet Laureate, Paul Laurence Dunbar. (Our grade school teachers used to read his dialect poetry daily to us.) […] 'Flood-tide' was loosely based upon the meter of Dunbar's 'The Corn Song,' which captured the syncopated rhythms of the 'Sankey' and other Pre-blues forms.
>
> (Touré 2004, online)

The poem presents the impoverished Southern farmers as survivors, withstanding the twin difficulties of a hostile environment and of virulent white racism, a survival embodied in their singing.

> "though sorrows completely
> bend them down.
> though butchered and maimed
> by nature and whitefolks,
> *they sing their songs,*
> *they sing their songs,*
> *they sing their songs,*
> and carry on."
>
> (*Umbra* I, 31)

Umbra's oscillation between Northern and Southern experience is succinctly illustrated by the juxtaposition of Touré's poem with Hernton's immediately following '125th Street (Harlem, new York)'. Dedicated to David Henderson, its list of products, names and bars; its use of racialized language and obscenity; and its pointed observations of cultural appropriation and the uptown-downtown dynamic recall Henderson's own observations of ghetto economics and urban alienation.

> Back into the street I roam
> This joint and that joint,
> Black man at the counter, white man own.
> (Dark man, a few; still
> What must I do and where must I go
> to escape this monolithic ghetto?) […]
>
> Down town white folks play
> (some black too)

> Wide lane, slick paved thoroughfares,
> *Showboat, How Green The Valley.*
> Up town niggers pay
> (Some Ofays too)
> Sugar brown gal in the alley,
> Bubblegum neon and processed hair [...]
> Civilization, culture, oh yes, I know!
> Muddy-water, sexy honky-tonk,
> White madness in a black cinema show.
>
> (*Umbra* I, 32–3)

Earlier in the issue, the more elusive poem 'The Long Blues' deploys Hernton's recurrent 'scarecrow' figure in an unspecified, pastoral landscape and addresses the dilemmas of belonging, return and psychological trauma that will inform much of his subsequent writing on the South.

> In sun or cold the weather picks scare-crow
>   bones clean
> I am tired of ghost-water and willow years
> Tired of pawn-shop dreams
> And the tumult of clashing swords
> Locked in my jawbones [...]
>
> My body totters, it reels ...
> And with the long blues riding my back
>   like a sweaty shirt
> I strut my agony out the door –
>
> Quickly, re-enter for more.
>
> (*Umbra* I, 19–20)

In these two poems, we find the classic poles of Hernton's work – the ability to render with specific detail the current urban environment but overlaid and juxtaposed with memories of the South that remain traumatic and vague. If, as we saw in the previous chapter, the urban malaise of New York feeds into Hernton's incendiary writings of riot, the South becomes the seat of an existential torment based on the gaps in memory resulting from trauma – what Hernton would later call 'a certain void' or 'an unnameable mood' relating to his Southern childhood and to incidents such as encounters with the police and the KKK (Hernton 1996, 140, 142; Oren 2006, 610).

Hernton had first visited New York in his second year at Talladega College and returned there during summers throughout his graduate education. Initially moving to Harlem for two years, he then 'returned to the South, and spent four years as an instructor of social science in four different Negro colleges' (Hernton 1993, 579). This initial return from North to South is triumphantly stated in his first published poem, 'Remigrant' (1954); yet Hernton felt himself 'unable to survive in those environments' and returned to New York in 1961 (Hernton 1993, 579). 'Ballad of a Young Jacklegged Poet' (1962, rev. 1976) reverses the journey in 'Remigrant', manifesting what Tom Dent calls 'a sense of the hopefullness [*sic*] that has never been completely absent from the migration from the South to the big city' (Dent 1980, 245).

> Wake up O jacklegged poet!
> Wake up dark boy from way down South!
> wake up out of Central Park [...]
> And walk defiantly
> Through streets of Harlem town.
>
> (*MM*, 13)[1]

The South was a vital part of Hernton's background and experience. But it was perhaps only in New York that Hernton could fully reckon with his past. Likewise, as Kalamu ya Salaam argues of Tom Dent, 'The New York years offered [Dent] a distance from his upbringing that, on his eventual return to New Orleans, allowed him to embrace his own blackness as never before' (Dent 2018, 23). In the following two chapters, I'll argue that neither Dent nor Hernton could have written the South in the way they did without the Umbra experience. I'll go on to explore Hernton's essays on his Southern upbringing, before focusing on his major poem 'Medicine Man' in which the encounter with memory, trauma and the link to a maternal tradition are wrenchingly explored.

As Dent noted, Umbra's group formation was based, in part, on rejecting associations with their parents' generation and the conservative political and cultural stance they represented.

> None of us – not Rolland [Snellings], not Ish[mael Reed], not David [Henderson], not Cal[vin Hernton], not me – could go back home, ever again. Nor have any of us been able to … I mean go back into the world of your parents and have them really understand what you're doing or why.
>
> (Oren 1984, 239)

For Dent, Umbra was a form of 'mutual support that came from severing ourselves [...] from the limitations and the expectations and the restrictions of our backgrounds'. In 'A Memoir of Mardi Gras' (1968), he further wrote of the distance between the goals of his generation and that of his parents.

> Sometimes it seems that the impact of this generational gap is as enormous as the physical and psychological severing and suffering of the forced journey from the Old to the New world: a tearing, ripping apart of everything a people, a generation, has known.
>
> The very ground we stand upon, the sky, the air we breathe, torn by each new generation proclaiming a new world, new terms of existence.

(Dent 2018, 322)

Opposing the discourse of 'racial uplift' and work-discipline foisted on him by the middle-class mores of his parents and teachers, Dent instead came to identify with the elder generation represented by his paternal grandmother, who raised him in his earliest years and who was, he notes, 'very poor, unlearned, born around slavery, [and had lived] in Georgia all her life' (90), or the local, freelance cook, Mrs Chatman, who had 'risen from [...] a hopelessness of rural poverty, a vague, gray, depressing eternity of involuntary servitude'.

> The act of identifying with the elders, the Mrs Chatmans, our grandfathers and grandmothers, and with what their lives might have been like was akin to travelling backwards in time along a river shore trying to discover where the shores had shifted, where was once land, where was once a muddy river. I knew instinctively I must attempt to perform that feat of disentangling, of historical delineation. (323)

Against the prohibition of idle dreaming as unconnected to work discipline, Dent cultivated a forbidden 'secret life': the world of the aesthetic, associated with dreams, secrecy, cross-generational identification and non-linear history, stood opposed to the world of labour, the black bourgeoisie and the discourse of racial uplift. Whether for Dent, struggling against the social expectations placed on him as a member of the 'talented tenth', or for Hernton, struggling to figure the brutality of Jim Crow experienced more directly in his impoverished Tennessee upbringing, the aesthetic provides a cross-generational link. Though Umbra rejected the mores of their parents' generation, theirs was also a work of cultural recovery, refusing the erasures accomplished, not only by the violence of American racism but by the black bourgeoisie's attempts to suppress black cultural traditions, often associated with the South (Hernton 1996, 146; Dent 2018, 57, 469).

In a 1980 review of Hernton's *Collected Poems*, Dent emphasizes that Hernton's early work is characterized by this tension between South and North, with the South simultaneously as a place of nostalgia and horror and the North as a place both of possibility – as cultural melting pot and as escape from Jim Crow – and of heightened, urban alienation (Dent 1980, 244–7). Though this interplay between South and North parallels the earlier Harlem Renaissance, the difference is that many of the Umbra writers were *from* the South. They write not as tourists, ethnographers or visitors seeking cultural rejuvenation but out of their own lives, charting the nourishing affection of family members and the psychological torments wrought by growing up in the era of Jim Crow.

'Chattanooga Black Boy'

Hernton's essay 'Chattanooga Black Boy' (1996) is an invaluable piece of autobiographical writing, lending valuable insights to the tormented ambiguities of much of his earlier work and to their political and personal stakes in particular. Hernton describes his grandmother as 'my first and deepest influence, mentor and teacher'. He lived with her for the first sixteen years of his life in Chattanooga, Tennessee, with a few years in the small 'countrified' town of Tullahoma (Hernton 1996, 140–3). There were no whites in the school Hernton attended as a child, and 'the white people who came to our house came only to collect money, such as rent, insurance payments, and to sell us things' (141). Hernton's relation to his grandmother constituted a formative microcosm, shaped by early experiences of racism and the resistance and resilience in its face which she embodied. 'From early childhood, I lived in a small world of my family (my grandmother and I), which was situated in a larger world of a town (Chattanooga) within the still larger world of the "Deep South", which, in turn, existed in the bigger world of the United States' (142).

Hernton's autobiographical account focuses on the traumatic effect of racial discrimination on his upbringing, and particularly, its effect on memory.

> In writing this piece, I am relying a great deal on memory, on recall, the hazards of which are ever present. Memory consists of recollections, in between which are blanks. This is especially true of childhood memory. But blanks occur throughout one's entire lifespan, and there is the mystery of why certain incidents, scenes, and episodes are remembered and others are not. We have memories that are hidden, they lie sleeping for many years, to be awakened by some triggering mechanism. There are blanks throughout my childhood years where I have no memory of myself whatsoever. (142)

Hernton's work often manifests an anguished encounter with this Southern upbringing and its often-suppressed trauma. In the essay, Hernton details two formative incidents: the first, when he recognized that his skin tone was lighter than that of his grandmother and his brother, and the second, when he was forbidden to play with a white friend after the KKK issued a warning to the boy's parents (Hernton 1996, 139–40). As Hernton notes, this

> caused a certain void to open up in me [...] that I would experience from time to time throughout my life. I felt a void open up inside whenever I felt rejected, scorned, or ridiculed. I would experience it, for example, every time a white person looked at me with what we call the 'hate stare'. I know that feeling of emptiness – of denial and pain – is part of the individual and collective emotional experience of all black people in America. (140)

Because memory is suppressed, the trauma of racism causing 'a certain void to open up in me', the blanks are filled by fantasy and invention. Hernton's poems of the South are often couched in a language freighted with mythic and private frames of reference. In a 1986 interview, Hernton argues that his goal is not always analytical clarity but an attempt to work through feelings, associated with his Southern childhood, that cannot be expressed directly:

> Some of those poems [...] were written of an unnameable mood, and the poem is giving a name to the mood that I was in, so some of it is elusive to me.

(Oren 2006, 610)

He does, however, cite the Great Depression, the Scottsboro Boys case and the Second World War as formative (Hernton 1996, 143-4). In the lengthy scene which takes up the middle of the novel *Scarecrow*, an early version of which is published in *Umbra Anthology* as 'The Yield', Hernton uses the vehicle of an LSD trip to stage a traumatic encounter with memories of the racism of the South and of New York: 'historical and biological time merge' as the 'great cataclysm' of the Great Depression occurs 'in the cells and genes and molecular spheres of the mind' (*Umbra Anthology*, 23; *Scarecrow*, 193). Fragments of Hernton's Southern past occur throughout the book, often as part of hallucinatory passages connected to psychological torment and the sudden eruption of traumatic memory. It is only upon departure for England that the narrator – who closely parallels Hernton – can fully reckon with these memories which, despite his sociological research into conceptions of sex and racism in the South, have remained suppressed. *Scarecrow* was written over a ten-year period between London, Sweden and Ohio: its returns to the South are staged from a distance, drafted and redrafted in the successive versions of the manuscript (Oren 2006, 616). If Hernton responds with speed to contemporaneous political events in the North, as seen in the last chapter, his encounters with the South are more fraught and extended.

'Medicine Man'

I turn now to Hernton's major poem 'Medicine Man', which lends its title to his 1976 *Collected Poems*. Staging an encounter with his grandmother, the poem is complex and ambivalent. Though it is one of the few of his poems currently in print, the poem has received virtually no critical attention (Nielsen/Ramey, 100–3; Ward, 272–5). In his review of the book for *Obsidian*, Tom Dent quotes from 'Medicine Man', calling it a 'sweeping metaphysical poem which address[es] the concerns of mother, identity, origin', but barely discusses the poem, instead concentrating on Hernton's presentation of race, class and urban poverty on the Lower East Side (Dent 1980A, 249). Meanwhile, Lorenzo Thomas's discussions of Hernton's work in *Extraordinary Measures* do not so much as register the poem's existence. Fittingly, for a poem concerned with the shameful erasure of historical memory, it remains something of a secret text, deep within the eclipsed shadows that gave Umbra its name.

Remaining unpublished until 1976, 'Medicine Man' was written at least a decade earlier. In a report on a reading given by Umbra poets to launch the BART/S, Clayton Riley notes: '[Hernton's] verse recollection of a trip to his former S. Carolina home was, in anguished intensity, a work of eminent beauty' (Riley, 19). Though he does not give the poem's title, the description strongly suggests that it may have been 'Medicine Man', in which case it may have been written by 1965. There are further textual clues: the poem's line 'Thirty red years contending with Satan' (*MM*, 48), and its references to April, the month of Hernton's birth, suggest that it may have been written in his thirtieth year, in 1962. The difficulties of dating this poem relate to the narrative it stages. As in *Scarecrow*, time and space are dizzyingly overlaid: 'thirty years' becomes 'thirty times ten' (48), the singular voice of Hernton's grandmother becomes 'ten voices' (50) and the poem's rural landscape is juxtaposed with the horror of the Middle Passage. Such displacements refuse Eurocentric notions of linear history which instate the violent erasure of memory, but they are also viscerally experienced repetitions of trauma.

Hernton's poem was published in the context of an increasing reclamation of Southern heritage on the part of writers like Dent, Alice Walker and Julia Fields (the latter of whom were both published in *Umbra Anthology*); it also connects to associations of the South with femininity drawn in foundational Harlem Renaissance texts such as Jean Toomer's *Cane*. A fundamental ambivalence inheres in such gendering of geography: Toomer mixes figures of fecundity and sexuality with the violence of lynching and sexual and racial ostracism. As Lorenzo Thomas notes, 'the South enjoys a continuing mythic presence in African-American thought and culture'. Yet, for Thomas, such a hold is 'problematic': 'the history of the region [...] offers ample evidence that anyone's attachment to the South might be as easily assumed to be haunted as fondly nostalgic' (*EM*, 165). Indeed, in his 1966 essay 'The Debt I owe', Hernton argued that 'the South is a psychocultural region of mixed personality determinants whose conflicting vectors completely immobilize the flexibility and continuing growth of the psyche' (Hernton 1966D, 8). Both this essay and the poem mark Hernton's attempts to reckon with this legacy. Accounts of the South have frequently been 'haunted' by its connection to the premodern, the traumatic association of landscape with violence, nostalgic imaginings of the pastoral and the ecstasy of religious practice. Falling somewhere between Thomas's poles of 'nostalgia' and 'haunting', Hernton's poem is a notable contribution to such traditions and should be reclaimed as a key exemplar of Southern writing. In what follows, I will read the poem through its framing trope of the medicine man, the reclamation of hoodoo folk practices, the traumas of the Middle Passage, and psychoanalytic figurations of mourning and melancholia.

'Dressed at last to kill'

Building around repetitive, circling phrases, the poem's formal structure, in which virtually every stanza finds a later analogue, mirrors its narrative of return, resolution and cyclical time. As the poem begins, Hernton places the titular persona in the 'kangaroo jungle' of America, removed from ancestral sources.

> North of Dark
> North from Shango
> In kangaroo jungle of West Lost
> Dressed in hide of fox
> Dressed at last to kill
> Thirteen grains of sand
> Seven Memories
> And Ten voices whispering in a rock.
>
> (47)

In 1970, Albert Murray wrote: 'When the Negro musician or dancer swings the blues, he fulfils the same fundamental existential requirement that determines the mission of the poet, the priest and the medicine man' (Albert Murray, 58). Hernton's self-framing as medicine man recalls the BAM use of hybrid, archetypal figures representing male independence, strength and a trickster aesthetic, from priest to *griot* to folk heroes such as Shine (Neal 1969; Hernton 1971, 18; Finn, 125). Drawn from hoodoo traditions often stamped out and replaced by the growth of Afro-Christianity (Hernton 1971, 125), the medicine man stands as a defiant reclamation of resistant 'conjure' practices in line with the 'Neo-HooDoo Aesthetic' developed by Hernton's close friend, Umbra member Ishmael Reed. Hernton is listed as one of the principal contemporary practitioners of 'Neo-HooDoo' in Reed's 1970 'Neo-HooDoo Manifesto', and his use of the medicine man strongly resonates with the 'Neo-HooDoo' aesthetic (Reed 2007, 35). Reed's 'Neo-HooDooism' insists that black Southern traditions can form the basis of a vital modernist aesthetic, linking them to Haitian voodoo and to West African, ancient Egyptian and South American religious and cultural practices, and stressing that they are an unacknowledged part of American culture as a whole (Reed 2007, 26–8). The Neo-HooDoo artist, as a trickster figure who speaks to suppressed traditions, channelling collective voices in the mode of voodoo possession, also refuses to subsume them to a singular focus on individual ego or ossified tradition: 'Neo-HooDoo believes that every man is an artist and every artist a priest' (Reed 2007, 27). Likewise, Hernton's self-figuration as medicine man serves as an investigative vehicle through which to channel multiple voices: the speaker adopts the voice of their own 'knee bones' and at times appears to speak in the voice of maternal and grand-maternal figures, refusing the stability of utterance suggested by BAM poetic self-figurations such as Baraka's 'a black priest interpreting/the present & future for my people' (*SP*, 212).

Yet, if Hernton's medicine man appears to depart from BAM archetypes, he also swerves from the confidence and verve of Reed's Neo-HooDoo personae. 'Dressed in hide of fox / Dressed at last to kill', the medicine man's costume is ironically posed as a fashion statement. Hernton's medicine man further contrasts with white poetic appropriations of shamanism, sparked in large part by Carlos Castaneda and taken up by the likes of Gary Snyder and Jerome Rothenberg (Snyder; Rothenberg; Hobson; Reed 1995, 151). While the 'white shaman' holds to the cultural-imperialist idea that they can unproblematically 'channel' religious and historical practices from a position of relative ignorance and cultural difference, Hernton does not assume an initiated understanding of shamanistic or folk cultures. Throughout the poem, as we'll see, Hernton's treatment of ritual practices is deliberately and consistently ambiguous – an ambiguity relating to fundamental feelings of shame and melancholic ambivalence.

Having located himself in the contemporary desert of 'West Lost', and assumed their costume, the 'Medicine Man' outlines the temporal dilemmas that the poem will centrally concern.

> Time medicine riddle
> Time rock disguised in evil bite
> In devil flight
> Time encloses cycles
> Voice memory
> Revolve.
>
> (48)

It has been suggested that the word 'shaman' derives in part from the Sanskrit *śram*, meaning 'to be tired' or 'to become weary' (Czaplicka, 197), and Hernton's shaman is as much exhausted by the 'riddle' of historical memory – 'Time medicine riddle / Time rock disguised in evil bite' (47) – as gifted with special wisdom by it. Memory provides the possibility both for shamanic imaginative flight and for the oppressive, enforced 'devil flight' of slavery and its afterlives.

Seeking to solve this riddle, the medicine man prepares to undertake a journey. As they speak to their 'knee bones', in an echo of James Weldon Johnson's iconic 'Dem Bones', itself a reference to a passage from Ezekiel presaging the liberation of the Children of Israel from slavery and exile (Johnson, 1; Ezekiel 37: 1–14), the poem moves from the 'rock[ing]' of time 'in evil bite' to the grandmother's rocking chair which comes to form the poem's central image.

> Then I said to my knee bones
> Teach me how to bend
> My knee bones hardening seven memories
> Recalled what I fail to know
> In an estranged familiar tongue
> Said:
> > If you must go
> > Go by the abandoned railroad yard
>
> The muddy ditch
> Rocking chair.
>
> (*MM*, 48)

The poem is in the tradition of African-American pilgrimage narratives, where, as Robert Stepto notes, the recurring trajectory is either of 'ascent' from South to North or of 'immersion' (descent) from North to South (Stepto, 67). Stepto's phrasing – 'the reversal of direction, back to the matrix or cradle of the South' – recalls Hernton's phrasing in 'The Debt I Owe': 'the mother-matrix out of which and in which the Negro's mind has been fashioned' (1966D, 9). For Stepto, while such journeys relate to historical patterns of migration or flight, they also assume a phantasmagorical resonance outside time. The 'confining social structure' of Southern slavery is neither

> a fixed geographic [n]or symbolic space; it is not quite simply powerfully 'Georgia' and 'Mississippi' [or, in Hernton's case, Tennessee] […] but, in its various dimensions and symbolic meanings, many states and regions, including that nebulous but universally known realm referred to as 'downriver'. (68)

In his review, Tom Dent calls the poem's location a 'landscape devoid of the familiar' (Dent 1980, 250), and this setting recalls Stepto's unfixed symbolic or geographic space, both 'estranged' and 'familiar', specific and general.

> Flank to the left where an old black woman
> With prayers for you in her wrinkled hands
> Cupped in an old-fashioned aproned lap
> Rocks eternally
> Eternal rock
> Rocking chair
> Pause, leave a tear
> Beneath the fallen viaduct.
>
> (*MM*, 47)

At this stage, the medicine man can only 'pause' to 'leave a tear'. The voice warns:

> But do not linger
> For the road back is never
> Home is never where you were born.
>
> (48)

By the poem's end, these instructions return transformed, the grandmother now associated with song and with a cyclical return that contains the possibility of transformation, rather than simply the replaying of trauma. Hernton picks up on a specific image – the old woman singing to herself in a rocking chair – and turns it into an analogue for the role of poetic memory, mourning for the suffering and celebrating the survival of an older generation this rocking expresses: '*Singing in that rock!*' (50).

Gris-gris

At first, however, the grandmother is associated not with song but with a physical object. The speaker addresses the old woman in the rocking chair directly.

> Oh Grandmother, figurine gris gris goddess
> Do I
> Should I
> Can I live so that I may die easily.
>
> (48)

Gris-gris, as it developed in South American, Caribbean and Southern hoodoo traditions, is somewhere between a religious and an artistic practice. Ritual objects, stories or verses, imbued with magical powers, were shaped into designed leather pouches and used either as protective lucky charms or to punish enemies, including slave-owners (Anderson, 28, 37, 51; De Salvo, 45, 111).[2] For Sylviane A. Diouf:

> Gris-gris were [...] more than a protection, they were a weapon of war that enabled the insurgents to be fearless, to defy danger, and challenge death. Thus, besides their personal significance to individuals who needed hope and a sense of security, the gris-gris served a communal purpose that was highly subversive in a situation of servitude [...] They were, in essence, the negation of slavery. (Diouf, 81–3)

As Paul Gilroy notes:

> Afrocentric spirituality and conjure [...] as well as the linguistic tropes which negotiate the boundaries of insubordination and insolence in slave cultures denied legitimate access to literacy, have all bequeathed distinct political legacies which may not, for example, have immediate equivalents in the epistemological repertoire of contemporary Marxism or social democracy. (210)

In their reclamation of the vocabulary of conjure, voodoo, magic and gris-gris, writers like Baraka, Hernton, Reed and Thomas tap into this political legacy, reacting against secular rationalist criticisms of folk beliefs. For Baraka, gris-gris is 'carrier of, or celebrator of, or homage to, whatever power kept us cool, kept the gray away', 'gray' inflected by its history as a term 'we used to call "white" people' (2009A, 6). Its use is both ameliorative and transformative, 'keep[ing] away' hostile groupings and cementing group identity as tool of protection and survival. Likewise, Reed's 'Neo-HooDoo Manifesto' mocks the Christian prohibition on '"false idols" (translated everybody's religion) or "fetishes"' (Reed 2007, 30). For Reed, gris-gris objects are somewhere between a representation, a magical object, a weapon and a book. In *Flight to Canada* (1976), he writes: 'A man's story is his gris-gris […] The thing that is himself' (Reed 1976, 8). Gris-gris is in turn an object, a story and a person: an act of refashioning and reconstruction which redefines narrative itself.

'Thirty times ten removed'

As Reed notes, voodoo is a maternal religion (Reed 2007, 26–7); Hernton's use of the medicine man is a way of channelling maternal voices, refusing the masculinist vocabulary of 'Dynamite', whereby the resolution of trauma was figured through the attainment of 'manhood'. Addressing his 'gris gris goddess' grandmother – both ancestor and maternal intermediary to ancestors – the speaker pours out their anguish. Yet this leads him to lament the loss of connection, through the paternal intermediary, to those ancestors, as an individual lifetime ('thirty red years') mingles with three hundred years of slavery (note that the poem was first published in the tercentennial year of the Declaration of Independence).

> Thirty red years contending with Satan
> The backbones breaking pain
> Thirty times ten removed from gods
> My fathers knew.
>
> (48)

Consequently, he calls on the male Yoruba deity Shango – associated with thunder, lightning, justice, dance and virility. This failed invocation turns to a startling image of cannibalistic brutality.

> Oh Shango, man of mothers
> Will you join us in trance
> In eating of the bowels of black man

> Who is our victim
> Who is no longer father of his man.

(48)

As Hortense Spillers notes, the Middle Passage saw African-Americans 'excluded from' or 'abandoned by' the group formations represented in West African religious practices by ancestral law (Spillers, 423). This break in part results from elders selling off juniors to slave traders – initiating them not into maturity, through generational links with ancestors, but into a radical condition of harm, into object- rather than subjecthood (425). The father figure who initiates the link with the ancestors is removed, the link broken – as in Hernton's 'who is no longer father of his man' (*MM*, 48). Whereas the original connection to ancestral law described by Spillers rests on a mythic schema, the Middle Passage is decidedly historical. Yet, due in large part to the lack of reliable historical records, apart from those of the slavers, it assumes the full weight of myth, of a shift in the symbolic order. Nonetheless, for Spillers, to confront this 'primal scene' must involve the non-mythic, breaking from the law of the dead and confronting the future to instate 'the circulation of a new social energy' (Spillers, 426). In Hernton's poem, the appeal to the paternal ancestor leads to grotesque acts of cannibalistic murder, rather than to restoration. The speaker calls on Shango to join 'us in trance', eating 'the bowels of black man / who is our victim' (*MM*, 48). The first-person plural subject appears to refer to white slavers, who mockingly ask the deity one might expect to protect *against* them to join in a cannibalistic rite suggesting the Black Power trope of emasculation. Facing a crisis of agency, the speaker claims, 'I have done somebody wrong', whether they 'approve' or 'do not approve': they can only witness the scene of slaughter, asking 'Why should I approve' (48).

'To those residing in evil bite': Cannibalism and incorporation

Following this crisis, the speaker returns to the maternal.

> Hence I put away old handed-down ailments
> Put away common motives that drive men
> To conventional madness
> And weep for the mother of my twin.

(48)

Yet this resolution, too, turns from 'weeping' to acts of conjuration, masturbation and cannibalism.

> And conjure Dance on pages of medicine book
> > of white hands
> And by ceaseless slapping on genital organ
> And by eating of embryo taken from ovaries
> > of the dead infant boy
> Leaping to meet me death
> If I weep at all.
>
> (48)

'Medicine book' once more suggests gris-gris – a representation which has come to life, an object with the power to contain spirits, to serve as a meeting place between the living and the dead (Thompson, 127–8). Like Reed's 'gris-gris [...] the thing that is himself', or the grandmother as 'figurine gris gris goddess', this ancestral link should allow mourning to take place. Yet the book is 'of white hands' and the 'dance' associated with descriptions of masturbation and cannibalism which appear as if lifted from racist anthropological texts or the primitivist depictions of Africa encountered in Hernton's weekly trip to the cinema as a child (Hernton 1996, 145). While the stanza begins with the speaker resolving to escape 'conventional madness', transitioning from melancholia to mourning through 'weep[ing]', by its end, they face death 'if I weep at all' (48).

These lines suggestively resonate with psychoanalytic accounts of mourning and melancholia. For Freud, individual melancholia arises from an initial feeling of ambivalence towards a lost object, one strongly related to a sense of guilt at having survived the lost subject (Freud, 249–50, 255–7). While melancholia 'cannibalises' the object by 'incorporating' it, the act of mourning externalizes and puts away the object, restoring the subject to psychic health. In Freud's account, such mourning is a metaphoric second form of death, killing that which has literally died or been otherwise lost; for the ego to live by expelling the object which it has incorporated into itself involves a kind of violence necessary to psychic health (Freud, 257). In 'Medicine Man', the process of mourning seems to be denied by the very process it 'conjure[s]': mourning violent death itself becomes associated with killing. Melancholic guilt here relates to the trauma, denigration and erasure of one's history, and a consequent feeling of shame, both for the absence of an adequate narrative and for the humiliation attendant on those fragments which are available – fragments characterized by defeat, powerlessness and helplessness in the face of systematic violence. Such guilt is not merely to do with individual narrative framings but with the collective histories of group formation that act as forms of racial inscription (Hernton 1966D, 37–9).

The poem continues:

> And if I approve
> Eating entrails of multitude of living victims
> It will not resurrect those already dead
> It will not heal ear and tongue of betrayal
> April is a time of betrayal
> And I do not approve
> I do not approve.
>
> (*MM*, 49)

At once a personal and a literary reference (Hernton was born in April 1932), 'April is a time of betrayal' adapts the opening line of T.S. Eliot's *The Waste Land*, 'April is the cruellest month', which figures wider civilizational discontents through an ironic spin on Chaucer's portrayal, in *The Canterbury Tales*, of April as a time of spring renewal and pilgrimage (Eliot, 49; *EM*, 135). Racializing Eliot's usage, such discontents in Hernton's poem have to do with the 'multitude of living victims' of the Middle Passage. Mirroring the preceding page in which they were trapped in a tortured decision over whether to 'approve' of acts of brutality, the speaker finally proclaims, 'I do not approve / I do not approve' (*MM*, 49). Yet this moral stance once again fails to reach resolution. Ancestral religion offers no help:

> And if I pray
> I pray not to God or Shango
> I pray to bellies of deep sea sharks
> And pray for us survived west lost
> North of dark in chains.
>
> (49)

The poem directs an ironic and despairing prayer to the sharks who eat slaves during the Middle Passage. In the face of such dispossession, this prayer provides no support; the only intercessor ironically becomes the very creature which has consumed one's ancestors. As in the earlier references to cannibalism – 'eating of the bowels of black man' (48) – these lines resonate with psychoanalytic figurations of the process of melancholic incorporation which forestalls the ability to fully mourn. Freud specifically uses the term 'cannibalism' to refer to this process, a term taken up and developed with important qualifications by Melanie Klein, Nicholas Abraham and Maria Torok (Freud, 248; Klein, 344–69; Abraham and Torok 1994, 125–38). Uniting Freud's initial metaphor with that of 'encryption' and entombing, Abraham and Torok argue that the ego is said to unconsciously 'consume' the lost or dead love object, taking it into itself as a means of preserving it and denying its loss (Abraham and Torok, 125–38; Ellmann, 40–1). Such accounts resonate with the poem's intense and often grotesque physicality: the speaker's grandmother 'liv[es] inside [his] wounds', sharks eat slaves and the speaker himself eats dead children (48–9). For Abraham and Torok, incorporation involves the process of 'demetaphorisation', where the subject is unable not to take things literally. The incorporative melancholia of Hernton's poem likewise lies in the gap between the literal and the metaphorical, yet its references to real historical violence challenge this linguistic theory of loss. Sharks really do eat the slaves who fall from the ship, even if the speaker's grandmother does not literally 'live inside my wounds'.

As we saw in the previous chapter, Hernton himself frequently plays on metaphorical relations between madness, poetry and revolutionary activity (see also Oren 1984, 240). In his introduction to *Medicine Man*, Joe Johnson writes: 'Hernton was/is mad and he stutters coherence' (*MM*, 5). Johnson's 'stutter' usefully corresponds to Nathaniel Mackey's notion of 'telling inarticulacy' in African-American poetry, 'which often arises from and reflects critically upon an experience of isolation or exclusion' and which 'symbolizes a refusal to accept damage done, a critique and a partial rejection of [...] a predatory coherence, a cannibalistic "plan of living"' (Mackey, 252–3). Via Mackey, Hernton's use of cannibalism in 'Medicine Man' can be read as a deliberate *détournement* of racist myths in order to refer to acts of violence, mourning and suffering as both cannibalistic and cannibalized. Imperial violence and enslavement were often justified through the figure of the cannibal who must be either pacified through religious conversion or destroyed by force. Turning the metaphor of cannibalism into a part of the development of human identification as such, as Freud does, mitigates this foundational racial othering. Hernton, however, goes further. In the 1962 'Statement' written for Paul Breman's anthology *Sixes and Sevens*, Hernton reverses progress narratives and presents the entirety of Western civilization as one characterized by 'death by hating and eating, general devolutionary slaughter' (Hernton 1962, 211). Similarly, in 'Medicine Man', racist myths of cannibalistic practices are turned back on the Western slavers 'eating of the bowels of black man' (48). The destruction of slaves is endlessly replayed as a suppressed, intergenerational trauma in which it is not always clear whether the speaker is cannibalizing or being cannibalized, slaver or slave.

Hernton also invokes the vexed question of gendered self-division within the African-American community itself, the figure of his grandmother serving as spur to remember the suppressed history of injustice against women. The speaker declares:

> So shameless black men speak blood of their sisters!
> And will it if I weep
> Drive away juju of the fox
> And if I pray
> I have done somebody wrong.
>
> (49)

Once again, they are trapped in uncertainty, unable to appeal to a deity without being complicit in harm. Yet, as the earlier questions of 'approv[al]' were resolved in mirroring stanzas, the speaker finally refusing to 'approve' centuries of slaughter, so here, turning on another paradox, they find resolution through the decision to redirect their prayers.

> And if I do not pray
> I pray for those who will live until moon
> And to those residing in evil bite
> And to the old black woman living in my wounds.
>
> (49)

Rather than to the 'bellies of deep sea sharks' who eat slaves or the 'shameless black men [who] speak blood of their sisters', the medicine man now prays to these victims and to his grandmother. While these prayers are still imbricated within intense suffering, unable to 'resurrect those already dead' (49), they nonetheless attest to an encounter with trauma that refuses historical forgetting.

'Singing in that rock!'

As we've seen, the poem begins with instructions for return to the South in which the speaker is told not to 'linger / For the road back is never / Home is never where you were born' (47). At its end, these instructions return, transformed.

> Wherefore I said to my knee bones
> Instruct me how to stand
> Teach me how to love and how to die
> And my bones wherein the hot oil
> Of the sun is contained
> Said:
>> Go by the abandoned railroad yard
>> Flank to the left your black mamma
>> Is rocking
>> Seven memories recall what
>> You know
>> North of the dark path in juju jungle
>> Age leaps upon the lips and caresses
>> The kiss of wisdom is love
>> Hold thirteen grains of sand
>> Look at the sun until it three-times
>> Blinds you, and listen
>> Listen to ten voices
>> Singing in that rocking chair
>>
>> *Singing in that rock!*
>> *Singing in that rock!*
>
> (49–50)

Whereas, in the first instance, the speaker's knee bones 'recalled what I *fail* to know' (48, my emphases), through their encounters with historical suffering, the speaker now comes into a condition of knowledge: 'Seven memories recall what / You know' (50).

Likewise, the 'ten voices' which earlier could only 'whisper [...] in a rock' (47) are released into song, punningly associated with the grandmother's rocking and rendering her singing collective. As Hernton recalls, while he was young, 'the light-skinned and middle-class blacks persisted in being ashamed of black folk culture and modes of entertainment [including the spirituals and blues], along with everything remotely connected with having been slaves' (Hernton 1996, 146). Hernton's grandmother informed him of slavery and of his African ancestry; she was a source of alternative histories, embedded in black cultural forms such as spirituals (Hernton 1996, 144–6).

'*Singing in that rock!*' suggests both the grandmother singing in her rocking chair and the songs she sings. In turn, their Christian symbols of fortitude and endurance transfer onto the grandmother herself – 'Eternal rock' (47) – recalling the earlier use of gris-gris in which physical objects associate with ritual traditions, attaining a living, spiritual power. Hernton draws from personal experience and transforms it into a broader cultural symbol of survival. Given that 'black folk culture' was 'connected with having been slaves', the pun on 'rock' also suggests work songs, timed to the rhythm of hacking at rocks. Whereas, earlier in the poem, such activity is turned against workers – 'The one who crushes the young men and smashes them' (49) – here, their song joins that of the grandmother, rocking between leisured activity and forced labour and across temporal divisions in an ensemble of remembrance and survival.

This conclusion is a kind of magical spell that finally releases the song contained within the rock. Yet, while the poem's cyclical structure appears to affect transformation and resolution, the spell is still trapped in ambiguity. 'Look at the sun until it three times / Blinds you' echoes Peter's three-time denial of Christ, harking back to the previous discourse of 'betrayal' (Matthew 26.69–75, Mark 14.66–72, Luke 22.54–62, John 18.13–27). The spell reaches blindness rather than (in)sight: the medicine man's efficacy in channelling ancestral 'voice memory' through an 'estranged familiar tongue' (47) echoes the poem's recurring 'betrayals'. While the poem's cyclical structure embodies the nourishing possibilities of witnessing and return, mitigating the violence of loss, dispossession, and trauma, it also prevents a clear movement from A to B, resolving only ambiguously in its endlessly rocking song. Its framing through refrains and parallel patterns remains a 'melancholic deferral of closure' (Luciano, 152) repeating trauma as much as it resolves it.

Conclusion: Mourning, melancholia and shame

As we saw in the second chapter, Baraka's 'Black Dada' worked through Damballah as 'shamed god'. The list of victim-dedicatees that concludes the poem includes his maternal grandfather, Tom Russ, who, as Baraka notes in a 1961 letter to Ed Dorn, was the 'first man to open a super market in [Dothan,] Alabama ... but run out with fire when he prospered', persecution which continued on his move to Newark, where he was virtually crippled in an accident engineered when he chose to break with the local Republican Party and run as an independent political candidate (Pisano, 60). Russ is the subject of one of Baraka's earliest published pieces, the short story 'Suppose Sorrow Was a Time Machine' (1958), in which the imaginative conceit of the time machine takes Baraka back to Dothan in 1858 as a means of reckoning with an older generation's suffering (Baraka 1958; *Fiction*, 1–4). Baraka's use of the time machine – attempting to break the boundaries of geographical, generational and temporal separation through an aesthetic frame – parallels Hernton's figuration of return through the medicine man. Both writers deal with the shame of erasure and the suffering of their grandparents which they witnessed as children who could barely understand it (*Autobiography*, 15).

In 'Chattanooga Black Boy', Hernton recalls an incident in which he and his grandmother waited for hours in segregated queues for food distribution as part of Roosevelt's welfare programme, only to be turned away, even though there was still food in the store (Hernton 1996, 143–4). Hernton notes the shame of seeing his grandmother, a respected woman who 'didn't take no stuff from nobody' being humiliated at the welfare station, the only response she could make being to sing the spiritual 'Sometimes I feel like a motherless child' on the way home (Hernton 1996, 144). More generally, as Hernton notes, growing up under Jim Crow, 'we were forever under the white gaze from which there was no escape. Our ways and modes of living and expressing ourselves, which reflected our culture of origin in Africa, were degraded and denied' (Hernton 1996, 144). This culture of shame forms the background to Hernton's deployment of his grandmother in 'Medicine Man'. Such shame is not a singular event but a trauma which cannot be named, even by its survivors, and is passed down through generations, 'old handed-down ailments' reinforced by the inscriptions of racism which 'moulds' race as a 'uniform' (Abraham and Torok 1994, 171–6; *MM*, 48; 1966D, 37). For Hernton, racial trauma is inextricably related to the formative psychic development of the black subject: to the 'blanks' of reaction to trauma which occur every time they encounter the 'hate stare' of white racism and to every humiliation suffered by loved ones (Hernton 1996, 140). Each of these encounters is a loss which reinforces the shame of original ancestral dispossession, and each potentially nourishing return – to the South, to the grandmother, to the ancestral survivals of West African religion present in Southern culture and its spirituals, its landscapes, its neo-hoodoo practices – re-enacts and relives trauma.

For Freud, the task of 'grief' or 'mourning' is complete when the ego is able to remove the previous libidinal investment in the lost object, which it had incorporated into itself in a new external object (Freud, 243). But what might this mean politically in the context of Hernton's poem and the contexts into which it opens out? Or to put it another way: what object of substitution is proffered that would offer an alternative, both political and psychical? Though 'Medicine Man' was most likely written and read during the initial period of Umbra and the BART/S, it was published during a period when the insurrectionary possibilities of the late 1960s had faded and the nourishing climate of collective poetic endeavour inhering in Umbra had diminished: its members geographically dispersed, their activities taken up with university teaching in often remote locations, their work frequently ignored. The poem's turn to melancholia speaks not only to Hernton's individual reckoning with family history and psychic trauma at the moment of composition, but – in its published afterlife – to the loss of a shared aesthetic climate and of nationwide political possibilities. This also relates to the split between South and North which, as discussed at the start of this chapter, forms a crucial part of the Umbra aesthetic. In the next chapter, I will move to another major poem which stages a Southern return: Tom Dent's 'Return to English Turn', which, like Hernton's poem, was first published in 1976. Dent's return to the South saw him bring the Umbra ethos of collective organizing to a New Orleans context, and the move from New Orleans to New York and thence back to New Orleans is key to his work. Examining Dent will suggest some of the ways that Umbra's continuing afterlife led not simply to melancholia, anguish and exile but to a productive sense of collective possibility adjacent to the main trends of the Northern-focused BAM.

6

'Return to English Turn': Tom Dent

Tom Dent: An introduction

Born to a successful middle-class family in New Orleans in 1932, Tom Dent's father was the president of the prestigious HCBU Dillard University from 1941 to 1969, and his mother a concert pianist. From early on, he had connections to Civil Rights activism, playing ball with Paul Robeson as a child (Dent 2018, 249). As Dent notes, 'though I was born in New Orleans, I have nevertheless always thought of myself as at home anywhere in the South' (385). His father was originally from a poor background in Atlanta, his mother from a more privileged background in Houston: the two met in Texas before moving to New Orleans. Dent was particularly fascinated by his paternal grandmother, who raised him as a small boy, and her connection to cultural practices excluded from the model of middle-class success espoused by his parents would prove an important influence (90–1, 385–6). Studying at Morehouse College in Atlanta, where he wrote journalism for and edited the *Maroon Tiger* in the early 1950s, Dent completed an MA thesis on political science and conducted graduate studies at Syracuse University, before joining 'that desert called the US army' from 1957 to 1959 (49). Leaving the South partly in order to defy his parents' middle-class aspirations, Dent came to New York to find himself as a writer; he initially found himself in Harlem, where he became involved in journalism and social work, working for Harlem weekly newspaper *The New York Age* in 1959 alongside Calvin Hicks and for the New York Welfare Department (437–8). Through Hicks, Dent became involved with On Guard; he had also met a number of the Umbra poets through readings organized by Raymond Patterson and by Raoul Abdul, Langston Hughes's secretary, and it was through these circles, which loosely united journalists, social workers and activists, that politically committed artists such as Dent, Archie Shepp and Askia Touré came together to form Umbra out of a sense of the necessity for On Guard's primarily activist focus to find an aesthetic extension (50). While Hernton was, through his highly dramatic readings, arguably the most visible *artistic* presence in the group, Dent was a key *organizational* presence, functioning as a 'convener' and 'social group leader': Umbra's weekly meetings happened in his East 2nd Street apartment, 'and because I didn't have any ideological constraints about how I dealt with people, I felt it was easier for me to deal with everybody and invite new people in' (461). Within Umbra, Dent's family background in Movement organizing and his membership of the 'talented tenth' were both important organizational assets and a source of resentment (Oren 1984, 244). As Margo Natalie Crawford writes, Dent in essence 'betrayed his class position', having been 'set up to be a part of the most privileged African-American class in New Orleans': first by becoming a writer and then by moving towards a more nationalist orientation than the current state of Southern Movement activism (Crawford, 309). Hence too, his focus on nurturing working-class, geographically marginalized aesthetic communities, and his rejection of the accepted, middle-class models of 'black success', and both the academic and the literary mainstream (Dent 2018, 469).

As Dent puts it, the Umbra aesthetic was inspired by the music of modern jazz innovators such as Coltrane, Miles Davis, Monk, Eric Dolphy and Archie Shepp, a member of the workshop. 'We were developing an urban sensibility, more critical of the potential of American democracy than the beliefs expressed in the Southern Civil rights movement' (Dent 1980, 244). Dent's own early poetry registers this focus – as well as poems with a more abstract, metaphysical focus such as 'Time Is a Motor', initially published in Langston Hughes's anthology *New Negro Poets USA*, and work influenced, like that of Baraka and Thomas, by European avant-garde writers such as Genet, Rimbaud and Kafka (Dent 1982, 14–15, 2018, 80) – early poems in *Umbra* and *Blue Lights and River Songs* concern Miles Davis, Thelonious Monk and 'Third Avenue, Near Fourteenth Street' (*Umbra* I, 7–9; Dent 1982, 14–18), with the city often presented as a hostile place, its 'cacophonous noise and light' graced by Monk's music, which 'details / the conundrum of my life', 'Death just around the corner / Of midnight' (Dent 1982, 13, 16). As with Calvin Hernton's early work, Dent's vocabulary touches on the topics familiar from Beat writing – jazz, the urban environment, the expression of alienation – but filters it through a voice at once more sardonic and metaphysically anguished. As he writes in 'The Offering: A Rose for Franz Kafka', 'Must I prove I really exist? / Out of control, walking on air, drink the poison' (Dent 1982, 15).

Dent's 'Nightdreams – Black', published in *Umbra*'s first issue, opens:

Being beat down,
I would fly away on the wings of a hawk.

(*Umbra* I, 7)

At once anguished and sardonic, the poem oscillates between figures of flight and encasement, of liberation through Harlem's thriving (albeit romanticized) black culture and the brute reality of the ghetto conditions from this culture emerges. While playfully allusive, suggesting Blake's Tiger and Rilke's Panther, such allusions are always filtered through the prism of racial representation and the relation of individual to community.

> were I a tiger!
> were I ever a tiger! [...]
> were I tiger roar a cry against my cage
> caged were my tiger [...]
>
> You tell me that my Harlem is jazz ... Black
> zoot-suited women with longer dangling dicks
> that eat barbecue and talk rhythm.
>
> You tell me that black shines in the silly
> Masturbating dream of some wet-sheeted night ...

(*Umbra* I, 7–8)

This tension reflects Dent's own turn to Harlem as a seat of black cultural rejuvenation in contrast to his middle-class background; yet it also suggests a sardonic address to the racial tourism of white 'Beat' writers who romanticize and appropriate this culture. Thus, the allusion to Ginsberg's 'Howl' in the following stanza:

> Oh, turn away, I see the narcotic weave –
> the estranged float on a thousand street corners
> of my generation – and now the weave is descending
> into a trickling, lazy fall – to the cold pavement
> where leaping roaches and muffled cries lie!

(*Umbra* I, 8)

Ginsberg famously wrote of 'the negro streets at dawn', and Dent implicitly asks: whose culture is this, and whose streets are these? The poem concludes:

> I would blackness, and love, and life go on
> forgetting, like an ant who eats only for today ...
>
>   Were I that simple: shoot me!
>   Were I that white: color me!
>
> Were I nowhere near heaven, being beat down,
> but nearer Paris, or Venus, or second base,
> or even the silly thin five-yard line of my dreams,
> I would float through the skin of my torture like
> Smoke rising, like clouds sliding, like bones
> Becoming dust, life becoming death ....

(*Umbra* I, 9)

Dent is intensely aware of the role of race and class in constructions of urban escape. The 'torture' here is individualized, but its address to the dilemmas of black life in the city has suggestive correlations with the work examined thus far by Henderson and Hernton in particular. Dent's poem calls for the speaker to 'turn away', and *return* proves the key figure for his subsequent work. While New York is an important locus for these early poems, it was specifically to New Orleans that he turned from the mid-1960s on, carrying the experience of New York's 'Umbra Days' with him to forge an aesthetic and a politics of collectivity, community and historical memory at once nationalist but non-partisan, regional but internationalist, Afro-centric but focused on the present. As Dent notes, 'for some [in Umbra], literary expression was too limiting to satisfy their more activist needs' (Dent 1980, 245). More than most, Dent himself felt the pull between a commitment to writing and the demands of full-time activism. His poetry cannot be examined without considering how it relates to the organizational problems he grappled with throughout his career: this chapter's concluding reading of his long poem 'Return to English Turn' aims to catch the dual focus in his career on Umbra and the North and on New Orleans and the South, while also emphasizing the particular aesthetic of his poetry, which is often neglected in favour of his work with the Free Southern Theater and his critical writing. (The recent, 500-page *Reader*, for example, contains only a handful of poems, numbering not more than forty pages, in early versions that he submitted for an MA in the early 1970s (Dent 2018, 264–300).)

New York to New Orleans

Though he was central to its organizational activity, Dent published relatively little during Umbra's active period: two poems (the aforementioned 'Nightdreams' and 'Ode to Miles Davis') appear in *Umbra*'s first issue, and two further poems ('Love' and 'Time Is a Motor') in Langston Hughes's 1963 anthology *New Negro Poets USA*, which also featured work by Baraka and by a number of other Umbra writers, including Hernton, Henderson and Ray Durem (Hughes 1963, 71, 80). It was only upon his return to New Orleans in 1965 that he found his mature poetic voice, and the majority of his slim corpus of poetic work concerns the city. Indeed, in his introduction to the recently published *New Orleans Griot: The Tom Dent Reader*, Kalamu ya Salaam calls him 'the single greatest New Orleans writer of all time' (Dent 2018, 19). In the section which follows, I'll explore the ramifications of Dent's return, outlining his work with the Free Southern Theater and *Callaloo*, among other projects, as well as the ways in which New Orleans contributed to his own poetics. Though these activities postdate Umbra, they are, as I'll show, important extensions of it, and telling Dent's story serves to illuminate not only what happened *after* the group's split but how its earlier activities continued to reverberate well into the century's final decade.

Dent's career can be divided into two principal periods. The early phase, from 1959 to 1965, saw Dent based around New York, focused around Umbra. Yet, during this time, Dent increasingly divided his time between New York and Southern States such as Mississippi, working as a press attaché for the NAACP Legal Defense Fund between 1961 and 1963 and subsequently with the Free Southern Theater in New Orleans in 1965. Dent keenly felt the pull between New York as organizational base and cultural focal point and the need to organize directly within Southern communities. During his time with the NAACP, he was friends with Medgar Evers, with whom he had worked in the NAACP's Legal Defense Fund. As Dent notes of Evers's brutal murder in 1963: 'I knew him personally and it cracked me up [...] I had known Medgar as a man whom I felt safest with, more than any other in Mississippi [...] my earliest mature memories of driving through Mississippi were with Medgar' (Dent 2018, 390). Such direct engagements with the brutality of the Southern experience parallel the violence found in the North, particularly that of the Harlem Riots, which, as we've seen, served to radicalize many of the Umbra poets. It was this background that led Askia Touré to co-write the SNCC's Black Power Position Paper in 1966; Dent's work in the South parallels that of Touré, who also worked in Mississippi. Though he was less ideologically focused than Touré, he would likewise adopt a broadly nationalist vocabulary, based on the concentration of black life in the South and the particular character of its landscape. In 1971, he wrote:

> And when we think of Mississippi we think of land, the beauty of the land in its variety of topography, which gives us a feeling of what Africa might be like. We think of land because it is this land that Black people will soon control, politically and economically [...] If there is any place in America where there can actually be a black nation, it is in Mississippi.

(Dent 2018, 126)

Dent's work in the NAACP manifested the twin pull throughout his career, between the demands and expectations of political activism and the necessity for the creation of aesthetic communities. Dent later recalled: 'John O'Neal once wrote that he was surprised how many people in the Southern Civil Rights movement considered themselves poets' (Dent 2018, 352). As indicated by the equal involvement of Umbra writers like Dent and Touré in aesthetic work (predominantly in the North) and activism (predominantly in the South), divisions between activism and art were perhaps more apparent than real, but Dent perceived a condescension – particularly among the older generation – towards those who believed aesthetic work to be an equal part of the struggle. In 'Running and Dipping Poem No.1', he sarcastically recalls

```
[...] all the organ
            zashun
ale
ideolo    gists
who told me I had to do some

thing
other than
                w
                 r
                  i
                   t
                    e
if I wanted to liberate
black people and forced
me to believe
in the worth
in honest
```

written
word
for my people.

(282–3)

Trying to balance the pull between his work as political activist and sense of writing's importance as a political tool, Dent's career would go on to unite the two, often at the expense of his own individual fame. The second major phase in his career saw him based in the South, following his return to New Orleans in 1965, where he remained for the rest of his life; Dent helped the FST transition from a New York–based company into one focused around New Orleans and developed institutions such as the Congo Square Writers Union, BLKARTSOUTH, *Nkombo* and the Southern Black Arts Alliance. Dent saw these two periods as a continuum. This is perhaps best encapsulated in the dedication to *Blue Lights and River Songs* (1982), which collects poems written over a period of more than two decades, dating back to as early as 1959: 'To the Umbra People and the Congo Square People'. (The Congo Square Writers' Workshop grew out of the FST, bringing Umbra's spirit of ethos of aesthetic openness and collective organization to New Orleans.) In numerous statements, poems and interviews, Dent continually emphasized the importance of Umbra to all his subsequent work: aesthetically, the experience of New York, at once alienating and enlivening, is registered in early poems and was vital for his ability to see the South from a different perspective. Organizationally, the Umbra experience was paramount: it provided a model for virtually all the activity in which Dent was to be subsequently involved.

This is a neglected part of Black Arts histories: the way in which earlier encounters with a broadly Northern, urban radicalism associated politically, with Malcolm X and with activism such as that of On Guard, and aesthetically, with the innovations in music, theatre and poetry that were to shape the BAM aesthetic, spread across the country, particularly in the often-ignored but hugely important building of a Black Arts aesthetic in the South. Furthermore, while the Umbra poets reacted with urgency to shifting and often divisive developments in contemporary politics, overly schematic periodizations are inadequate barometers of such a history, as indicated by Dent's simultaneous involvement with Umbra in New York and the NAACP in the South during the early 1960s and Askia Touré's with Umbra, BART/S, RAM and the SNCC during the mid-1960s. From the 1960s through to the 1970s and beyond, Dent's work serves as crucial index of this spread: despite Umbra's germination in New York, this also constitutes a vital part of the group's legacy.

As we saw in the previous chapter, Umbra's internationalist and New York–based focus was mirrored by many of its writers' concern with the American South as a site of cultural renewal, nationalist sentiment and a connection to ancestral memory. Following Umbra's dissolution, Dent joined the Free Southern Theater in April 1965. Founded by Gilbert Moses, John O'Neal and Doris Derby two years previously, the group's tours around Mississippi – fraught with financial difficulty and encounters with redneck communities – were always directed from New York. Likewise, though he had travelled widely across the South as part of his NAACP activities, and continued to do so with the FST, Dent at this stage still considered New York as his base. Yet, on a visit home to New Orleans in 1965, Dent found himself unexpectedly staying in the city where he would concentrate his artistic, personal and political activity for the rest of his life As Dent puts it, 'Somehow I just never returned to New York' (Dent 1997, 2). Ironically enough, Dent moved away from the city at the very moment that the opening of BART/S initiated a new phase of Black Arts activity, drawing attention to New York as a centre for radical black writing. (There are parallels here to Hernton's departure from New York for England in 1965 and Baraka's for Newark the following year.) While less extreme in its rhetoric than that of the BART/S, Dent's New Orleans work was if anything *more* embedded in the black community than the often fractious and short-lived experiment in Harlem.

Yet seeking to develop the FST as a specifically New Orleans–based ensemble, with actors and technicians taken from local working-class communities rather than New York professionals, caused conflict with those, such as Gilbert Moses, who believed that the only efficient way to run the theatre was from New York. The North–South tensions in the group manifested particularly in terms of race – as indicated by the departure of key white members such as Richard Schechner and Murray Levy – but the accusations of New York-centrism also had a class dimension which related to profound shifts in the ways that Movement activists understood their organizational role. As Dent wrote: 'The FST took itself seriously as a *southern* theatre, but continued to run tours from New York while hooking its fund-raising to the white liberal / New York / benefit complex' (Dent 2018, 123). Dent felt hat adopting this model, borrowed from activist groups such as the SNCC (for whom original founders Derby and John O'Neal had worked), meant that aesthetic and political movements could not be linked up nationwide. Despite the group's intentions, the development of a touring company which drew most of its participants from New York, rather than nurturing artistic development in the South, reinforced, rather than bridging, regional divides. In a letter to the FST's board of directors from October 1970, Dent notes of the clash that arose during this period:

> The most central issue in this conflict, which through the course of our existence appeared in many manifestations, was a disagreement or fundamental indecision over whether the FST should be fundamentally a New York oriented theater, with its main ideas, structural controls, finances and personnel emanating from there, or whether it would be a New Orleans southern oriented theater [...] It seems to me that the original idea of the theater encompassed the first alternative, and the southern tours of the FST were originally conceived in a fashion that would relate to New York and northern support in the same manner that SNCC, CORE and other civil rights movement activities related to such support in the early and middle sixties. On the other hand, a southern-based theater had of necessity to spend more time *building* something, satisfying the needs of New Orleans first.

(Dent 1970, n.p.)

The company's initial move to New Orleans saw it align itself with the middle-class communities surrounding Tulane University, but, under Dent's aegis, the FST further relocated to the 9th Ward's Desire Street Housing Project in 1966 (Dent 1969, 111). The location for Tennessee Williams's play *Desire* was a predominantly black area, one of the poorest in the city, and the attempted airing of a controversial TV programme on 'The Ghetto of Desire', organized by Dent, led to clashes with the city authorities, and, though shown nationwide, the programme was blacked out in New Orleans (Dent 1969, 123–32). The relocation to *Desire* also saw a gradual shift in emphasis on what plays the company should stage. The group initially presented material by the likes of Beckett, Ionesco and Brecht – material which, as Dent notes, was often unsuited to the cultural environment of the poor rural communities where the FST toured. As he concludes in *The Free Southern Theater by the Free Southern Theater*, the sourcebook he co-edited with Gilbert Moses and John O'Neal in 1969:

> To bring [...] white theatre as it exists today in America to the black community is most irrelevant. It is a statement of negation, if taken too seriously. [...] It is saying, 'What you have ain't shit. If you want to be "cultured" you got to dig *Godot*.' Well I say, goodbye *Godot*, we'll stick with Otis. We'll expand, and develop, from that. And the hell with what the white critics say or expect. It's as simple as that.

(Dent 1969, 233)

Given this, the FST increasingly began to focus on plays specifically about the communities in which they were performed, often incorporating poetry and music in multimedia shows which parallel Baraka's own contemporaneous work at Spirit House in Newark. As early as 1964, the company had produced some material which moved away from the focus of their earlier repertoire. Focusing instead on incorporating political questions relevant to the communities in which they performed, such material drew on the aesthetic resources of Southern culture, rather than bringing 'high art' to communities who found it simply irrelevant (Neal 1970, 171–2). Yet tellingly, when Bobbs-Merrill published the substantial (and invaluable) sourcebook on the FST, such material, as Larry Neal noted in his review of the book, was left out (172). Notable examples later included Dent's own *Ritual Murder* (1976), a stark portrayal of intramural violence from multiple perspectives, the plays of Val Ferdinand (Kalamu ya Salaam), and a highly successful touring version of Baraka's *Slave Ship*, directed by Gilbert Moses in 1969. As Dent notes, while the latter production was far more widely noted when presented in New York, it in fact had more impact in the South. Whereas, in the North, the play was contained within the forms of bourgeois theatre and was not focused on 'the igniting of the Black community itself', in the original, Southern production, it was truncated and presented in community contexts where audience participation in the concluding, communal ritual made it genuinely explosive (Dent 2018, 128). Indeed, as ya Salaam notes, a performance in Greenville, Mississippi, very nearly caused a riot (Elam, 122; ya Salaam 1970, 28).

Facing financial pressures due to the increasingly radical content of the plays they produced, which often focused on local political issues, the FST's activities began to decline around the mid-1970s, though the group was officially in existence until 1985. But, out of the specifically New Orleans–based elements of the FST, Dent plunged his organizational capacities into developing the Congo Square Writers Workshop and, with ya Salaam, the literary journal *Nkombo*, which published seven issues between 1968 and 1974. In 1976, he, Jerry Ward and Charles Rowell co-founded *Callaloo* as a journal specifically dedicated to Black Southern writing. Umbra formed a strong presence in the journal's early stages: poetry by Dent and Lorenzo Thomas appeared in the first issue, and Thomas's crucial essay 'The Shadow World', on Umbra and the origin of the BAM, appeared in the fourth issue in 1978 (Thomas 1978). Dent's first issue editorial is an important statement of his focus on the South and deserves quoting at length.

> CALLALOO was born out of a specific desire to give expression to the new writers in the Deep South area [...] Writers from the Deep South have traditionally felt they had to go northward and eastward to pursue their literary careers & get

published. This was because the publishing industry was concentrated in the Northeast and because all the other accoutrements of a literary career were also there. For the first time now there has developed a coterie of Black Southern writers who have sunk their anchors in the South, and who see the Black Southern experience with its rich history of both oppression & and the struggle against oppression as the fulcrum of their literary work. This perspective is further enriched by strong African cultural survivals – the motheroot of our families and communities in America. Some of these writers, like myself, developed from strong affiliations with community theaters & activist groups – some have stayed fairly close to the traditional university scene, the main source of economic support available to black creative and critical artists. [...]

So many of our literary friends are tired of & disgusted with the New York scene. New York has become an even more inhuman city than it was, & it was always bad. Most of my friends (though not all) realize that if they place any value on the quality of their lives & on their mental health they must get out of New York. The resurgence (really the surge) of the Black South economically, politically & culturally could be looked upon merely as a facet of the flight from the Apple, but it would have happened anyway; eventually NY will be looked upon only as a place where writers go to attend to the necessary details of getting published. So one of the things we are about is the redressing of the balance between so-called advanced, progressive NY & the backwards, countrified South. In this case backwards could mean the excitingly healthy exercise of looking closely and without fear at our history, not only in America but from the perspective of our African & Caribbean origins. And of course the country is the land, a more positive image when we own and control some of it, and use it to remind us of nature's great truths – buttressing us against the illusions & deprivations of the cities. We, more than any other people in America, have experienced an all-encompassing exposure to the garbage & excrement of the twentieth century city.

(Dent 1976b, v–vi)

Dent further notes the material reality of this split:

There isn't any money behind this journal [...] [We] are broke and exceedingly foolish for trying to begin another magazine in such a wretched financial state. We have gratefully received small gifts from people we know who believe in us & believe in the idea. We need more & will be happy for your support. Do not expect us to be businesslike. Businesslike people don't undertake literary journals without money. Do expect – in fact, demand – that we do something worthwhile. Most of all enjoy, read, write, let us hear from you, & believe.

(vi)

Dent's apparently 'localistic' focus on the South in fact reveals the localism and parochialism of regarding New York as the necessary epicentre of black writing. Moreover, in his study, in his own contemporaneous writings, of cultural practices in New Orleans such as the Mardi Gras Indians and voodoo, Dent emphasizes the city's stronger West African cultural survivals amid the melting pot of jazz, carnival culture and interconnections with the Native American population. Poetically, the collections *Magnolia Street* (1976) and *Blue Lights and River Songs* (1982), as well as uncollected works from the same period, often focus on contemporary political developments in the city. But these are always linked up to histories dating back to the Middle Passage. As Lorenzo Thomas notes: 'The time of the poems is always this moment, though snippets of ancient and recent history constantly appear', and 'the dimensions of a more profound historical tragedy are sounded' – what Dent calls 'terror of the centuries we romance / back to haunt us in ours' (Dent 1982, 74; Thomas 1985, 90). Dent's New Orleans is, in Thomas's words, 'both vibrantly present tense and aggressively nostalgic' (*EM*, 175). As his comments in the *Callaloo* editorial suggest, Dent's later work also focuses on 'our African and Caribbean origins', through the influence in particular of his mentor Keorapetse Kgositsile – the highly influential South African poet-in-exile who was a key part of the BAM – and of Kamau Brathwaite, who would later advise Dent on portions of his in-progress manuscript, *Southern Journey*, and who dedicated his 1995 lectures 'New Gods of the Middle Passage' to his 'friend and comrade' Dent (Dent 1997, 384, 2018, 261, 292–3; Brathwaite 2005). One of Dent's last major projects, unfinished at his death, arose from a trip he had undertaken to West Africa following original slave roots (Dent 2018, 257–58).

It is an irony of the histories of figures such as Dent that, due to his focus on organizational activity and on nurturing Southern writing at the expense of pursuing of individual literary fame, he published little, though the collection of his writings at the Amistad Research Centre numbers some sixty linear feet (Dent 2018, 7, 17). Until the publication in 2018 of the *Tom Dent Reader* edited by Dent's New Orleans comrade and BAM historian Kalamu ya Salaam, very little of his work was in print. Tellingly, Dent left *Callaloo* due to the magazine's new university affiliation and its move away from an initial focus on Black Southern writing:

> My vision of it was that it would be an extension of *Nkombo*, and that we would develop writers [...] But Charles [Rowell] wanted to develop a national, high quality journal with an emphasis on scholarly works, which he did.
>
> (Dent 2018, 489)

Despite the journal's subsequent rise as a hugely important resource in linking African-American writing to that of the Global South, Dent's role appears long forgotten. Nonetheless, he continued to do thriving cultural work in New Orleans. In particular, during the 1970s, Dent began working on a number of oral history projects. From 1978, he began the oral interviews, tracing the afterlife of the Civil Rights Movement in Southern States, that would become perhaps his best-known work, the book *Southern Journey* (1997); collaborated with photographer Roy Lewis to depict isolated Louisiana Black communities along the Mississippi River; worked as a consultant on the autobiography of his childhood friend, the activist and politician Andy Young; and served as executive director of the New Orleans Jazz & Heritage Foundation during the late 1980s. Dent's concern from the 1970s through to the 1990s had been with the broader political implications of the history of the Civil Rights Movement, particularly the role of the South, as well as with the continuing effects of racism. He was particularly attentive to this as it manifested in his home town of New Orleans, noting, in poetry, plays and essays, the ways in which the appointment of black mayors and the celebration of the city's black culture as part of the tourist trade merely covered over the continuing poverty of working-class African-Americans in housing projects such as the Desire Ghetto. What Dent took from his experience with Umbra in New York was an emphasis on community, a refusal of incorporation into the literary mainstream and a working through of the personal dilemmas which, as indicated by an important long letter to his psychoanalyst, published in the *Reader*, were felt as much in political as in personal terms (Dent 2018, 81).

Dent's slim corpus of poetry addresses such concerns through specific figures and places: this is an orally inflected poetry of community in which Dent's own tendency towards introspection sits alongside the imperative to document forgotten figures – as in 'Magnolia Street', addressed to 'Miss Lucas' – to pay tribute to artistic and activist peers to whom poems are dedicated – from John Buffington, to Louis Armstrong, Keorapetse Kgositsile, Victor Hernandez Cruz and Sarah Webster Fabio – and to chart what he called the 'survival instinct' of black cultural practices such as parades and music in the face of their commodification and of urban 'regeneration' (Dent 2018, 45–7, 271–2, 285, 291, 292–3, 298–9). Acknowledging that such practices were often co-opted by white politicians to 'polish the images of New Orleans glamour' (239), at the expense of the black workers and artists who are exploited as part of the tourist industry, Dent's New Orleans writings nonetheless emphasize the figure of the carnival parade in particular as a part of what he calls 'a theatre of the street', connected to 'the strong positive legacy of African cultural retentions, especially in music, dress, the various racial societies, dance, cooking, parades, funerals' (240; see also 235–6). In the 1973 prose text 'Report from New Orleans', Dent figures music and carnival as revolutionary forces which might transform the space of the city. Recalling Baraka's 'The Screamers' (1963), he imagines a parade which

> never ends – it marches right on to City Hall [...] through the courts, through Parish Prison and Central Lockup, then winds its way through the library, up and down Canal Street, through Maison Blanche and Holmes, through Mr. Tee's taking a few diamonds with it, and right over to Tulane and Broad to the police station bursting the eardrums of the polices so that their brains fly right out the side of their heads in both directions and the music oozes in to impart finally some sense. [...]
>
> And there were no more niggers because the niggers *were* the city: what his people had learned long before him was the order and the music was the law.
>
> (235–6)

As Dent notes in 'A Memoir of Mardi Gras' (1968), the commercialized aspects of New Orleans parades were a 'hustle' that

> resurrect[ed] glorified images of the Old South where things are under control, specifically the niggers – as long as enough of them are dancing for coins, how can they ever become a threat? Despite the demonstrations, the urban explosions on the television screens elsewhere, we are assured New Orleans will never really change, aren't we?
>
> (316–17)

Dent asks:

> How did our dance, drumming, music – traditions so deeply embedded in the mother culture – become distorted into a dance for spare coins from New World neo-Europeans? [...] Whatever we thought the 'New' South had the potential to become, it could never achieve until some of this perversion ceased.
>
> (317)

Discussing Sidney Bechet's recollections of his grandfather Omar, a fugitive slave, Dent writes: 'Memory was the key. Memory invoked through dance, drumming, music [...] there but buried deep deep into the subconscious' (318–19). The lines Dent quotes from Bechet serve as an encapsulation of his own poetic ethos with its concerns, turns and returns, insisting on the connections between the local and the international and on a forward movement out of conditions of degradation, which refuses to disavow local specificity or to forget the legacy of historical trauma.

The only thing they had that couldn't be taken from them was their music [...] It was bewildered, this part of them. It was like it had no end, nowhere even to wait for an end, nowhere to hope for change in things. But it had a beginning, and that much they understood ... it was a feeling in them, a memory that came from a long way back.

(Bechet, quoted in Dent 2018, 319)

There are correlatives and contrasts to Hernton here. Paradoxically, as we've seen, though Hernton's work was often highly politicized, his poetry of the South tends more towards the personal and the metaphysical. While Dent's engagement with community was based in part on the opportunities afforded him as an organizer by his 'talented tenth' background – as well as by the guilt this manifested – his role as an organizer gave him a clear sense of the collective stakes involved in writing the history of the region and its cultural survivals. In his New Orleans poetry, Dent serves at once as historian and musician, filtering the voices and stories of community in an echo of the traditional African function of the *griot*. As he writes: 'In the African tradition it was the role of the poet to record and interpret events. His place in the tribal community was an honoured one more basic and functional than the literary career of twentieth century european america' (quoted in Thomas 1985, 89). While firmly connected to the spaces of national and international politics, Dent sees the function of the community-based poet-*griot* as recording 'the terms of our existence in these times – the little sacrifices, the small births & the small deaths' (89).

'Return to English Turn'

Dent's major poem 'Return to English Turn' traces a history of New Orleans, from the slave ships to the present, which pivots around the figure of bends of the river and the 'barren levee called / English turn' – the spot at which, in 1699, explorer and future Louisiana governor Jean-Louis Bienville 'convinced english / this land french', leading to the establishment of the city twenty years later (Dent 1978, 10). First written in 1974 and submitted as part of Dent's MA thesis, the poem was printed, following substantial revisions, in Dent's privately printed collection *Magnolia Street* (1976) and in *Callaloo* in 1978. (Dent 1976A, 1978, 2018, 264–70). In his MA notes, Dent calls it a 'long poem about Louisiana history with the Mississippi river as a central symbol' (Dent 2018, 261). As Lorenzo Thomas puts it, here, 'the broad river at the heart of America becomes the "great river" of three continents' traditions – the Atlantic Ocean that simultaneously links and separates "New World" Africans and their ancestral homeland' (Thomas 1985, 90). Dent's uniting of local geography with historical memory and a strange sense of the international ramifications of Louisiana history – in particular, the trade routes that form part of the river's traumatic history – exemplify his mature style. The poem is in three parts: the first turns from the 'English turn' to the conditions of slavery which accompanied it; the second, 'to you in the city project' (Dent 1978, 13), the contemporary dwellers of urban New Orleans – in particular, 'the project called Desire' (10) where, as we've seen, Dent had relocated the FST in 1966 – before calling for a (re)turn to African roots; the third serves as a shorter epilogue in which the 'clear music' of 'the song an old griot sings' symbolizes this notion of African survivals and 'the uprooting of / european markers' (14).

The poem begins with Dent meditating on the sign commemorating the transfer of land from one colonial force to another. He pauses to ask:

… and us?

us in the hull
chained
confused
torn
in the hull
the musics of our ruptured memory
clashing with the grating roar
of chains.

(10)

Music, as in Hernton's 'Medicine Man', serves as index of memory and, as contrast with the sounds of machinery, will unite the slave ship with modern commercial ships where black labourers are still exploited. As ya Salaam notes, Dent's poems of this period saw him move from a primarily narrative focus to an orally inflected engagement built around short lines and refrains (Dent 2018, 259). 'Chains' and 'chained' serve to link physical landscape to history: a material account which, like Hernton's, refuses to separate its materialism from the spiritual survivals of more intangible cultural forms. The 'songs' and 'shouts' which Dent celebrates cannot be disentangled from the conditions of slavery and modern servitude which produce them: like Hernton's 'rock', they both attest to the 'rupture' of memory and the possibility of linking to a past at once traumatic and sustaining. Dent's poem focuses on labour: on the

> chain-forced hull energy
> forging the neo-european progress
> chain-forced hull energy
> sustaining the languorous civilization

(11)

The poem's oral quality – emphasized in its rewriting, which expands the more impressionistic earlier draft to a multisectioned poem which carefully builds and returns to its refrains – subtly impacts its meaning. 'Chain-forced' moves to 'chained-forced': the chains which attach to boats become the chains by which slaves are tied and forced to produce the 'hull energy' which will control the river for the purposes of commerce and the dollar.

> chained-forced hull energy
> trying to bring this river under control
> control commerce control
> control machine control
> control dollar control.

(11)

Dent proceeds to link this force of labour to music.

> and even our music was stolen
> made circus show for drunk
> whiskey dreams not ours

(11)

This music, which records the suffering and survival of such labour, becomes mere entertainment for white listeners – a constant concern, too, of Dent's New Orleans writings on artists from Professor Longhair to 'Slow Drag' Pavageau and his time as director of the New Orleans Jazz and Heritage Foundation. Music which reacted against labour becomes itself a form of labour, 'our dance, drumming, music [...] become distorted into a dance for spare coins from New World neo-europeans' (Dent 2018, 317): the 'hull songs' of the slave ships and riverboat labour connect to the songs performed in Mardi Gras parades for tourists. Yet these songs were not made for those tourists: they are

> hull songs for us alone
> songs of hulldom for us

> yeah oh yes ...
> warming the heart of congealed years.
>
> those songs our only way of saying
> what we could not afford to say
> those songs our only understanding
> of what we could not comprehend
>
> (Dent 1978, 12)

In the forced erasure of memory accomplished by the splitting, during slavery, of families and tribal units, and the concomitant prohibition of African cultural forms, music attempts to express the inexpressible. Yet, as with Hernton: 'It will not raise those already dead/It will not heal ear and tongue of betrayal' (*MM*, 49). Dent briefly echoes the despair of Hernton's medicine man and the slaves whose cries to Shango go unanswered.

> & even when we beseeched our god of
> rivers
> it seemed he had forgotten us
> and there was no escape
> no turning back.
>
> (Dent 1978, 13)

But Dent's poem throughout aims to juxtaposes its catalogue of historical abuses and forgetting with a countervailing impulse to resistance and survival. Unlike Hernton, Dent deploys the second-person plural throughout. Even the opening lines, which appear to concern the individual speaker 'travelling along / river road' and discovering the sign for English turn, deliberately omit a pronoun until the appearance of the 'we' who 'begin our neo-european forced journey' (10). Likewise, as Hernton's grandmother, '*singing in that rock*', swings back and forth between past and present, humiliation and survival, so Dent's 'turn' builds up to a defiant statement of collective identity at the end of the poem's second section.

> let us return to english turn
> rip up the signs
> wipe out the legacies
> pledge no more forced journeys
>   no more english turns

> no more spanish turns
> no more french turns, portuguese
> or german turns
> rip the markers of neo-european conquest from
> > their roots
> plant a new one marking:
> > > *our turn.*

(13-14)

Dent's conclusion emphasizes the transitional pivot on which the poem turns – the 'place called english turn' and the 'neo-european' civilization that founded multicultural New Orleans on conquest, trade and forced labour. In response, Dent calls for a new turn towards African ancestry and nationalist resolve. Emphasizing futurity but, like Hernton, acknowledging the importance of memory, he refuses what he would later call the 'smooth, bright mask of posttrauma adjustment to racial and economic conflict' which imagines that the achievements of the Civil Rights Movement have erased the continuing ravages of racism (Dent 1997, 77).

> our turn to flow out of the hulls, on to the decks,
> > take control of the pilot wheels, choose the
> > direction of our own journeys for the first
> > time in this valley
> our turn, but never forgetting the forced journeys

(14)

What, in this poem, is presented as collective resolve is also about Dent's own return: about his struggles with childhood, class and culture in the divided cities of New York and New Orleans and his decision to (re)turn to the South in order to make an artistic, personal and political reckoning. As he notes in the preface to *Southern Journey*, the river which forms the central figure for this, and many other of his poems, had earlier been associated with escape from the city (Dent 1997, 1-2).

> One generation before the maze of legal obstructions that delineated racial segregation in the South was dismantled piece by piece [...] my family expected that I would seek my fortune elsewhere, because possibilities in the South were far too limited [...] The necessity that I leave the South for the sake of a more promising future was rarely explicitly stated, but it was strongly implied [...]

> Immense changes were not expected in their lifetimes, nor did they think the younger generations should depend too heavily on massive changes during our lifetimes.
>
> (Dent 1997, 1)

Consequently, Dent 'began a rich dream life built around leaving for destinations so far from, so different from the South, the two worlds would never recognise each other' (1). Fixating on the Mississippi River which ran through the centre of the city, Dent came to associate the past with downriver, the future upriver: 'the great highway out into the world beyond the street corners, beyond the limitations and boredoms of the world I was growing up into'.

> For me and others like me, those dream roads – fuelled by books, movies, and legends – led to a non-racial world, where we would find solace from the exclusively black world we were confined to, where the colour of our skin, our racial heritage, did not matter. But then, that was truly a dream world – a world, I have come to believe, that does not exist.
>
> (2)

While Dent remained clear-eyed about the possibilities for the 'New South', following the gains of the Civil Rights era, his experience as an activist saw him fully aware of the continuing selling-out of black communities by politicians and the continuing exploitation of their culture while they continued to live in conditions of poverty. More broadly, he was aware that this reflected a trajectory across the South. *Southern Journey*, in which he retraces his steps through sights of 1960s Civil Rights activism, is in many ways a melancholy book. Acknowledging the enormous gains by which 'changes we hardly believed were possible have occurred' (2), Dent's journey through Southern towns revealed that, while the overt signs of segregation had disappeared, economic divisions along racial lines remained. Furthermore, they were, paradoxically, *harder* to challenge with a less visible enemy to fight against: 'you can choose to be aware of an underclass, or you can look away, not noticing any blemishes at all' (Dent 1997, 76–7). But Dent's determination to document and agitate against this is crucial. Dent's return to New Orleans reproduces the resolve of Hernton's early poem 'Remigrant' to stay and fight in the South. Having earlier refused both the middle-class pathways planned by his parents and the temptations of literary fame for the hard work of community arts organization and political engagement, Dent's poetic working through of personal relations to New York and the South, and to their filtration through issues of race and class, increasingly moved into a collective dimension. Matured by the experience with Umbra in New York, his enduring legacy was to continue that process back home. Sometimes, as Dent suggests in his engagement with New Orleans (or, for that matter, Baraka in Newark), home *can* be where you were born.

As we'll see in the next chapter, both Dent's and Hernton's reckonings with memory inform the work of another Southern-based Umbra writer, Lorenzo Thomas. Writing on the cusp of the 1970s, in the era of the Vietnam War – in which he served – and the transformation of the Civil Rights Movement during the preceding decade, Thomas's poem 'The Bathers' – one of the major statements of Black Arts writing – likewise seeks to link ancestral survivals with the anguished questions facing present political action.

7

Memory and Myth in Lorenzo Thomas's 'The Bathers'

Introduction

In this concluding chapter, I focus on a single poem by Lorenzo Thomas. Written in 1970, 'The Bathers' serves as an encapsulation of the Umbra project and of the scope of this book. Addressing events from early 1963 – the height of the Umbra period – but written after the group's dispersal, the poem's arguments about history, myth and memory encapsulate the Umbra ethos. Like the work analysed in the book's first chapter, the poem addresses the problematics of representation and strategy surrounding moments of public protest; its urban setting recalls those of Baraka, Henderson and Hernton addressed in the middle chapters; and its address to memory, mourning and mysticism within a Southern context link to Dent's and Hernton's writings on the South in those immediately preceding. 'The Bathers' is an urgent and vital exploration of defeat and survival. It attests to the existence of Umbra not only as a vital organizing force but as a collective spirit that persisted long after the workshops and readings had collapsed: transferred to other arenas, and continued in the lives of individual members, Umbra serves as index of the same kinds of continuance, survival and resistance that the poem charts.

Born in Panama in 1944, Thomas moved to New York at the age of five. While still a teenager, he was involved with various Civil Rights peace organizations and, importantly, in a poetry workshop led by the Belgian-Jewish labour organizer Henri Percikow in which he met David Henderson. With Henderson, he then became an important part of the Umbra circle, as well as associating with New York School writers, primarily through workshops held by Ted Berrigan (Dent 1985; *EM*, 142; Smethurst 2005, 141; Thomas 2006). As we saw in the first chapter, his earliest poems address the political activism around On Guard with a keen eye to the frames of media reportage, and the other work he published in this period – in *Umbra*, in New York journals such as *Lines, C* and *The Rivoli Review*, and in radical magazines like *Liberator*, the French Maoist journal *Revolution*, and Margaret Randall's *El Corno Emplumado* – combines the conversational approach characteristic of New York School writing with a keen sense of racial politics and the intersections of the political and the personal. These poems are sharp analyses of the traps of stultifying racist representation, encapsulated in the epigraph from Aimé Césaire which opens 'The Unnatural Life' – 'What I am is a man alone / imprisoned in white' (*TB*, 17) – in which the speaker's self-presentations of black militancy drip with a fierce irony. Typical of these is the long, sectional 'Broadway-Lafayette Espadrille'.

> The Broadway number jumbled up in my brain.
> My mind's dream of Walt Frazier
> And/or Black Revolution And *rifa*
> All down to my feet moving swift
>
> In my sneakers. Is this the wrong Broadway?
>
> Swoop back downtown. The same burthen
> Too much reefer
> On my head backward and forward
> Through the City all day.
>
> (Thomas 1979, 28)

During the late 1960s, Thomas was drafted under Vietnam conscription laws, which, as many noted at the time, disproportionately targeted African-Americans (Bibby, 54–5; Thomas 2008, 119). In a complex position due to his status as a first-generation immigrant, Thomas debated whether to flee to Canada to escape the draft. After deliberation, he joined the navy in 1968 and was posted to Vietnam as a 'military advisor' in 1971 (Poulos; Thomas 1983, 2–3, 2001A; *TB*, 69–85).

'The Bathers' was written in 1970, during Thomas's time as a navy conscript, and the fact that it was not published until 1975 – and not in book form until 1981 – attests to the difficulties he faced at this time, in which connections with his poetry colleagues – within Umbra or the St Marks Poetry Project – of necessity waned (Thomas 1975A; *TB*, 59–62). Thomas's friend Anne Waldman – who published his pamphlets *Dracula* and *Fit Music* with Angel Hair in 1972 and 1973, respectively – punningly writes in a little-known poem addressing his conscription: 'You get sent [...] go out of circulation, blood turns cold' (Waldman, 75; see also Thomas 2001A). Though they collect material dating back to the early 1960s, his first full-length collections, *Chances Are Few* and *The Bathers*, did not appear until 1979 and 1981, respectively. Thomas's work, particularly during this era, reckons with modes of division and defeat that damage the collective potential found in the early days of Umbra. In choosing not to avoid the draft, Thomas risks being the 'envoy of a monstrous epic / Or saga of Western corruption' (Thomas 1983, 2–3, 2001A; *TB*, 84). As seen in previous chapters, Umbra's presence among the bohemian communities of the Lower East Side offered a space of both possibility and social contradictions on which they reflect with sharpness and anguish. Likewise, in the wake of his Vietnam service, Thomas experienced a further alienation upon returning to New York, charted in the section of *The Bathers* entitled 'Slum Days after the War' (*TB*, 86–132). The 'Proem' to Thomas's *Fit Music*, written in California the same year as 'The Bathers', characterizes the perceived lack of political solidarity among those bohemians in the face of the draft. (See also Thomas 1983, 2–3.)

> [...] There should be a Lord
> If there must be a Proem you thought.
> But there was none. Only your drunkard
> Friends your dope fiends and pimps
> Demon lovers and lovers.

(*TB*, 69)

In this light, Thomas's attempt in 'The Bathers' to reclaim the waning political agency of a moment of political struggle from earlier in the decade takes on an added significance.

Before moving on to the poem itself, a further aspect of Thomas's career should be noted. Like Dent, Thomas left New York a few years after his return from Vietnam, moving to Texas in 1973 as writer-in-residence at Texas Southern University and, subsequently, as professor at the University of Houston-Downtown, where he remained for the rest of his life. Given this, the poem's Southern location has an added significance. Continuing the Umbra ethos of collective encouragement, Thomas served a vital role in mentoring young black writers in Texas. Moreover, he carved out a highly successful career, tracing radical traditions of cultural and political practices erased in conventional accounts: most notably, his analysis of the work of Fenton Johnson,

William Stanley Braithwaite, Umbra, the BAM and black Louisiana writers in *Extraordinary Measures* (2003). Yet his position was fraught. As Patricia Spears Jones notes, Thomas

> became one of the first Black writers to work in the poets in the schools programs in Texas and Arkansas. As an Arkansan, I know how complicated that must have been for him – lone Black man travelling all across what is a mostly white (outside the Delta) state.
>
> (Jones, online)

Following the experience of double alienation (as a black soldier) in Vietnam and double alienation (as a black veteran) in New York, Thomas now faced the double alienation of being an African-American academic in the still racist culture of the South. During this time, African-American writers were often appointed on short-term contracts as 'guest professors' in newly established Black Studies departments. While given (albeit precarious) employment and teaching opportunities, they were also confronted with the complacent racism of white academics. (See also Reed 1972A, 77–81.) 'My Office', which opens Thomas's second collection, *Chances Are Few* (1979), addresses the precarious position of tenure and racial marginalization within the academy, where 'gestures of assurance [...] Floated haphazardly on possibles / As slight as handshakes [...] And got nowhere' (Thomas 1979, 10–11). Likewise, in a characteristic blend of irony and hope, 'Wheeling' – initially published in the first issue of *Callaloo* in 1978 and republished in a feature on Umbra edited by Tom Dent two years later – sees the speaker driving with friends across Texas. As Harryette Mullen, whom Thomas had met and mentored in Texas in the 1970s, writes:

> The impossibility of finding a jazz or R&B station on the radio alerts the weary traveller to the threat of being stranded as a black stranger in white territory or the danger of falling asleep at the wheel while driving at night with the only available stations carrying country western music or fundamentalist sermons.
>
> (Mullen, 64)

Music here indexes racial divides and the real threat of racist violence. Because of this, music is also the place where they might be fought, as the speaker tries to find 'soul' – not just as a genre of music but as the embodiment of a whole philosophy, a whole way of life, a whole set of cultural survivals that speak of collectivity and resistance.

> That's redneck music man just wait
> You awake just in time
> To see the next exit
> And remark similar signs
>
> You have seen somewhere
> Before. This awakens
> The driver and evoked
>
> Gratitude from the death seat
> Where I been riding
> Alone with the bland view [...]
> Welcome back to God's country
> Wait. I'm *trying* to find the soul.

(Thomas 1979, 30–1)

Thomas's geographical trajectories – from Panama to New York to Vietnam and thence to Texas – embody Umbra's identity, at once attesting to the vitality of internationalism and to the exilic pain of displacement. When Thomas moved to New York, he could not speak in English; having, as he notes, mastered the language, and begun his poetic career when still a teenager, he faced another disruptive transition when drafted to Vietnam, before moving to Texas, historically one of the most racist states in the American South (1981B, 19–20). 'The Bathers' exemplifies this: the poem was written on a personal and historical cusp, between New York, Vietnam and Texas, in a year when the Black Power movement perhaps reached its peak, seeing a Black Power revolution in Trinidad and Tobago, and activists such as Stokely Carmichael and Eldridge Cleaver travelled around the world. (Cleaver was a guest of honour of the North Vietnamese government, where he urged black GIs to join the Black Liberation struggle over the Voice of Vietnam radio station in Hanoi (Bloom, 320–1).) Yet signs were already apparent of the fault lines which would open up in the BPP early the following year between the 'survival programmes' espoused by Huey P. Newton and Eldridge Cleaver's insistence on immediate armed struggle, and while, as we've seen, Vietnam had been on the Umbra writers' consciousness since the mid-1960s, Thomas acutely registered the irony of his own position in relation to the ongoing conflict. Though Thomas's poem addresses events from almost a decade before, and was not published for a number of years after, it participates in the complex debates that surrounded this historical moment. Initially published in an obscure Southern journal, which is virtually impossible to locate, and then in a collection which is long out of print, the poem's absence is a depressingly familiar story as regards Umbra. Yet the poem itself stages a confrontation with historical memory and seeks to hold to a collective possibility that offers an alternative model, offering a glimpse of what the Umbra writers all in different and sometimes contradictory ways struggled for: from the personal to the mythic to the historical, a focus on black survival, a collective black presence and the central role of poetry as a place where these could be expressed and brought together.

'The Bathers' measures the distance from an earlier moment of political possibility, caused by subsequent political defeat and the waning of a symbolic moment. Deploying West-African, Islamic, Afro-Christian and Ancient Egyptian symbology in relation to an iconic representation of a recent political event, Thomas destabilizes Eurocentric historiography, indicating its incommensurability and ideological complicity with a history of African-American suffering to which it refuses to give voice and exploring the political efficacy of alternative systems. The poem does not recreate non-Western ritual systems but deploys them as shifting parts of an ensemble linked against anti-black state violence, which, the poem argues, operates within and reproduces a symbolic economy. Linking back to Hernton's 'Medicine Man', it presents mourning 'through the tear of a mother', with the ancestral link to Africa serving as an index of survival and of the combination of mourning and militancy (*TB*, 62). But whereas Hernton's grandmother appears in the context of personal reflection, Thomas's maternal figure is placed in a more explicitly political context, addressing one of the most famous incidents in the Civil Rights Movement, the fire-hosing of protestors by the Birmingham City Police Department in May 1963.

Umbra and Birmingham

In 1963, Birmingham was one of the most racially divided cities in America; five months later, four young black girls would be murdered in a KKK-affiliated bomb attack on the Sixteenth Street Baptist Church, an important centre for Movement organizing over the spring and summer. In May, the city was in the middle of a sustained campaign of non-violent activism, organized predominantly by the Southern Christian Leadership Conference (SCLC) and known as Project 'C' (the 'C' stood for 'Confrontation'). This series of sit-ins and marches, designed to provoke mass arrests, met with brutal repression from Birmingham's 'Commissioner of Public Safety', Theophilus Eugene 'Bull' Connor, who had control over the city's Fire and Police Departments. In her history of the Birmingham Campaign, Susan McWhorter argues that the SCLC's campaign had, at this stage, begun to fade in part because of fear inspired by the jailing of Martin Luther King. Such fear lay not only in the threat of imprisonment – crowding jails with protesters was, after all, one of the movement's tactics – but of activists losing their jobs if they continued to publicly protest (355–7). At this point, SCLC leader Jim Bevel came up with a new strategy of deploying children in marches, later dubbed 'the Children's Crusade'. On May 3, the second of these marches took place, consisting mainly of teenagers aged between twelve and eighteen (369). In response, Connor ordered fire hoses and police dogs to be set on the marchers, with brutal results (370–1). Indeed, future *New York Times* war correspondent Johnny Apple Jr. would later maintain that none of the many war zones he had covered frightened him as much as Birmingham (374). As we'll see, photographs of this incident by Charles Moore were credited as instrumental in shifting public perception and the emergence of Civil Rights legislation, forming a key reference point for Thomas's later poem.

Like the death of Lumumba in 1961 and the Harlem Riots in 1964, Birmingham also formed the subject for a number of important Umbra poems early on. Removed from the New York context that shaped much early Umbra work, Birmingham instead resonated with its Southern dimension. Perhaps the closest of these poems to Thomas's 'The Bathers' is Ishmael Reed's 'The Ghost in Birmingham', an important early predecessor. Reed considers this his first mature work; opening his collected poems, it was written, as he notes, 'under the influence of the Umbra workshop' and published in the November 1963 issue of *Liberator* (Reed 1972A, vii). As we've seen throughout, many of the major Umbra poems are in dialogue with each other, picking up on recurring figures and turns of phrase within the individual context of their writers' distinctive styles. Such dialogue happens not only between writers and friends but between poetry and politics, mobilizing and troubling the normative standards of current political discourse in productive ways. Reed's deployment of mythic elements in relation to the Birmingham Civil Rights protests of 1963 is, like Thomas's, ironized yet crackling with collective potential, however nebulous. A kind of spirit of rebirth, the titular ghost floats among the crowds and flashbulbs of Birmingham, parodying and challenging both the Judeo-Christian focus of Civil Rights campaigners and the accusations of 'outside agitation' made by police chief 'Bull' Connor. The poem begins with the *loa*-like spectre of Denmark Vesey, leader of a slave revolt and one of the dedicatees of Baraka's 'Black Dada Nihilismus', moving among the crowd as a figure of Rinehart-like invisibility who nonetheless becomes politically visible. Deploying the Afro-Christian self-figuration against 'pharoah', Reed ultimately rejects Christianity for a fusion of esoteric mythologies and political radicalism.

> The only Holy Ghost in Birmingham is Denmark Vesey's Holy Ghost, brooding, moving in and out of things. No one notices the figure in the antique cloak of the last century, haunting the pool games, talking of the weather with a passerby, attending mass meetings, standing guard, coming up behind each wave of protest, reloading a pistol. No one notices the antique figure in shabby clothing, moving in and out of things – rallies of moonshine gatherings – who usurps a pulpit and preaches a fire sermon [...] going somewhere, haranguing the crowds, his sleeves rolled up like a steel worker's, hurling epithets at the pharoah's club-wielding brigade, under orders to hunt down the first born of each low lit hearth.
>
> (Reed 1972A, 3)

Reed goes on to attack Connor's statement on outside agitation, used to justify the deployment of dogs, fire hoses and federal troops on protestors.

> There are no bulls in America in the sense of great symbols, which preside over resuscitation of godheads, that shake the dead land green. Only the 'bull' of Birmingham, papier maché, ten dollars down monthly terms, carbon copy mock heroic American variety of bullhood, who told a crowded room of flashbulbs that there was an outsider moving in and out of things that night, a spectre who flashed through the night like Pentecost.
> He's right, there was.
> Not the spook of the Judaic mystery, the universal immersed in the particular [...] but the nebulous presence hidden by flashbulbing events in Birmingham, Metempsychosis stroking the air.
>
> (3)

Touching on the questions surrounding self-sacrifice that form the central dilemma of Thomas's poem, Reed asks, 'When will Osiris be scattered over 100 ghettoes?' (4) The poem concludes on the recurrent figure of metempsychosis (deployed prominently in the LSD 'rebirth' at the heart of Hernton's novel *Scarecrow*), uniting with Vesey's ghost to suggest, in the words of the Civil Rights anthem, that 'a change is gonna come':

Tin wreathed heroes are followed by the figure in antique
  clothes, obscured by the flash-bulbing events in Birmingham.
Metempyschosis in the air.

(4)

Calvin Hernton's 'Terrorist', again printed in *Liberator*, addresses the bombing of the 16th Street Baptist Church by a KKK-affiliated terrorist group on 15 September 1963. Ironically registering the language and ideology of Christianity, the death of the child 'innocents' is ironically celebrated as sacrifice and communion ritual:

> To die young, before the rodent of exchange
> Imperils the flesh, when you are innocent
> And immaculate to the paranoid itch
> Is lamb's blood
> Is bread trans-substantiated
> To galaxy.

(*MM*, 98)

In *The Black Panther* newspaper in 1971, Angela Davis would argue that the bombing itself illustrates the 'dialectical' situation of the Black Church, which was in the course of being transformed into a politically radical force:

> The attack on the church must be seen within the framework of the role of religion in the historical development of the oppression of black people. It then becomes immediately clear that the attack was objectively a response to the fact that Black people were beginning to transform an institution, which had been originally designed to serve as a weapon of oppression, into a weapon of resistance. The increasing participation of certain sectors of the Black church community in social struggles was a clear demonstration of the historical dialectics of oppression.

(Davis 1971, 13)

For Davis, the fact that, in Birmingham, the church itself became a target indicates its increasing politicization: the 16th Street Baptist Church was attacked precisely because it had become a rallying point for Civil Rights protests earlier that year. Hernton's poem initially appears to lack this dialectical view and to reject Christianity altogether. Refusing the Christian notion of sacrifice, seen as an act of grotesque cannibalism, the poet imagines himself as the father of the children, taking revenge on their murderers:

> If I were loin from whose pain
> The ecstasy of those four little girls
> Leaped, I would wail and weep,
>
> Seek revenge; fly, with shotgun,
> Through the streets.
>
> (*MM*, 99)

Yet, by the poem's conclusion, elements of Christian vocabulary return, transformed. Like Touré and Baraka, Hernton deploys a register of apocalyptic justice, moving from fantasies of individual revenge to collective upsurge, while drawing on the biblical tradition of cursing an entire city.

> *A revolution must draw blood.*
>
> […] blood will heave
>
> In your shattered streets,
> Birmingham!
>
> And God, the tornado
> Shall rave down on you like an angered
> Black fist, merciless
>
> And violent!
> Unto the blazing sun.
>
> (*MM*, 99)

The Umbra poets register the ambivalence of this moment. Critiquing Christianity's sacrificial economy, while partaking of its apocalyptic vocabulary, Hernton's and Reed's poems are complex mediations on the representational systems through which the SCLC campaign was figured. It should also be noted that, a few days after the infamous fire-hosing incident of May 3, and several months before the church bombing in September, Birmingham was the site of one of the first major black urban uprising of the 1960s: the so-called Birmingham Riot, which took place in response to the 11 May 1963 bombing of Martin Luther King's brother's house and of the Gaston Motel by members of the KKK, aided by the Birmingham police, and which saw a white policeman stabbed by black protestors. Birmingham Civil Rights leader Abraham Woods saw the disorder as the 'forerunner' to the riots of the 'long, hot summer' of 1967, while Nick Bryant argues:

> It was the black-on-white violence of May 11 – not the publication of the startling photograph [by Charles Moore] a week earlier – that represented the real watershed in [John F.] Kennedy's thinking, and the turning point in administration policy. Kennedy had grown used to segregationist attacks against civil rights protesters. But he – along with his brother and other administration officials – was far more troubled by black mobs running amok. (Raines, 165; Bryant, 393)

As Timothy Tyson puts it, 'the violence threatened to mar SCLC's victory but also helped cement White House support for civil rights. It was one of the enduring ironies of the civil rights movement that the threat of violence was so critical to the success of nonviolence' (Tyson 1997, 150). The violence found in the earlier Umbra poems on Birmingham thus had an immediate material precedent and grappled with similar issues of strategy, representation and resistance. In 'The Bathers', Thomas likewise negotiates between figures of suffering, revenge and spiritual rebirth. Incidents such as the fire-hosing of the Birmingham protestors, and the subsequent murder of the four young girls, pushed many towards a non-violent, nationalist vocabulary with the later rebellions of Harlem, Watts and the 'long, hot summer' echoing the anticipatory Birmingham riots that May. Writing a number of years later, Thomas registers this shift within the further context of the Vietnam War and his own sense of complicity and collective fracture. Umbra emerged, at the start of the decade, from a moment of collective fury at the American State; Thomas's poem, at its end, illustrates both how much and how little has been achieved.

'The Bathers'

The poem centres on an iconic photograph taken by Charles Moore in Birmingham on 3 May 1963, reproduced on the book's inside cover, in what appears to be a painted version by Thomas's brother Cess, and followed by a collage including another of Moore's photographs from the same series. Moore's now-iconic image captures three of the teenaged protesters, leaning against a wall with their faces turned away in order to brace themselves against a jet of water from one of the fire hoses. The photograph initially appeared in a *Life* magazine feature by Moore, widely credited as precipitating the changes in public opinion that led to the 1964 Civil Rights Act (they were reportedly cited on the floor of Congress during debates on the bill), and was subsequently named by *Life* as one of '100 photos that changed the world' (Durham, 32; Sullivan).

Thomas puts Moore's image to a use at once ironic and empowering. As the poem's title suggests, its central conceit converts this image of powerlessness into one of baptism, shot through with references to Christian and non-Christian religious traditions. The boy who 'transform[s] into a lion' – reminiscent of the Egyptian sun god Horus (Budge, 473–4) – and the vodoun *orisha* – who 'walk [...] amid the waters with hatchets' – suggest a more militant stance (*TB*, 59, 62). Meanwhile, 'Allah's useful white men' (62) alludes to the vocabulary of the NOI, also referenced in Thomas's 'The Unnatural Life'. (Popularized by Malcolm X, NOI terminology had entered into the BAM through writers such as Baraka, Touré, Sonia Sanchez and Marvin X (Marvin X 1969; Touré 1969; Sanchez 1974; *Autobiography*, 266–8, 273).) Likewise, in 'Fātiha' (1972), the call of a cell-block *muessin* serves as politically inflected sign of solidarity and 'technology / Of liberation' (*TB*, 132).

The poem begins 'We turned to fire when the water hit / Us', sarcastically referencing that the hoses turned on protestors belonged to the local fire department (*TB*, 59). Fire was a frequently deployed trope of BAM writing, suggesting political action – the oft-repeated 'Burn, Baby, Burn!', taken as the title to a 1965 poem by Marvin X – and spiritual illumination, most notably in *Black Fire*, where X's poem was anthologized (*BF*, 269). In 'The Bathers', the rage of the protesters who 'turn to fire' sees 'their anger [...] drawing the water' (*TB*, 61): 'Something / Berserk regained / An outmoded regard for sanity' (59). This 'outmoded regard' – the tone suggesting misplaced *politesse* – appears to be satirically *détourne* language which appeals for calm against continuing state violence, characterizing such calm as the 'sane' and 'rational' response or, conversely, that sees such violence enacted in the name of a supposedly rational public order. Yet for 'something / Berserk' to 'regain [...] sanity' suggests that the militant anger provoked by violence is in fact the sane response.

In Thomas's poem, the fire hose 'baptises' its victims into a mode of 'regain[ed]' consciousness shot through with nationalist sentiment – 'In the nation coming your children will learn all about that' (59) – and with a bluntly expressed contempt for the police and the state – 'we hate you' (61) – that also satirizes the Christian language of redemption centred on the river 'Jordan' as the entry into 'the new land' (62). The poem's register as a whole could be read as bitterly ironic, even sarcastic, in its appropriation of such Christian language: 'Some threw the water / On their heads. / They was Baptists' (62). However, it also uses this language, alongside that of ancient Egyptian history and mythology, to suggest images of nation-building, fertility and harvest – as in the yoking of modern-day technology with Egyptian irrigation systems in the apostrophe 'O electromagnetic Light shadûf!' (60). In particular, the recurrent figure of Horus – the god of death and rebirth, whose body is ritualistically scattered across the land in order to ensure the harvest and who, as the sun god, daily ascends to and from the ocean of chaos – echoes the sacrificial logic of Afro-Christianity, encapsulating this complex discourse of ambivalent transformation through cyclical mythology (Lurker 1980, 77–8; Krämer 2012; Budge, 473, 493, 520–2).

While Thomas deploys mythological discourse, he also insists that the 'new land' be implemented in the present, rather than deferred to the heaven of a Christian imaginary or located in an idealized past. At the same time, he mocks the notion that the new land could be reached through non-violence, based on Christian ideals of self-sacrifice and suffering. In particular, like Hernton in 'Terrorist', Thomas critiques the controversial use of child protestors which rebounded, with bitter irony, in the church bombings later in 1963, registering debates over non-violent strategy and, specifically, the role of children in situations of public protest.[1] This being said, the Birmingham Campaign – let alone the aforementioned riot of May 11 which followed – was not exclusively 'non-violent'. Noting that, in response to the use of fire hoses, the crowd mocked and pelted the police with debris, Susan McWhorter argues: '[P]aradoxically, "creative tension" – the Gandhian dynamic [Martin Luther] King had spelled out in his [letter from Birmingham jail] – became truly creative at the moment it threatened to become destructive' (374). Such tension was erased through the textual framing of Moore's photographs in *Life*, where, as Martin Berger notes, they were presented as encounters between white activity and black inactivity (15–18). For Berger, 'the white penchant for spectacle, comfort reporting from the perspective of white actors, and even their liberal politics led white reporters and editors to downplay the bravery and accomplishments of blacks as they conjured a fantasy of black passivity in the face of white aggression' (22). Thomas's poem captures this complication, reinscribing a notion of black agency from which even sympathetic liberal observers shied away.

The poem concludes by arguing that the fire hoses' 'baptism' has actually formed the (River) Jordan over which the people have crossed into the new land in an apparently ironic hymn of praise:

> And orisha walked amid the waters with hatchets
> Where Allah's useful white men
> Came there bearing the water
> And made our street Jordan
> And we stepped into our new land
>
> Praise God. As it been since the first time
>
> Through the tear of a mother.
>
> (*TB*, 62)

In his essay 'The Changing Same' (1966), Baraka argued for a 'social spiritualism' in which the vocabulary of the new land was tied not to a heavenly city but to the current struggle for black political control in Newark: 'a mystical walk up the street to a new neighborhood where all the risen live' (1967A, 210, 1971B, 79–80). Similarly, Thomas refigures the Birmingham street as a transitional stage *en route* to the 'new land' – albeit one in which the leisurely 'walk up the street' is replaced by the dangerous crossing of a fire-hose 'river' created through police violence.

To claim the existence of the 'new land' satirizes the distance between the Christianized promises of redemption made by political leaders and the continuing experience of coercive state violence. The poem's ironic transformation of fire-hose water into baptism – one also deployed in Hernton's writings on the Watts Riots (*MM*, 94; 1966c) – suggests that the redemptive language of Christianity, predicated on a temporal model of deferral, *intersects* with the continuing fact of state violence, rather than providing an alternative. Such language is of a piece with the fatalistic, sacrificial logic central to the suppression of African-American dissent. When the poem concludes by welcoming this fatalistic sacrifice with the call to 'Praise God', the irony is palpable.

> Praise God. As it been since the first time
>
> Through the tear of a mother.
>
> (62)

Yet, this is only one dimension of the poem's Christian imagery. The final line – 'through the tear of a mother' (62) – adds to the injunction to 'Praise

God' the sorrow which precedes praise, the mother's tear echoing back to the woman who 'washes gas tears / from her man's eyes' (61). Thomas's use of the maternal figure links back to Hernton's 'Medicine Man', where the maternal embodies both historical suffering and ancestral survival. Whereas Hernton figures his grandmother primarily through hoodoo practices, Thomas parodies the Christian vocabulary of Civil Rights. But bearing in mind Angela Davis's dialectical characterization of the black church, Thomas also finds a moment of possibility in the mourning and the hope that Afro-Christianity expresses.

In the account of the 1965 Watts Riots which concludes his 2007 autobiography *Black Radical*, African-American Communist Nelson Peery, who was living in Watts at the time, again figures urban unrest through the maternal and through Christina mourning. The passage in question ends Perry's political analysis of the riots as potentially revolutionary movement on a quieter, emotional note. During the riots, Leonard Deadwyler was murdered by police while taking his pregnant wife to the hospital; visiting Deadwyler's widow, Peery juxtaposes the silent words of a Christian spiritual with her grief-stricken rocking, presenting this grief through an index of trans-historical suffering and as a spur to end the conditions that caused it.

> She sat numbed, rocking her torso in the straight-backed kitchen chair, lips pursed, crying the lament of our dreary past. Oh Sweet Jesus, hear my cry. Rocking, rocking, sorrow too sad for tears. As when she stood in humiliating terror on the auction block. *Sweet Jesus, hear my cry.* […] As when the baying redbone hounds picked up the scene of her man gone for glory. *Sweet Jesus, hear my cry.* As when she wrapped the greasy sheet around the lashed and bloody body. […] *Sweet Jesus, hear my cry.* And when the white-helmeted, hate-crazed cops blasted out the life of her man, she sat numbed, lips pursed, sorrow too sad for tears, rocking, rocking, crying the dirge of the helpless, the lament of our dreary past. *Sweet Jesus, hear my cry!*
>
> Blinking back tears, I turned toward our little apartment. There was work to be done.

(Peery, 232)

Thomas's 'Praise God' appears a good deal more ambivalent. Yet it has more in common with Peery's spur to action – 'there was work to be done' – than might at first appear. The use of Christian apostrophe throughout the poem contains political possibility. At the beginning of the poem, the nation is presented in the future tense – 'In the nation coming your children will learn all about that' (59). But at its conclusion, the protesters are said to have *already stepped* into the 'new land' (62). In different ways, both references function as prefigurative nationalist calls: the call for a new land to actually be established and for black self-determination to be at last achieved. In his extensive biographical essay on Thomas, Tom Dent argues that the 'new land' is a metaphor for a 'spiritual' concept as much as a material one: 'a new, more positive concept of self as a people distinct from territorial identity as Americans, thus helping to shed the psychological shackles of slavery' (Dent 1985, 320–1).

Nonetheless, while Dent's insistence on the metaphorical, 'spiritual' and psychological significance of the term 'new land' is helpful, it should not be entirely removed from the issue of actual space. Thomas's assertion that the Birmingham protests have already created the new land is in part ironic, but this is not a defeatist, fatalistic irony aiming to undercut the efforts of the protesters. Rather, it is precisely the distance between the condition of the protesters on the segregated streets of Birmingham and the desired new land that, seven years later, might inspire redoubled efforts for its creation. When the street becomes Jordan and the protesters step into the new land, Thomas at once draws on the power of the Christian rhetoric central to the Birmingham campaign and distances himself from its shortcomings, inflecting them instead with a vocabulary that he would later define as 'positional Afrocentricity': 'a cultural frame of reference regarding history', challenging Eurocentric 'misrepresentation of Africa and Africans [which] helped justify or rationalize slavery, and provided the foundation for subsequent social and economic oppression [...] an unexamined aberration purporting to be universal' (*EM*, 100–1).

By the time the poem was written, this symbolic shift was central to the Black Nationalist political programmes which increasingly took precedence over Martin Luther King's Christian model and were often explicitly anti-Christian. Choosing to write of 1963, rather than of more recent events, Thomas polemically refigures of Birmingham as one of the spurs that shifted such programmes towards a more militant stance. As with Angela Davis's dialectical figuration of the church the following year, Christian rhetoric both enables and is an inadequate, or even restrictive, expression of sorrow and struggle.

> As the street's preachers
> Have a good understanding hear them
>
> > O israel this O israel that
>
> Down here in this place
> Crying for comfortable privilege
> In a comfortable land.
>
> (*TB*, 61)

Certainly, if this shift occurred most notably among African-American political movements, Moore's coverage also inspired a perspectival shift for a white liberal audience, outraged by the gap it revealed between American democratic ideals and the reality of Birmingham. In his analysis of 'The Bathers', Aldon Lynn Nielsen goes so far as to argue that Moore's images of Birmingham formed 'one of the great ruptures in hegemonic discourse in our time' (155). However, what is more important in Thomas's poem than the change of consciousness for white observers is the shift of perspective for African-Americans, allowing them to reframe their own collective subjectivity. Yet the poem's 'we' is far from monolithic: including Baptists, preachers, Egyptian and Arabic gods, the woman washing away gas tears, warriors, children, and *orisha*, Thomas's ensemble of human and mythological figures are united by their exclusion from the 'American Dream', an exclusion based on historical erasure and on the social construction of race as a category of naturalized moral judgement.

However, even as it excludes them, this system could not be sustained without a partial *inclusion* based on their labour power. The poem's second stanza reads:

We did them a fortune. We did
Them a favor just being
Ourselves inside of them.

(*TB*, 59)

These lines can be read in the following fashion. The collective subject, as African-Americans, contributes and has contributed to America's 'fortune' through their labour (and, as Thomas argues in the long poem *Dracula* (1966), their culture). Realizing that, through contributing to this 'fortune', 'we did them a favour' allows one to realize one's own potential collective power in a condition of apparent powerlessness. This realization is, in part, economic. Rather than being 'done' to or for someone else, a fortune is generally said to be 'made' by an individual capitalist, the labour power through which they have built up their capital implicitly written out of the verbal structure. Thomas's transformation of 'making' to 'doing' exposes the collective action behind America's amassed 'fortune'. 'Favor' is apparently a sarcastic assumption of power on the part of the powerless: how are the victims of the fire hoses in a position to do anyone a 'favour'? Yet it also suggests that a future debt is owed: the 'favour' will be returned. The poem's notion of baptismal rebirth plays on the twin sense of labour as work and labour as (child-)birth – 'Consumed in the labors of comfort / That cries for the balm / Of all that is natural' (*TB*, 61). These labours both (like fire) 'consume' human bodies and cause those bodies to cry out – as, again, in the poem's closing line, 'through the tear of a mother'. Against current conditions of labour, the protesters seek to be born instead into new life and into a 'new land'.

These economic implications are crucial, but what is uppermost in the poem is the collective voice of victims regaining their *symbolic* heritage, paving the way for a political future characterized by self-determination and -representation. As Nielsen puts it: 'When Birmingham's civil authorities sent the water crashing against the massed demonstrators, they could not have imagined the symbolic power they were transferring to the objects of their hatred' (157–8). However much this 'symbolic power' has been subsequently recuperated – modern conservatives use the Civil Rights Movement as a historical touchstone – it was undeniable both in 1963 and 1970 that, as Thomas writes:

It was in Birmingham. It happened.

Week after week in the papers
The proof appeared in their faces

Week after week seeing the same moment grow clearer.

(*TB*, 60)

In this moment, even the agents of state violence can be figured as 'Allah's useful white men' (62), provoking those they persecute to strive against them. This is not because they teach them the 'virtues' of suffering; rather, they are, in Marx and Engels's terms, producing their own gravediggers (Marx and Engels 2002, 233). The incident in Birmingham is of a piece with American history, built on the violent exploitation of African-Americans. But it also marks what Nielsen calls 'a rupture' in that history (159). And, for Thomas, it is out of this rupture that history might be rewritten both backwards and forwards, bringing with it a new sense of representational clarity and collective power.

Yet the declaration – 'It was in Birmingham. It happened.' – would be unnecessary if these events had indeed entered the national consciousness, contributing to a chastened sense of self-figuration. Thomas suggests that the incident must be re-performed – re-framed – beyond its original moment. The poem's visual appearance within *The Bathers* reads as an ironic comment on what 'Framing the Sunrise' (1975) punningly names as the condition of '[being] framed' (*TB*, 126–31). To 'frame' is to surround a picture with a decorative border – as is done on the book's front-cover illustration – or to 'frame' a shot in photography, film or television. It is also to fake evidence and pin a crime on an innocent party. For Thomas, this 'framing' has consistently taken place throughout American media and popular culture, serving to mute political dissidence, whether in relation to the Civil Rights Movement or the Vietnam War, and stigmatizing the very victims of systematic political violence as responsible for such violence.

As Susan Vanderborg notes, building on the framings of 'Framing the Sunrise': 'the danger [...] is indeed that we were visually framed: the newsreel images of embattled civil rights protesters, atomic explosions, and Vietnam-bound troops have become stock postwar icons in a way that radically diminishes their original impact' (105). Here we might contrast a more famous artistic use of Charles Moore's images, that of Andy Warhol's ten silk-screen paintings from 1964, (mis)named the *Race Riot* series (the images are of police violence against non-violent protesters, rather than of the kind of urban uprising commonly stigmatized as a 'race riot'). (See also Dale Smith, 91–2.) In May 2014, a single one of these paintings sold for $62,885,000 at Christie's in New York (*Race Riot*: Sale 2847, Lot 23). Christie's anonymously authored *Lot Notes* argues that the painting 'reveal[s] Warhol's unerring, almost prophetic ability to select, isolate and transform a single image into a provocative and quizzical icon that stands as a symbol for an entire area of contemporary culture'. Despite the otherwise detailed and sensitive treatment of the painting's contextual background, this conclusion reduces the sphere of political activity to a merely artistic concern, packaged for consumption within the inflated prices of an art market from which working-class African-Americans – such as those depicted in the photo – are always-already excluded. It thus reinforces precisely the conditions of profiting from African-American suffering that the Birmingham protesters and Thomas's poem sought to change. A moment of actual struggle becomes an item of cultural capital for a white artist far removed from that struggle, presented for other white people removed from that struggle. Like Warhol, Thomas is concerned with issues of advertising, media representation and appropriation. However, Warhol's method removes any explicit or even implicit 'judgement' from such work. As the *Christie's* writer notes:

> [He] imb[ues] one of the most contentious, up-to-the minute and also divisive, subjects in 1960s American politics with the same ambiguity and sense of authorless indifference he bestowed on the Soup Can, Brillo Box or other consumer products.

By contrast, Thomas is resolutely concerned with reclaiming political agency and critiquing exactly the appropriation and flattening out of affect that Warhol mimics.

In 'Collective Poems' (1972), dedicated to Ishmael Reed, Thomas writes:

> Made like I tolerated antagonism
> Only to uplift the defamed
> My people sing and dance it
> I made 'bards' of my excluded brothers
> When the bigots refused me my name.
>
> Born so poor, but a magnet with my shamed English
>
> I have reclaimed the legends.

(Thomas 1975B, 37–8)

To 'reclaim the legends' is at once to reassert the importance of 'Afrocentric' cultures and belief systems that have been stigmatized, ignored or suppressed by a white supremacist civilization, and to history itself, as part of an ongoing process of political emancipation. The incident addressed in 'The Bathers' has become a part of the 'legend' America tells itself – one in which noble suffering is followed by achieved political integration. Thomas insists on telling the story from a different angle, deploying alternate temporal and symbolic models in a manner that is both poetic and political. The most visible images of American media culture are made to reveal a truth hidden in plain sight.

Thomas imagines a reconciliation or rebirth – at least in the symbolic space of the poem – between the cowed status of African-Americans 'in a comfortable land' (*TB*, 61) and the reawakening of an Afrocentric consciousness inseparable from political activism. In 'The Bathers', neither Egyptian nor Christian mythology is flawless model. Though 'the street's preachers / Have a good understanding', the words they speak are mockingly reported as 'O israel this O israel that' (61). Yet they are still 'crying for common privilege' (61): their words contain the hopes and traumas associated with a history of suffering and might even spark political mobilization. To associate the Birmingham protesters with Christian baptism, the Egyptian myth of ascent from water to sun and the shadûf irrigation system is at once to ironically point up the real misery of their plight and to suggest the possibility for political emancipation that their act of public protest instates. By refusing to straightforwardly memorialize the protestors' sacrificial suffering, and by deploying Afrocentric and Black Nationalist–tinged rhetoric to describe them, Thomas rewrites history in order to ensure that they might still retain a living presence. Thomas's own later deployment of the term 'positional Afrocentrism', as discussed earlier in the chapter, is useful here. As

Michael Magee writes: 'Thomas insists […] that Afrocentrism is not a "truth" about Africa but a polymorphous and effective form of symbolic action which draws on African as well as African-American sources' (Magee 1999).

In a 1995 lecture on the 'Origins of the Black Avant-Garde', Thomas cites Clyde Taylor's *The Mask of Art*, recommending 'Taylor's insistence that we grasp what he calls "the ironies of discourse"', his call for a 'radical practice' which 'analyse[s] the ironies sedimented in unequally weighted discourses to better understand the semiotic manipulations of power, and the rhetorical strategies available to improve the odds' (2001c, 59). To be sure, the circulation of 'The Bathers' – first in an obscure literary magazine and then in a small-press edition published by Ishmael Reed – is hardly an entry into public life capable of fully combating the distributed recuperation of Charles Moore's photograph – or even of Andy Warhol's gallery-based version of that photograph. Thomas was very much aware of this, in the 1978 interview with Charles Rowell exhibiting caution at the BAM's belief in 'the functionalism of poetry', at poetry's direct capacity to enact actual political change (Thomas 1981B, 24). Nonetheless, if, as the title to his 1979 collection put it, 'Chances Are Few', 'The Bathers' is at least an attempt to 'improve the odds'.

Conclusion: 'If Our Heads Are Harder'

In 'Dada Zodji', a poem of the early 1960s which juxtaposes the hulls of Middle Passage slave ships with those of US warships in the build-up to the Vietnam War, Baraka writes of 'a continuous history of defeat', one in which the speaker can foresee 'no future past memory' (*BM*, 62). The speaker of this poem does not act, but can only report, with various measures of irony and satirical despair on the racialized conditions which delimit their existence, sarcastically pleading: 'Let me / seriously lose my mind'. As we saw in the second chapter, Baraka's work would soon move from such ironized self-laceration into a highly publicized poetics of revolutionary action. Likewise, the address to and participation in urban insurrection and public protest was a key motivating factor in the Umbra poets' early work, from the poems that emerged from On Guard by Reed, Thomas and Touré, addressed in the first chapter, to Henderson's and Hernton's texts on riot and urban space, addressed in the third and fourth. Energized and mobilized by events such as the 1964 Harlem Riots, the incendiary language of such writing leads Hernton to call for 'the total destruction of America as we have known it in the past and as we largely know it today' (Hernton 1971a, 103). Yet these texts also engage with the strategic dilemmas that problematize the accomplishment of revolutionary goals.

As Kalamu ya Salaam notes of the BAM: 'there is no easy way to write about a difficult period within which the reversals, conversions, conflicts and internal contradictions were an ineradicable part of the process of making history' (ya Salaam 2016, 107). Following the moment of possibility named in the work of the mid- to late 1960s, the entry into the 1970s was also an entry into widespread political defeat through external and internal pressures: the crushing failure of what Baraka called 'the desired explosion' (Pisano, 106). Ya Salaam dates the implosion of the BAM to 1974, the year of Baraka's much-publicized turn from nationalism to Marxism and the year which also saw David Henderson publish the final issue of *Umbra* magazine by which point the members of Umbra had dispersed across the country (ya Salaam 1997, 74).

The appointment of black poets to teaching positions in universities, often resulting from the creation of Black Studies departments, was a notable gain of political activism, enabling certain aspects of material security and recognition. The careers of Umbra poets within the academy – Thomas in Texas, Touré in San Francisco, Hernton in Ohio, Reed and Henderson in California – were to a greater or lesser extent productive ones. Thomas's two-decade career as a teacher and scholar at the University of Houston-Downtown resulted in works of scholarship which remain invaluable reference points, most notably, the vital *Extraordinary Measures*, whose history of 'Afrocentric Modernism' centrally includes Umbra. But the appointment of African-Americans, often on short-term contracts as 'guest professors', saw them initially encountering ingrained and institutional condescension and racism. Ishmael Reed's caustic 1969 poem 'badman of the guest professor' responds to the criticisms made of his teaching programme by colleagues while undertaking a guest professorship at the University of Washington that year. As Reed sardonically notes: 'One of them, because I wasn't teaching his kind of reading list, mischievously placed a copy of the *MLA Style Sheet* among my student's textbooks at the bookstore. (I found its discussion of the semicolon to be quite weak.)' (Reed 1972A, viii). Critiquing 'd red faced university' (78), Reed figures himself as an outlaw who robs the academy of its treasures:

> i know u didn't want me to
> come here but here i am just
> d same; hi-jacking yr stagecoach,
> hauling in yr pocket watches & mak
> ing u hoof all d way to
> town. black bard, a robber w/an
> art [...] (77)

Responding to his opponents, Reed rejects the academy's standards of propriety and its insistence on the white literary canon (here represented by T.S. Eliot and William Faulkner).

> dats why u didnt like my reading list – right?
> it didnt include any one on it dat u cd in
> vite to a cocktail party and & shoot a lot of
>   bull – right?
> so u want to take it out on my hide – right? (80)

The poem's dozens-like catalogue of attack ends by insisting that Reed has other goals.

> as i said, im passing thru, just sing
> ing my song. (81)

Though he was denied tenure, Reed would teach on and off at the University of California, Berkeley, for thirty-five years, also teaching at numerous other institutions including Yale, Columbia and Harvard (*Conversations*, 111–27). Yet his main activities were focused on the Before Columbus Foundation and on the nurturing of a multicultural aesthetic which may have used the resources of the academy when it was able but was more akin to Umbra's non-institutionalized ethos. David Henderson, to whom Reed's poem is dedicated, had long experience with radical education projects such as the Teachers and Writers Collaborative and had initially joined Reed in California to take on an academic position. In a 1972 interview, however, he explains how he came to reject the academy.

> I came out here to teach in the English department at Cal; then I taught in the black studies department; and then I quit, which I had intended to do after leaving the English department. It's no place for me. [...] It denies black people their ethnicity in approaching wisdom their own way; it denies ethnicity to all people who are not in the ruling class. (Middlebrook, 39)

Likewise, while Tom Dent taught creative writing at the University of New Orleans from 1979 to 1981, he also singularly refused academic affiliation, preferring to work in community-based projects and on the Southern oral histories that would become his increasing focus. As Dent notes, during the 1950s, 'the whole module of black success we were programmed toward was doctor, lawyer, preacher, teacher, and that was it' (Dent 2018, 469). During the 1960s, in working as activists and artists, the Umbra poets had rejected such models: their entire ethos had a class dimension. In conversation with Dent, Kalamu ya Salaam stresses that while 'the two major avenues [for writers] were the academic, scholarly pursuit and the commercial root', Umbra and Dent's projects in New Orleans rejected both. 'We didn't care about whether it was commercial or not; we did care whether it reached the intended audience of black people in our community. When you are not writing to impress critics but rather to reach a specific audience that you know, the work comes out different' (Dent 2018, 491). This, however, meant that, as Dent replies, 'we were actually swimming against the tide [...] By 1980, the definition of success was back to where it was before the sixties' (491). During the era of Nixon and Ford, and into that of

Reagan, geographical dispersal, teaching commitments and the fading visibility of self-organizing black consciousness movements, whether in art or politics, combined with a broader sense of the diminution of collective possibilities for transformation. Given the ways in which such diminution mirrors, even as it differs from, the failures of the Left to enact broader social change earlier in the century, we might be encouraged to view such a development as part of Baraka's 'continuous history of defeat'.

Means of figuring this condition of defeat, as well as the limitations of the new discourses associated with Black Power and the BAM – the rhetoric of violent, often gendered affirmation, frequently used to figure and propose that which was defeated –become central in such text as those addressed in the book's final three chapters. While the first half of the book focused on the experience of New York during the 1960s, these chapters focused on texts published during the 1970s, concerning Southern experience. Hernton's 'Medicine Man' mourns the violence and dispossession which transplanted Africans to America, seeking to move beyond the delimiting constructions of racialized subjecthood in order to better figure traumatic yet disavowed processes of historical formation. Dent's 'Return to English Turn' likewise reckons with the histories of the slave trade through the central figure of the Mississippi River, calling for a 'turn' towards nationalist collective consciousness, focused on futurity and the gaining of political control but 'never forgetting the forced journeys' (Dent 1978, 14). Meanwhile, Thomas's 'The Bathers' seeks a transformation of consciousness that will mirror an earlier transformation, associated with a political event whose temporal distance has appeared to render its transformative potential dulled. This attempt to 'change the odds,' like Hernton's in 'Medicine Man', disrupts linear temporality in order to reconfigure historical understanding through a creative practice of reinscription.

Emerging from a nourishing and pioneering climate of collective endeavour, such work is still remarkably prescient. Just as the Black Power movement was an often internally confrontational blend of disparate ideologies and strategies – from the religious frameworks of the NOI to the internationalist Marxism of the BPP – so the literary currents and strategies practised by the writers considered in this study are as disparate as the African diaspora itself. Contradiction and ambivalence, as well as polemical insistence and attempts at political mobilization, inhere not only in the relation between different writers but in the work of individuals, as shown by the preceding analyses of Baraka, Henderson, Hernton, Dent and Thomas. Attempts are made to force connections between such diverse fields as ancient Egyptian mythology, Southern hoodoo beliefs and polemical figurations of political events: the creation of what Baraka, in his 1964 essay 'Gatsby's Theory of Aesthetics', calls 'difficult meanings, meanings not already catered to' (*BM*, 41). Yet these attempts always register the diasporic gap which must necessarily inflect any totalizing attempts at knowledge. Given the political defeat of the movements with which such aesthetic practices are aligned, these attempts also reflect the ultimate failure to find a form of tactics which might alter those systems against which they struggle.

This does not mean that the 1960s were a period of political possibility which it is impossible to rekindle. Reckoning with and mourning moments of defeat must also inform continuing struggle. As Douglas Crimp would later argue in relation to the AIDS crisis:

> There is no question but that we must fight the unspeakable violence we incur from the society in which we find ourselves. But if we understand that violence is able to repeat its horrible rewards through the very psychic mechanism that make us part of this society, then we may also be able to recognize – along with our rage – our terror, our guilt, and our profound sadness. Militancy, of course, then, but mourning too: mourning *and* militancy. (Crimp, 18)

Mourning, rather than melancholically incorporating loss, does not disavow the possibility of future transformation. Furthermore, mourning loss and its corollary, learning from defeat, evince a dynamic relation to the past and to history saliently expressed by a poem such as 'The Bathers', poised as it is between irony, despair and an affirmation of collective possibility. As Baraka wrote in his autobiography[1]:

> For myself I think that struggle and defeat finally are useful if our heads are harder, our grasp of reality firmer. I think they are. (*Autobiography*, 462)

As argued in the introduction, what is instructive in Umbra's case is not simply its success but the very factors that destroyed it. This dialectic between possibility and defeat inheres not only in the organizational structure of the group but in the works of the writers themselves.[2] Emerging from one period of political defeat – the era of McCarthyism – and segueing into another – that of 1960s black radical formations – the creation of *Umbra* magazine as a publication and of the Umbra workshop as a social entity offered its writers a nourishing climate of collective possibility which was nonetheless not sustained as a simple, long-lasting group formation. Though the combined members of the group went on to produce over forty books (Dent 2018, 489), major publication and archival traces tend to appear well after the principal period of what Calvin Hernton calls the group's 'physical existence', and the available narrative accounts of the group's fractious breakdown are themselves anecdotal and conflicting (Hernton 1993, 581). Yet the very conditions of difficulty present in writing about such issues are also ones we can use to analyse their work and which that work itself illuminates.

Furthermore, while Umbra's fractious split was experienced as a keenly felt loss and defeat by the majority of its members, the move of many of its key participants away from New York also left a broader, more diverse and positive legacy. In contrast to nationwide journals such as *Black World*, Dent argues:

> The objective was not to build the magazine to a profile that would become nationally renowned, but to build writers. (Dent 2018, 489)

As Dent put it, Umbra was not simply a workshop, a reading series or a publication:

> 'Umbra' began to take on a meaning not limited to the magazine or workshop – it meant the soul, the spirit of what we were into, a kind of presence […] anywhere we were. (Dent 2018, 56)

Umbra's narrative of intense group activity in a particular location, followed by a split, followed by a move to different area as a new locus of collective organization, parallels both Baraka's career and the nationwide spread of the BAM. As Baraka would later write in his autobiography, his move from New York to Newark after the violent breakdown of BART/S was initially experienced as a profound defeat:

> I felt that I had failed in New York. The last days at the Black Arts had thoroughly disgusted me […] I had opted to cut out […] I needed to know the art and science of politics and how to run an institution. It was a long time before I learned either. (*Autobiography*, 230–2)

However, it was this second move which would in fact lead not only to Baraka's career of political and aesthetic grass-roots organizing in Newark but to the spread of the BAM across the country. As James Smethurst puts it:

> By 1970, it becomes possible to talk about a Black Arts Movement that truly spanned the United States […] as the movement, like Black Power, spread to virtually every city and many smaller towns in which there was a discernible African-American community […] Black artists and intellectuals […] really felt that they were part of an emerging nation as well as a mass movement. (Smethurst 2005, 367)

Though 'Umbra' per se was at best a sporadic presence by this stage, the Umbra members participated in this spread. Dent would do key cultural work with the Free Southern Theater across the South, and in particular in New

Orleans, where he had settled in 1965. As well as the FST, for whom he remained director until 1970, Dent organized the journal *Nkombo* and the Congo Square Writers' Union, co-founded the literary workshop BLKARTSOUTH with Kalamu ya Salaam, and established the Southern Black Cultural Alliance and, with Jerry Ward and Charles Rowell, the journal *Callaloo*, initially dedicated to Black Southern writing and still in existence at the date of writing. Hernton moved to England the same year that Dent relocated to New Orleans, where his involvement with the Caribbean Artists Movement suggests internationalist links between writing of the British Imperial diaspora and the BAM. Reed would relocate to Oakland and do key and continuing work to promote contemporary American multicultural writing with the Before Columbus Foundation, *Yardbird Reader* magazine, and Reed, Cannon, and Johnson publishing company (with Umbra members Joe Johnson and Steve Cannon). Thomas would promote black writing through workshops and membership of cultural organizations in Texas. As well as spending time in California, Henderson would remain an important presence in New York, establishing alliances with the Nuyorican Poets Café, as well as working with the Teachers and Writers Collaborative. Umbra thus served as something of a model for all kinds of collective organizing across – and even beyond – the United States, organizing which in some sense can be counted as part of the BAM but also as adjacent to and prior (at least in origin) to it. Ya Salaam argues with regard to the independent publishing efforts of Umbra writers like Dent, Henderson and Reed: 'The reality of their life work has been to support the development of viable and self-determined Black writing and to emphasize the connection of that writing with a larger body of progressive writing worldwide' (ya Salaam 2016, 88). For ya Salaam, Henderson's editorship of the *Latin/Soul* issue of *Umbra* – the magazine's fifth and final issue, containing poems by Nicolas Guillen, Cesar Vallejo, Pablo Neruda and a feature on 'Guerrilla Poetry of South America' – and Ishmael Reed's editorship of *Yardbird* magazine demonstrate that 'the focus was not simply "color blind" interracialism but instead a prescient confluence of writings from communities of color whose commonality was struggle for self-determination and self-defense more than on behalf of a liberal sense of abstract humanism' (88). Making an active effort to publish writers from African America, Africa, the Caribbean, Asia and South America along the model of the 'Bandung World', such Umbra and post-Umbra activity charted a 'non-aligned and independent course'.

Thomas's 'The Bathers' first appeared in print in 1975, the year of the final defeat of US military intervention in Vietnam: a symbolic setback for global imperialism and, as Max Elbaum and others have suggested, a motivating force for the Maoist-inspired New Communist Movement with whom Baraka became involved following his shift to Marxism (Elbaum, Simanga). Yet, though he elsewhere draws parallels between African-American urban insurrection and the guerrilla tactics of the Vietcong (*TB*, 119–21), for Thomas and other African-American veterans such as Yusuf Komunyaaka, faced with indifference and even outright hostility on return, as well as the realities of post-traumatic stress disorder for those who had witnessed combat, such a moment could not fully be experienced as victory. The return from Vietnam was also a moment of trauma for those African-American soldiers who, like Thomas, had served in that war and thus consciously or unconsciously served as what he calls, in a poem of the period, 'envoy of a monstrous epic / Or saga of Western corruption' (*TB*, 84). Such dilemmas relate to the dialectic of victory and defeat set up in 'The Bathers' by which the public humiliation and brutality faced by Birmingham's child protestors in 1963 (a 'defeat') is turned into a symbolic 'victory' with resultant legislative gains for the Civil Rights Movement, yet, subsequently, such moments of radical potential are subject to recuperation and 'defeat'. Likewise, in many poems from this period, Thomas finds in the complex experience of the solider in Vietnam, and, subsequently, the veteran returning to New York, mingled moments of guilt, defeat, solidarity and the possibility that 'we will have us a better world, here' (1976B); 'we shall conquer without a doubt' (*TB*, 89).

During the period at which these writers produced their major work, the necessity to find new political and aesthetic forms was fraught with the contradictions, both productive and wrenchingly despairing, attendant on the history of anti-capitalist and anti-imperialist struggle. Earlier in the 1960s, Baraka had lamented that he had 'no tongue / to give my children their names'; likewise, Thomas addresses the dilemma of 'sp[eaking] the ancient words / in shameful English' at the end of the decade (*BM*, 62; *TB*, 59). To these writers, both present and past forms, whether political or aesthetic, seemed inadequate, yet those which emerged to replace them – whether in the literary and political organization engaged in by these poets or the aesthetic strategies they adopted in the work itself – contained sometimes seemingly irresolvable dilemmas of their own. Whether in 1963 or 1970, 1968 or 1976, New York, Newark, Birmingham or Vietnam, poetry served as a key tool to work through paradoxes which might of necessity have to be simplified and put aside in the nitty-gritty of political action. This was a historical moment in which the international project of decolonization with fluctuating resources saw a sometimes bewildering, high tempo of change and artistic development, rendering Umbra's work uncomfortable within the bounds that more prescriptive models of Cultural Nationalism require. Such work forces us to look at this moment and at the literary texts that came out of it through a new lens. As Tom Dent recalled in 1983: '[Umbra] was so deep that it lasts to this day with all those people, with all of them. We share that and I think that we all realize that never before or ever again in our lives will we go through such a period, because we couldn't sustain that kind of intensity for very long' (Dent 1981, 3).

As Margo Natalie Crawford notes, the final, 1974 issues of *Nkombo* (under Tom Dent's editorship) and *Umbra* (under the collaborative editorship of David Henderson, Barbara Christian and Victor Hernandez Cruz) came out in the same year. Both aesthetics serve as continuations and developments in different contexts – New Orleans for Dent and multi-ethnic New York and California for the others– of what Umbra had started a decade earlier. Modified by the increasing contexts and nationwide cultural prestige afforded the BAM – there were, simply, *more writer*s, often nurtured by Umbra members – these are still very much a part of the Umbra ethos. As Crawford writes: 'Rooted wandering [...] is the editorial practice that makes Tom Dent's early years as an editor of *Umbra* flow into his later editorial work with *Nkombo* and into Henderson's editing of *Umbra*' (Crawford 2017, 133).

As this suggests, though much of his subsequent work focused on the communities of New Orleans with which he engaged in the post-Umbra period, as he constantly emphasized, Dent's earlier struggles in the North and South, and the formative experience of Umbra as collective enterprise, informed his entire career. Indeed, for Dent, Umbra serves as an alternative model to the BAM. It is this diversity that makes it hard to write about Umbra as a group but also serves as its strength.

> I see nothing wrong with the fact that members of the group have moved in directions as distinctly different as those represented by, say, Askia Touré and Ishmael Reed. [...] After all, black life in America is rich and varied and must be rendered specific if it is to be real, to be felt – as specific and varied as is our music. (Dent 2018, 58–9)

This can be exemplified through a reading of Dent's poem 'Ten Years after Umbra', briefly discussed in the introduction. First published the same year as Hernton's collected poems, it appears in a feature on Umbra that Dent edited for *Black American Literature Forum*, which featured Dent's invaluable, aforequoted essay 'Umbra Days' and photographs by Alvin Simon taken at one of the group's meetings on 242 E. 2nd Street in 1963. The issue also contains a selection of poetry by Thomas, Touré, Henderson, Hernton, Joe Johnson and Dent that encapsulates not only where all the individual members of the group were by 1980 but how Umbra had informed their concerns. Poetry by Thomas (the poem 'Wheeling', discussed in the previous chapter) and Askia Touré ('Cornrow 3', a tribute to black Southern femininity) concerns the South; the other poems concern different cities, from Joe Johnson's street-wise 'Harlem' ('strut yo stuff, stuff against walls'), Hernton's 'Hands', a virtuosic run-through of the figure of hands as emblem of the strength of labour and black survival ('brown hands belonging / To brown people') and Henderson's 'Third eye/world', expressing his emphasis on diasporic connections in the modern city between Egypt, Bangkok, Brazil, Azania, Namibia and Zimbabwe: 'third world american / english speaking with roots in the ancestral lands / like everybody else / just about / belonging to a new world / yet of an older one / but with the perception of both' (Dent 1980B, 109–14).

Dent's poem was first published in the collection *Magnolia Street* in 1976 with a dedication to his fellow *Umbra* editors: 'For David [Henderson] and Calvin [Hernton]' (Dent 1976A, 21). It attests to the sometimes fractious atmosphere of the Umbra workshops and the traumatic impact of the group's dissolution.

> we had seen
> > our fingertips recoil
> > our minds reel
> > from the impact
> > of our tongued knives
>
> > but then
>
> we were naked then
> and we stripped our souls
> easy as the sun rose
> and what went on
> in that tenement prison
> was something in us
> bursting free like
> a flash fire.
>
> (Dent 1980B, 114)

The poem goes on to reference the Lower East Side context, both public and private, in which Umbra emerged – Stanley's was the bar where the workshop would repair to continue discussions after leaving Dent's apartment (Hernton 1993, 581) – and to ask:

> do you too now feel
> the drag of too many jammed years?
> Stanley's fades into dream
> and so without touching
> our hurting...

(Dent 1980B, 114)

Dent hints at his own sense of isolation from the New York context of the group, both during the period when he divided his time between New York and Movement activism in the South and since his 1965 move home to New Orleans:

> as for me
> the dirt roads of Mississippi
> are a long way
> from anywhere.

(Dent 1980B, 114)

Yet Umbra is nonetheless maintained as a space of possibility with the second person addressed as one who might 'feel' the frustration of 'too many jammed years' now urged to 'join' with the speaker in the poem's closing:

> but then the sun will rise
> just as easy tomorrow
> over this black earth
>
> join me there.

(Dent 1980B, 114)

This conclusion opens out its space of collective possibility from the specific grouping(s) of Umbra itself: 'lazy smoke on Friday nights / taste the wine'; 'what went on / in that tenement prison'. In its *Black American Literature Forum* printing, the Dent's poem is juxtaposed with Alvin Simon's 1963 photographs of the workshop. As these photographs both freeze a moment of time and allow its reproduction beyond the initial moment of inception, so Dent's poem creates a textual space which memorializes without entirely closing off that moment of collective possibility. The poem's two refrains – 'we had seen' and 'but then' – establish its temporality: primarily a nostalgic reflection on a moment of past collectivity, which nonetheless, by the poem's end, turns into the image of a recurring sunrise which will appear just as 'easy tomorrow' and in which the reader might 'join' the poet (114).

In 1976 and 1980, the space where the reader might join Dent could be the space where Umbra members concentrate their current organizational and poetic activities – whether Dent in New Orleans, Reed in California, Henderson in California and New York, Hernton in Ohio, or Thomas in Texas. In that sense, Dent's poem is not only 'for' Henderson and Hernton, its original dedicatees, but for *all* the other members of the workshop while also maintaining the workshop's own openness – a refusal to close down borders, an openness to all-comers and ideologies – so that it is also 'for' others who might continue in that spirit. It was Umbra that opened up this collective space, but it was Umbra too that enabled writers to develop very individual aesthetics in which the psychological as well as the political complexities of the burning issues they addressed could be treated: the relation of North to South; the role of urban insurrection; the role of political organization, aesthetic practice and cultural work; the figuration of defeat, from the Congo to Harlem to Birmingham to Watts and the Lower East Side. The space of Dent's poem mirrors that of his East 2nd Street apartment on the Lower East Side, where Umbra's workshops were held, and where, we might speculate, many of the poems addressed in this book were first read, and where in any case the ideas from which it germinated swirled like Dent's proverbial wildfire in an atmosphere of comradeship and fractious debate. As, retrospectively, these spaces are overlaid with the complex and often traumatic workings of memory, they nonetheless remain *poetic* spaces from which to breathe.

And poets have continued to breathe from these spaces. Umbra's influence carries forward not just into subsequent collective enterprises organized by Umbra members such as Reed, Dent and Henderson but into the collaborative ethos espoused by more recent groups such as the Dark Room Collective and the Cave Canem Foundation, whom Thomas places in the tradition of Umbra and other collective endeavours which tend to fall under the radar of academic scholarship (*EM*, 222). A recent revival of interest in Umbra has seen a number of conference panels and poetry readings taking place, including 'Giant Night – Umbra: A Living Archive', organized at the Poetry Project in New York in December 2016, in which Umbra poets Henderson and Rashidah Ismaili appeared alongside poet-scholars Ammiel Alcalay and Genji Amino and writer-musician Jace Clayton (aka DJ Rupture). Organized by the younger African-American poets Simone White and Tonya Foster, the event's subtitle – 'A Living

Archive' – suggests the way that such events cross both generational divides and scholarly and poetic lines.

Umbra's influence also extends to individual writers such as Patricia Spears Jones, Giovanni Singleton and, in particular, Harryette Mullen, arguably one of the most prominent of all contemporary African-American poets. Mentored by Lorenzo Thomas, who discusses her work in *Extraordinary Measures* – a favour returned in Mullen's *The Cracks between What We Are and What We Are Supposed to Be* – Mullen references the 'slumming Umbra alums' in a poem from her 1995 chapbook *Muse and Drudge*.

> slumming umbra alums
> lost some of their parts
> getting a start
> in the department of far art.

(Mullen 2006, 147)

Mullen's punning description alludes both to the breakup of the group ('lost some of their parts') and, through the oxymoronic 'slumming [...] alums', to Umbra's insistence on the vernacular and on auto-didacticism as against institutional affiliation or academic legitimation – encapsulated in her coinage 'the department of far art'. Somewhere between 'far out', 'fine art' and 'fart', Mullen's deliberate blurring of the boundaries of respectability captures something of Umbra's spirit: a collective organization not tied to institutional space and conducted in a spirit of combative but comradely exploration. Writing with jokey affection on the transmission of tradition, Mullen's own mentorship by Thomas and her significant influence on contemporary African-American experimental writing is a living embodiment of the Umbra ethos. Both in terms of their continuing influence – an undercurrent nonetheless powerful for its relative lack of visibility – and their significance in their contemporaneous moment, the Umbra writers should be afforded their rightful place in narratives of African-American avant-garde and activist lineages.

As noted in the introduction, this book has had to exclude as much as it has included. Regrettably, I have not had space to offer readings of the work of important Umbra members such as Lloyd Addison, Rashidah Ismaili, Oliver Pitcher, N.H. Pritchard, Joe Johnson or Steve Cannon; in particular, more work needs to be done on the gender dynamics of the workshop and the important role of its female participants. Likewise, there is far more to be said about the work of all the writers I do discuss, both in terms of their individual poetics and their organizational work: from Calvin Hernton's engagement with anti-psychiatry to Lorenzo Thomas's poetry of the Vietnam War, from Askia Touré's work within the BAM to Tom Dent's with the Free Southern Theater, Ishmael Reed's with the Before Columbus Foundation, and David Henderson's with the Nuyorican Poets Café. For all of these writers, the role of the artist negotiating their way between the difficult positioning of bohemian communities, the vicissitudes of intimate friendship, the demands of activism, the complexities of international politics and the forms that a creative but politically committed poetry might take were not merely 'aesthetic' or 'academic' questions but the central tasks of their life work, and we owe it to them to pursue the questions they asked with an equal commitment. Far from merely an exercise in nostalgic historical recovery, the work is only just beginning.

Notes

Introduction

1 References to the magazine, rather than the organization, are indicated by italics throughout.
2 Readers will note the heavily male-orientated nature of this list. This reflects the gendered publishing bias and social dynamic which characterized the group, an issue I address further in Chapter Four. Needless to say, more work is required on this, not only in critiquing the gendered dynamics of writing by male members of Umbra, but in reclaiming and restoring the work of the women who also participated in these circles, such as Ree Dragonette, Ann Guilfoyle, Mildred Hernton, Nora Hicks, Rashidah Ismaili, Jane Logan [Poindexter], Florence Squires, Maryanne Raphael and Brenda Walcott. In the light of this, I acknowledge that the focus of the present study reflects the male bias within Umbra itself, and intend to correct this imbalance in future work on Umbra.
3 Nora Hicks and Art Berger, an older white leftist, were the only official white members. Berger requested to join the group and was voted in; his printing connections were of great practical value (Oren, 206).
4 Umbra members (including Tom Dent) interviewed Ellison several times. Intended to appear in the magazine's third issue before the group's dissolution, the final text (in which Ellison was interviewed by Steve Cannon, Lennox Raphael and James Thompson), eventually appeared in *Harper's* in 1967 (Oren 1984, 170; Cannon et al.).
5 This phrase was the title of a reading given by Hernton, Reed and Henderson at the St Mark's Church in New York (Hernton 1993, 283).
6 I take this term from Hill 1984. See also Nelson 1989.
7 The recent UNESCO definition characterizes a pamphlet as any publication under forty-eight pages.
8 My use of the term 'ensemble' throughout draws on Moten 2003.

Chapter 1

1 Baraka here refers in particular to Mae Mallory (Tyson, 237).
2 Examples of such testimony are those of Ismaili, Rosa Guy, Hicks and Walter Bowe, quoted in (Wood 2004 and Smethurst 2005).

3   In terms of On Guard's gender dynamics, it should be noted that this sidelining of female participants is symptomatic of that which occurs in broader narratives of the period in general. Such accounts of already marginalized activities perform a further marginalization, leaving a narrative absence. For valuable correctives, see Hogishida, especially 54–5, and Karageorgos, 123–53. For the debates between On Guard activists and Malcolm X, principally around the issue of interracial sexual relations, see Hentoff; see also Maya Angelou's discussion with Rosa Guy of their attempt to involve X (Angelou 1989, 227–9).

Chapter 2

1   It should be noted that, while *Muhammad Speaks* was the newspaper of the Nation of Islam, it was edited by black Communists and former Communists hired by Elijah Muhammad, and its editorial stance (other than Muhammad's own column) tended towards left-nationalism (Smethurst 2005, 46, 116, 181–2, 387, n.41).
2   For Baraka's positive mention of 'Fresh Air', see *Autobiography*, 159. 'The strangler' reappears in the later 'Das Kapital' (*SP*, 266).
3   Though not an intentional allusion to Spicer's work, Baraka acknowledges that it may have functioned as such on an unconscious or serendipitous level (Smethurst 2005, 393, n.73).

Chapter 3

1   Delany first used the term 'nation within a nation' in 1859; the term was taken up in Du Bois's article of the same name in 1934. (Woodard 17; Du Bois 1935) Komozi Woodard dates the political formulation of American black nationalism to 1830 (Woodard, 15). Harold Cruse referred to 'domestic colonialism' in 1962, and the concept of 'internal colonialism' is outlined in Stokely Carmichael and Charles V. Hamilton's highly influential *Black Power: The Politics of Liberation* (Cruse 1967, 76); Carmichael and Hamilton – Chapter One in general, but especially 5, 16–17). For recent work on internal colonialism, see Howe; Wang, 78–80.]

Chapter 5

1   As Lauri Ramey notes, 'jacklegged' replaces the word 'Negro' from the original printing (Ramey 2008, 119).
2   Clarence Major dates the word's use from the 1700s to the 1940s (Major 1994, 211).

Chapter 7

1 For BAM figurations of children and militancy, see Baraka 1968B; BF, 103; Sanchez 1971.

Conclusion

1 Baraka, *Autobiography*, 462.
2 The term 'possibility' is here inflected by Houen 2012.

Bibliography

'2 mars 1960: massacres au Cameroun'. *Rebellyon.info*. Available online: http://rebellyon.info/2-mars-1960-massacres-au-Cameroun.html. Accessed 31 March 2015.

Abraham, Nicholas and Maria Torok. *The Wolfman's Magic Word: A Cryptonomy*. Trans. by Nicholas Rand. Minneapolis: University of Minnesota Press, 1986.

Abraham, Nicholas and Maria Torok. *The Shell and the Kernel: Renewals of Psychoanalysis, Volume 1*. Ed. and trans. by Nicholas T. Rand. Chicago: University of Chicago Press, 1994.

Allen, Walter. 'What's New?' [Rev. of *The Moderns* (Baraka 1963F)]. *New York Review of Books*, 9 January 1964: 11.

Amidon, Bill. 'Where Have All the Hipsters Gone?' *The Village Voice*, Vol. XVII, No. 32, 10 August 1972: 1, 12, 14.

Anderson, Jeffrey E. *Conjure in African-American Society*. Baton Rouge: Louisiana State University Press, 2005.

Angelou, Maya. *The Heart of a Woman*. New York: Random House, 1981.

Angelou, Maya. *Conversations with Maya Angelou*. Ed. by Jeffrey M. Elliott. London: Virago, 1989.

Anyangwe, Carlson. *Imperialistic Politics in Cameroun: Resistance & the Inception of the Restoration of the Statehood of Southern Cameroons*. Bamenda, Cameroon: Langaa RCPIG, 2008.

Apollon, Willy. 'Vodou: The Crisis of Possession'. Trans. by Peter Canning and Tracy McNulty. *Jouvert* 3, nos. 1–2. Available online: http://english.chass.ncsu.edu/jouvert/v3i12/apollo.htm. Accessed 15 July 2015.

Austin, J.L. *How to Do Things with Words*. Oxford: Oxford University Press, 1962.

Baldwin, James. 'A Negro Assays the Negro Mood'. *New York Times Magazine*, 12 March 1961: 25, 103–4.

Baraka, Amiri. 'Suppose Sorrow Was a Time Machine'. *Yūgen*, Vol. 2 (1958): 9–11. Reprinted in *Fiction*, 1–4.

Baraka, Amiri. 'How You Sound??' In *The New American Poetry, 1945–1960*. 1960. Ed. by Donald Allen. 424–5. Berkeley: University of California Press, 1999. Reprint.

Baraka, Amiri. *Preface to a Twenty Volume Suicide Note*. New York: Totem/Corinth, 1961.

Baraka, Amiri. 'The Politics of Rich Painters'. *Floating Bear*, No. 22 (1962): 246–7. Reprinted in *TDL*, 32–3. (1962A)

Baraka, Amiri. 'Present Perfect'. *Kulchur*, Vol. II, No. 8 (Winter, 1962): 95–8, 100–1, 103–5. (1962B)

Baraka, Amiri. 'A Contract (for the Destruction and Rebuilding of Paterson)'. *Beloit Poetry Journal*, Vol. XIV, No. 1 (Fall, 1963): 6–7. Reprinted in *TDL*, 11. (1963A)

Baraka, Amiri. 'Black Dada Nihilismus'. *Evergreen Review*, Vol. 7, No. 29 (March–April, 1963): 85–7. Reprinted in *TDL*, 61–4. (1963B)

Baraka, Amiri. 'A Poem Some People Will Have to Understand'. *Wild Dog*, No. 1 (13 July 1963): 11. Reprinted in *BM*, 6. (1963C)

Baraka, Amiri, ed. *The Moderns: An Anthology of New Writing in America*. New York: Corinth Books, 1963. (1963D)

Baraka, Amiri. 'What Does Non-violence Mean?' *Midstream*, Vol. IX, No. 4 (December, 1963): 33–44. Reprinted in *H*, 155–78. (1963E)

Baraka, Amiri. 'Black Dada Nihilismus'. Reading, Asilomar Negro Writers Conference, Pacific Grove, California, early August, 1964. Pennsound, University of Pennsylvania. Available online: http://media.sas.upenn.edu/pennsound/authors/Baraka/Asilomar-1964/Baraka-Amiri_06_Black-Dada-Nihilismus_Asilomar%20 1964.mp3. Accessed 2 February 2016. (1964B)

Baraka, Amiri. *The Dead Lecturer*. New York: Grove Press, 1964. (1964C)

Baraka, Amiri. 'The Roots of Violence: Harlem Considered'. [Symposium featuring Baraka, Kyver Blumstein, James Booker, Kenneth B. Clark, Sidney Lanier and Reinhold Neibuhr.] *Negro Digest*, Vol. 13, No. 10 (September 1964): 16–26. (1964E)

Baraka, Amiri. 'The Revolutionary Theatre'. *Liberator*, Vol. V, No. 7 (July 1965): 4–6. Reprinted in *H*, 236–41.

Baraka, Amiri. *Black Art*. Newark: Jihad, 1966. (1966A)

Baraka, Amiri. 'Black Art'. *Liberator*, Vol. VI, No. 1 (January, 1966): 18. Reprinted in *BM*, 116–17. (1966B)

Baraka, Amiri. 'Philistinism and the Negro Writer'. In *Anger and Beyond: The Negro Writer in the United States*. 1964. Ed. by Herbert Hill. 51–61. New York: Harper and Row, 1966. (1966D)

Baraka, Amiri. *Black Music*. New York: Morrow, 1967. (1967A)

Baraka, Amiri. 'LeRoi Jones Speaking at UCLA'. Reading, UCLA, Los Angeles, 5 April 1967. UCLA Communications Studies Department Channel, YouTube. Available online: https://www.youtube.com/watch?v=jVkv3Bbxkwg. Accessed 25 March 2018. (1967B)

Baraka, Amiri. 'Slave Ship: A Historical Pageant'. *Negro Digest*, April 1967: 62–74. (1967C)

Baraka, Amiri. 'What the Arts Need Now'. *Negro Digest*, April 1967: 6–7. (1967D)

Baraka, Amiri. 'Three Poems'. ['Leroy'; 'Black People!'; 'The Black Man Is Making New Gods'.] *Evergreen Review*, Vol. XI, No. 50 (December 1967): 48–9. Reprinted in *BM*, 217, 225, 205. (1967E)

Baraka, Amiri, eds. with Larry Neal. *Black Fire: An Anthology of Afro-American Writing*. New York: William Morrow, 1968. (1968A)

Baraka, Amiri. 'Board of Education'. 1968, typescript, Box 1, Amiri Baraka Collection of Playscripts, Manuscripts, Archives and Rare Books Division, Schomburg Center for Research in Black Culture, The New York Public Library. (1968B)

Baraka, Amiri. 'Communications Project'. *The Drama Review*, Vol. 12, No. 4 (Summer, 1968): 53–7. (1968c)

Baraka, Amiri. 'Home on the Range'. *The Drama Review*, Vol. 12, No. 4 (Summer, 1968): 106–11. (1968d)

Baraka, Amiri. *Black Magic: Collected Poetry, 1961–1967*. Indianapolis: Bobbs-Merrill, 1969. (1969a)

Baraka, Amiri. *Four Black Revolutionary Plays*. Indianapolis: Bobbs-Merrill, 1969. (1969b)

Baraka, Amiri. 'Islam and Black Art: An Interview with LeRoi Jones'. Interview by Marvin X and Faruk. *Negro Digest*, January 1969: 4–10, 77–80. Reprinted in *Conversations*, 51–61. (1969c)

Baraka, Amiri. 'Letter to the Editor'. *New York Times*, 11 May 1969: 132. (1969d)

Baraka, Amiri. *Raise Race Rays Raze: Essays since 1965*. New York: Random House, 1971. (1971b)

Baraka, Amiri, ed. *African Congress: A Documentary of the First Modern Pan-African Congress*. New York: William Morrow, 1972. (1972a)

Baraka, Amiri. *Selected Poetry of Amiri Baraka/LeRoi Jones*. New York: William Morrow, 1979. (1979a)

Baraka, Amiri. *Selected Plays and Prose of Amiri Baraka/LeRoi Jones*. New York: William Morrow, 1979. (1979b)

Baraka, Amiri. *The Autobiography of LeRoi Jones/Amiri Baraka*. New York: Freundlich Books, 1984. (1984a)

Baraka, Amiri. *Daggers and Javelins: Essays, 1974–1979*. New York: Morrow, 1984. (1984b)

Baraka, Amiri. [Interview by Lorenzo Thomas, 21 June 1984.] Umbra Poets Workshop Oral History Transcripts, Schomburg Center for Research in Black Culture, New York Public Library. (1984c)

Baraka, Amiri. *Conversations with Amiri Baraka*. Ed. by Charlie Reilly. Jackson, MS: University Press of Mississippi, 1994.

Baraka, Amiri. *Blues People: Negro Music in White America*. 1963. London: Harper Perennial, 1999. Reprint.

Baraka, Amiri. *The Fiction of LeRoi Jones/Amiri Baraka*. [Contains *The System of Dante's Hell* (1965), *Tales* (1967), *6 Persons* (1974) and uncollected work.] Chicago: Lawrence Hill Books, 2000.

Baraka, Amiri. 'On 40th Anniversary of Newark Rebellion: A Look Back at Historic Unrest That Changed the Nation'. Baraka, Larry Hamm and Grace Lee Boggs interviewed by Juan Gonzalez and Amy Goodman. *Democracy Now*, 13 July 2007. Transcript. Available online: http://www.democracynow.org/2007/7/13/on_40th_anniversary_of%20newark_rebellion. Accessed 1 February 2016. (2007b)

Baraka, Amiri. *Digging: The Afro-American Soul of American Classical Music*. Berkeley: University of California press, 2009. (2009a)

Baraka, Amiri. *Home: Social Essays*. 1966. New York: Akashic Books, 2009. Reprint. (2009b)

Baraka, Amiri. 'The Black Arts'. [Original draft of 'Black Art', n.d.] Typescript, box 2, folder 4, Amiri Baraka Collection of Unpublished Poetry, Manuscripts, Archives and Rare Books Division, Schomburg Centre for Research in Black Culture, New York. (N.d.A)

Baraka, Amiri. 'Black Rules'. n.d., typescript, box 2, folder 1, Amiri Baraka Collection of Playscripts, Manuscripts, Archives and Rare Books Division, Schomburg Centre for Research in Black Culture, New York. (N.d.D)

Barlow, William. *Voice Over: The Making of Black Radio*. Philadelphia, PA: Temple University Press, 1999.

Ben-Jochannan, Yosef. *African Origins of the Major 'Western Religions'*. New York: Alkebu-lan Books Associates, 1970.

Benjamin, Philip. '400 Picket U.N. in Salute to Castro and Lumumba'. *New York Times*, 19 February 1961: 1, 18.

Benston, Kimberly, ed. *Imamu Amiri Baraka (Leroi Jones): A Collection of Critical Essays*. Englewood Cliffs, NJ: Prentice-Hall, 1978.

Benston, Kimberly. *Performing Blackness: Enactments of African-American Modernism*. London: Routledge, 2000.

Berger, Art. 'Negroes with Pens'. *Mainstream*, Vol. 16, No. 7 (July 1963): 3–6.

Berger, Art. [Interview by Michel Oren, n.d.] Umbra Poets Workshop Oral History Transcripts, Schomburg Center for Research in Black Culture, New York Public Library.

Berger, Martin A. *Seeing through Race: A Reinterpretation of Civil Rights Photography*. Berkeley, CA: University of California Press, 2011.

Bibby, Michael. *Hearts and Minds: Bodies, Poetry, and Resistance in the Vietnam Era*. New Brunswick, NJ: Rutgers University Press, 1996.

The Bible: Authorized King James Version. Oxford: Oxford University Press, 1997.

Bigart, Homer. 'Hashish-Mad Rebels Kill 74 in Cameroon'. *New York Times*, Thursday, 25 February 1960: 1.

Bloom, Joshua, and Waldo E. Martin, Jr. *Black against Empire: The History and Politics of the Black Panther Party*. Berkeley: University of California Press, 2013.

Bonney, Sean. *Tensions between Aesthetic and Political Commitment in the Work of Amiri Baraka*. PhD dissertation, unpublished, University of London, Birkbeck, 2012.

Brathwaite, Edward Kamau. 'The Caribbean Artists Movement'. In *Writing Black Britain 1948–1998: An Interdisciplinary Anthology*. Ed. by James Procter. Manchester: Manchester University Press, 2000: 167–70.

Brathwaite, Edward Kamau. 'The Mmusiowatuunya dream mountain (for Tom Dent)'. *Black Renaissance / Renaissance Noire*, Vol.2, No.3, (Winter 1999/2000): 38–49.

Brinkman, Elizabeth. 'Calvin C. Hernton. Biography/Administrative History'. Oberlin College Archives. Available online: http:/www.oberlin.edu/archive/holdings/finding/RG30/SG326/biography.html. Accessed 11 January 2015.

Brutus, Dennis. *The Dennis Brutus Tapes: Essays at Autobiography*. Ed. by Bernth Lindfors. Woodbridge, Suffolk: James Currey, 2011.

Bryant, Nick. *The Bystander: John F. Kennedy and the Struggle for Black Equality*. New York: Basic Books, 2007.

Budge, E.A. Wallis. *The Gods of the Egyptians; Or, Studies in Egyptian* Mythology, *Vol. 1*. London: Methuen & Co., 1904.

Cannon, Steve, Lennox Raphael, and James Thompson. 'A Very Stern Discipline: An Interview with Ralph Ellison'. In *Conversations with Ralph Ellison*. Ed. by Maryemma Graham and Amritjit Singh. 109–10. Jackson: University Press of Mississippi, 1995.

Carmichael, Stokely (Kwame Ture) and Charles V. Hamilton. *Black Power: The Politics of Liberation in America*. New York: Random House, 1967.

Cole, Terry Joseph. 'David Henderson'. In *Dictionary of Literary Biography, Vol. 41: Afro-American Poets since 1955*. Eds. by Thadious M. Davis and Trudier Harris. 315–26. Detroit: Gale Research Co., 1985.

Chevalier, Tracy. 'Calvin Hernton'. In *Contemporary Poets*. Ed. by Tracy Chevalier. 414. Chicago, IL: St. James Press, 1991.

Cleaver, Eldridge. *Soul on Ice*. 1968. New York: Random House, 1992. Reprint.

Collum, Danny Duncan and Victor A. Berch, *African-Americans in the Spanish Civil War: 'This Ain't Ethiopia, But It'll Do'*. New York: G.K. Hall & Co., 1992.

Committee on Poetry. 'LeRoi Jones'. Letter to the Editors, *New York Review of Books*, 25 April 1968. (A handbill version of the document is dated 6 January 1968.)

Committee on Un-American Activities. *Annual Report for the Year 1964* (88th Congress, 2nd Session). Washington: U.S. Government Printing Office, 1965.

Committee on Un-American Activities. *Subversive Influences in Riots, Looting, and Burning. Hearings, Ninetieth Congress, First[-Second] Session*. Washington: U.S. Government Printing Office, 1968–69.

Corbett, John, ed. *The Wisdom of Sun Ra: Sun Ra's Polemical Broadsheets and Streetcorner Leaflets*. Chicago: WhiteWalls, 2006.

Crawford, Margo Natalie. *Black Post-blackness: The Black Arts Movement and Twenty-first Century Aesthetics*. Champaign: University of Illinois Press, 2017.

Crimp, Douglas. 'Mourning and Militancy'. October, Vol. 51 (Winter, 1989): 3–18.

Cruse, Harold. *The Crisis of the Negro Intellectual: From Its Origins to the Present*. New York: William Morrow, 1967.

'Cuba: A Declaration of Conscience by Afro-Americans'. *New York Post*, 25 April 1961: 9.

Czaplicka, Maria. *Aboriginal Siberia: A Study in Social Anthropology*. Oxford: Clarendon Press, 1914.

Dace, Letitia. *LeRoi Jones (Imamu Amiri Baraka): A Checklist of Works by and about Him*. London: The Nether Press, 1971.

Davis, Angela Y. 'Eight Years since Birmingham'. *The Black Panther*, Vol. III, No. 4 (18 September 1971): 4, 13.

Davis, Angela Y. *Woman, Race and Class*. New York: Vintage, 1981.

Dent, Tom, Calvin Hernton and David Henderson. 'Umbra'. [Rev. of *Umbra* I] *Liberato*r, Vol. III, No. 4 (April 1963): 13.

Dent, Tom, Calvin Hernton and David Henderson. *Umbra, I*. Winter, 1963.

Dent, Tom, Calvin Hernton and David Henderson. *Umbra, II*. December, 1963.
Dent, Tom, eds. with Gilbert Moses and Richard Schechner. *The Free Southern Theater by the Free Southern Theater*. Indianapolis and New York: Bobbs-Merrill, 1969.
Dent, Tom. 'Tom Dent to the Board of Directors of the Free Southern Theater, 23 October 1970'. Typed letter, Tulane University Online Exhibits. Available online: http://library.tulane.edu/exhibits/items/show/650. Accessed 26 January 2017.
Dent, Tom. *Magnolia Street*. New Orleans: Tom Dent, 1976. (1976A)
Dent, Tom. 'Preface'. *Callaloo*, No. 1 (December 1976): v–vi. (1976B)
Dent, Tom. 'Return to English Turn'. *Callaloo*, No. 4 (October 1978): 10–14.
Dent, Tom. 'A Voice from a Tumultuous Time'. [Rev. of Hernton's *Medicine Man*.] *Obsidian: Black Literature in Review*, Vol. 6, Nos. 1 & 2 (Spring–Summer 1980): 244–50. (1980A)
Dent, Tom, ed. 'Umbra Poets'. *Black American Literature Forum*, Vol. 14, No. 3 (Autumn, 1980): 109–14. (1980B) Contains Dent's essay 'Umbra Days' and the poem 'Ten Years After Umbra'.
Dent, Tom. [Interview by Michel Oren, 25 December 1981.] Umbra Poets Workshop Oral History Transcripts, Schomburg Center for Research in Black Culture, New York Public Library.
Dent, Tom. *Blue Lights and River Songs*. Detroit: Lotus Press, 1982.
Dent, Tom. 'Lorenzo Thomas'. In *Dictionary of Literary Biography, Vol. 41: Afro-American Poets since 1955*. Eds. by Thadious M. Davis and Trudier Harris. 315–26. Detroit: Gale Research Co., 1985.
Dent, Tom. *Southern Journey: A Return to the Civil Rights Movement*. New York: William Morrow, 1997.
Dent, Tom. *New Orleans Griot: The Tom Dent Reader*. Ed. by Kalamu ya Salaam. New Orleans: University of New Orleans Press, 2018.
De Salvo, Debra. *The Language of the Blues from Alcorub to Zuzu*. New York: Billboard, 2006.
Diouf, Sylviane A. 'African Muslims in Bondage: Realities, Memories and Legacies'. In *Monuments of the Black Atlantic: Slavery and Memory*. Eds. by Joanne M. Braxton and Maria I. Diedrick. 77–89. New Brunswick, NJ: Transaction Publishers, 2004.
Dockray, Sean Patrick. *Containment: The Architecture of the 1967 Newark Riots*. PhD dissertation, unpublished, Princeton University, 1999.
Douglass, Frederick. *Narrative of the Life of Frederick Douglass, An American Slave, Written by Himself*. 1845. Cambridge, MA: Harvard University Press, 2009. Reprint.
Du Bois, W.E.B. *The Souls of Black Folk*. 1903. Oxford: Oxford University Press, 2007. Reprint.
Du Bois, W.E.B. *John Brown*. Philadelphia, PA: George W. Jacobs and Co., 1909.
Du Bois, W.E.B. "A Negro Nation within the Nation," *Current History*, No. 42 (June 1935): 265–270.
Duncan, Robert and Denise Levertov. *The Letters of Robert Duncan and Denise Levertov*. Eds. by Robert J. Bertholf and Albert Gelpi. Stanford, CA: Stanford University Press, 2004.

Durem, Ray. *Take No Prisoners*. London: Breman, 1971.
Durham, Michael S. *Powerful Days: The Civil Rights Photography of Charles Moore*. Tuscaloosa: University of Alabama Press, 2002.
Dworkin, Ira. *Congo Love Song: African-American Culture and the Crisis of the Colonial State*. Chapel Hill: University of North Carolina Press, 2017.
Eavis, Ros and Salima Ikram. 'Nun'. *The Encyclopaedia of Ancient History*. Available online: http://onlinelibrary.wiley.com/doi/10.1002/9781444338386.wbeah15308, Wiley, 2012. Accessed 13 July 2014.
Eberstadt, Isabel. 'King of the East Village'. *New York Herald Tribune*, 13 December 1964: 14–15, 18, 20.
Elam, Harry J. *Taking It to the Streets: The Social Protest Theater of Luis Valdez and Amiri Baraka*. Ann Arbor: University of Michigan Press, 1997.
Elbaum, Max. *Revolution in the Air: Sixties Radicals Turn to Lenin, Mao and Che*. London and New York: Verso, 2002.
Ellison, Ralph. *Invisible Man*. New York: Random House, 1952.
Ellmann, Maud. *The Hunger Artists: Starving, Writing, and Imprisonment*. Cambridge, MA: Harvard University Press, 1993.
Eliot, T.S. *The Complete Poems and Plays of T.S. Eliot*. London: Faber and Faber, 2003.
Epstein, Andrew. *Beautiful Enemies: Friendship and Postwar American Poetry*. New York: Oxford University Press, 2006.
Fanon, Frantz. *Black Skin, White Masks*. 1952. Trans. by Charles Lam Markmann. London: Pluto Press, 1986. Reprint.
Fanon, Frantz. *The Wretched of the Earth*. 1961. Trans. by Constance Farrington. New York: Grove Press, 1963. Reprint.
Feinstein, Sasha. 'The John Coltrane Poem'. In *Jazz Poetry: From the 1920s to the Present*. 115–42. Westport, CT: Praeger, 1997.
Fejto, Francois. 'A Maoist in France: Jacques Vergès and *Revolution*'. *The China Quarterly*, No. 17, January–March 1964: 120–7.
Filreis, Alan. *Counter-revolution of the Word: The Conservative Attack on Modern Poetry 1945–1960*. Chapel Hill: University of North Carolina Press, 2008.
Finn, Julio. *The Bluesman: The Musical Heritage of Black Men and Women in the Americas*. London: Quartet Books, 1986.
Flynn, Meagan. 'Making an Impact as a Responsible Global Citizen'. [On Calvin Hicks] *The Times Delphic*. Available online: https://timesdelphic.com/2012/04/23/making-an-impact-as-a-responsible-global-citizen. Accessed 13 December 2017.
Fox, Robert Elliott. 'Ishmael Reed'. In *The Oxford Companion to African-American Literature*. Eds. by William L. Andrews, Frances Smith Foster and Trudier Harris. 624. Oxford: Oxford University Press, 1997.
Freud, Sigmund. 'Mourning and Melancholia'. In *The Standard Edition of the Complete Psychoanalytic Works of Sigmund Freud, Vol. 14*. Trans. and ed. by James Strachey. 237–58. London: Hogarth Press, 1955.
Fuller, Hoyt. 'The Negro Writer in the United States'. *Ebony*, November 1964: 126–35.

Fuller, Hoyt. 'On the Writers' Conference Beat'. *Negro Digest*, June 1965: 57.
Gan, Vicky. 'The Story behind the Failed Minstrel Show at the 1964 World's Fair'. *Smithsonian Magazine*, April 2014. Available online: https://www.smithsonianmag.com/history/minstrel-show-1964-worlds-fair-180951239/#llff2h4WKZrc2uxu.99. Accessed 12 March 2018.
Gardiner, Alan. *Egyptian Grammar: Being an Introduction to the Study of Hieroglyphics.* Oxford: Clarendon Press, 1927.
Gates, Henry Louis. *The Signifying Monkey: A Theory of African-American Literary Criticism.* Oxford: Oxford University Press, 1988.
Gilroy, Paul. *There Ain't No Black in the Union Jack: The Cultural Politics of Race and Nation.* 1987. New York: Routledge, 2002. Reprint.
Glass, Loren. *Counterculture Colophon: Grove Press, the Evergreen Review, and the Incorporation of the Avant-Garde.* Stanford, CA: Stanford University Press, 2013.
Goffman, Ethan. *Imagining Each Other: Blacks and Jews in Contemporary American Literature.* New York: State University of New York Press, 2000.
Grier, William and Price Cobbs. *Black Rage.* New York: Basic, 1968.
Griffin, Farah Jasmine. *'Who Set You Flowin'?': The African-American Migration Narrative.* Oxford: Oxford University Press, 1995.
Hale, Thomas. 'From the Griot of *Roots* to the Roots of Griot'. *Oral Tradition*, 2003. Available online: http://journal.oraltradition.org/issues/12ii/hale. Accessed 22 February 2015.
Hall, James C. 'On Sale at Your Favorite Newsstand: *Negro Digest/Black World* and the 1960s'. In *The Black Press: New Literary and Historical Essays.* Ed. by Todd Vogel. 188–206. New Brunswick, NJ: Rutgers University Press, 2011.
Halsted, Fred. *Harlem Stirs.* Prologue by John O. Killens. New York: Marzini and Munsell, 1966.
Hare, Nathan. 'Behind the Black College Student Revolt'. *Ebony*, August 1967: 58–61.
Harper, Michael, 'History as Cap'n Brown'. In *Debridement.* New York: Doubleday, 1973.
Harper, Phillip Brian. *Are We Not Men? Masculine Anxiety and the Problem of African-American Identity.* Oxford: Oxford University Press, 1996.
Harwood, Edwin. 'Urbanism as a Way of Negro Life'. In *Life Styles in the Black Ghetto.* Ed. by William McCord, John Howard, Bernard Friedberg, and Edwin Harwood. 19–35. New York: W. Norton, 1969.
Hayden, Robert. 'John Brown'. In *Collected Poems.* Ed. by Frederick Glaysher. 149–153. New York: Liveright, 1985.
Haywood, Harry. *Black Bolshevik: Autobiography of an Afro-American Communist.* Chicago: Liberator Press, 1978.
Henderson, David. '"The Ofay and the Nigger"; "Black Is the Home"'. *Umbra* I (Winter 1963): 41–4.
Henderson, David. 'They Are Killing All the Young Men'. *Fuck You: A Magazine of the Arts*, Vol. 5, No. 9 (June 1965): 28 (supplement, 5pp.). [Reprinted in altered form in *FOTSF*]. (Henderson 1965A)

Henderson, David. 'Keep on Pushing'. *National Guardian*, 10 July 1965: n.p. (Henderson 1965B). Reprinted in *Black Fire*, 239–44 and (in slightly altered form) *DMOH*, 31–6.

Henderson, David. 'Yin Years'. In *Poems Now*. Ed. by Hettie Jones. 100–9. New York: Kulchur Press, 1966. [Reprinted in altered form in *FOTSF* and *DMOH*.]

Henderson, David. *Felix of the Silent Forest*. New York: The Poets Press, 1967.

Henderson, David. *Umbra Anthology, 1967–1968*. No. 3.

Henderson, David. *De Mayor of Harlem*. New York: E.P. Dutton, 1970.

Henderson, David. *Umbra: Blackworks from the Black Galaxy*. No. 4, 1970–71.

Henderson, David, Barbara Christian and Victor Hernandez Cruz. *Umbra: Latin/Soul*. No. 5. 1974.

Henderson, David. *The Low East*. Richmond, CA North Atlantic Books, 1980.

Henderson, David. [Interview by Michel Oren, n.d.] Umbra Poets Workshop Oral History Transcripts, Schomburg Center for Research in Black Culture, New York Public Library.

Hentoff, Nat. 'Through the Racial Looking Glass'. *Playboy*, July 1962.

Hernton, Calvin C. 'Remigrant'. *Phylon*, Vol. 15, No. 1. 1st Qtr. (1954): 89. Reprinted in *MM*, 101.

Hernton, Calvin C. 'Statement'. In *The Heritage Series of Black Poetry, 1962–1975: A Research Compendium*. 1962. Ed. by Lauri Ramey. 211. Aldershot: Ashgate, 2008.

Hernton, Calvin C. 'White Liberals and Black Muslims'. *Negro Digest*, Vol. 12, No. 12 (October 1963): 3–11.

Hernton, Calvin C. *The Coming of Chronos to the House of Nightsong: An Epical Narrative of the South*. New York: Interim Books, 1964. (1964A)

Hernton, Calvin C. 'Is There *Really* a Negro Revolution?' *Negro Digest*, December 1964: 10–22. (1964B)

Hernton, Calvin C. 'Jitterbugging in the Streets'. *Streets*, Vol. 1, No. 2 (May–June 1965): n.p. Reprinted in *BF*, 205–9, and *MM*, 83–6. (1965A)

Hernton, Calvin C. *Sex and Racism in America*. New York: Doubleday, 1965. (1965B)

Hernton, Calvin C. 'Going Back South'. *Dissent*, May 1966: 265–74. Reprinted as part of 'The Debt I Owe' in Hernton 1966D. (1966A)

Hernton, Calvin C. 'How I Came to Write the Filthiest Book Ever Written'. *Fact*, Vol. 3, No. 5 (September–October 1966): 46. (1966B)

Hernton, Calvin C. 'On Racial Riots in America'. *Peace News*, 25 March 1966: 3. (1966C)

Hernton, Calvin C. *White Papers for White Americans*. New York: Doubleday, 1966. (1966D)

Hernton, Calvin C. 'The Witchcraft of LeRoi Jones'. *Peace News*, 15 April 1966: 5–6. (1966E)

Hernton, Calvin C. 'Dynamite Growing out of Their Skulls'. In *Black Fire: An Anthology of Afro-American Writing*. Eds. by Amiri Baraka and Larry Neal. 78–104. New York: William Morrow, 1968.

Hernton, Calvin C. *Coming Together: Black Power, White Hatred and Sexual Hang-ups*. New York: Random House, 1971.

Hernton, Calvin C. 'Hate Poem'. *Umbra: Latin / Soul*, No. 5 (1974A): 85.
Hernton, Calvin C. *Scarecrow*. New York: Doubleday, 1974B.
Hernton, Calvin C. *Medicine Man: Collected Poems*. New York: Reed, Cannon & Johnson, 1976.
Hernton, Calvin C. [Interview by Michel Oren, 11 August 1982.] Umbra Poets Workshop Oral History Transcripts, Schomburg Center for Research in Black Culture, New York Public Library.
Hernton, Calvin C. 'Les Deux Mégots Mon Amor [sic]'. In *Light Years: An Anthology on Sociocultural Happenings. Multimedia in the East Village, 1960–1966*. 1985. Ed. by Carol Bergé. 291–306. New York/Santa Fe, NM: Spayten Duyvil/AWAReing Press, 2010.
Hernton, Calvin C. [Interview by Michel Oren, 12 April 1986.] Umbra Poets Workshop Oral History Transcripts, Schomburg Center for Research in Black Culture, New York Public Library.
Hernton, Calvin C. *The Sexual Mountain and Black Women Writers*. New York: Anchor/Doubleday, 1987.
Hernton, Calvin C. 'Umbra: A Personal Recounting'. *African-American Review*, Vol. 27, No. 4 (Winter, 1993): 579–84.
Hernton, Calvin C. 'Chattanooga Black Boy'. In *Names We Call Home: Autobiography on Racial Identity*. Eds. by Becky Thompson and Sangeeta Tyagi. 139–52. New York: Routledge, 1996.
Hernton, Calvin C. 'Between History and Me: Persecution, Paranoia and the Police'. In *Even Paranoids Have Enemies: New Perspectives on Paranoia and Persecution*. Ed. by Joseph Berke. 166–76. London: Routledge, 1998.
Hicks, Calvin. 'Cuba and the Struggle for Afro-American Liberation'. *On Guard*, Vol. 1, No. 2 (May 1961): 1.
Hickner, Jamie Elizabeth. *'History Will One Day Have Its Say': Patrice Lumumba and the Black Freedom Movement*. PhD dissertation, Purdue University, West Lafayette, Indiana, 2011.
Higashida, Cheryl. *Black Internationalist Feminism: Women Writers of the Black Left, 1945–1995*. Urbana, Chicago: University of Illinois Press, 2011.
Hill, Christopher. *The Experience of Defeat: Milton and Some Contemporaries*. London: Faber and Faber, 1984.
Hobsbawm, Eric. *Echoes of the Marseillaise: Two Centuries Look Back on the French Revolution*. London: Verso, 1990.
Hobson, Geary. 'The Rise of the White Shaman as a Figure of Cultural Imperialism'. In *Y'bird*, 1977: n.p.
hooks, bell. *Killing Race: Ending Racism*. New York: Henry Holt, 1995.
Houen, Alex. *Powers of Possibility: Experimental American Writing since the 1960s*. Oxford: Oxford University Press, 2012.
Howe, Stephen. 'Afro-America as Nation, and as Internal Colony'. In *Afrocentrism: Mythical Pasts and Imagined Homes*. 87–100. London: Verso, 1998.

Hudson, Theodore R. *From LeRoi Jones to Amiri Baraka: The Literary Works*. Durham, NC: Duke University Press, 1973.

Hughes, Langston. 'Simple Declares Be-Bop Music Comes from Bop! Bop! Bop! Mop!' *The Chicago Defender*, 19 November 1949: 6.

Hughes, Langston. *Ask Your Mama: Twelve Moods for Jazz*. New York: Knopf, 1961.

Hughes, Langston, ed. *New Negro Poets U.S.A.* Bloomington and London: Indiana University Press, 1963.

Hughes, Langston. 'The Twenties: Harlem and Its Négritude'. *African Forum*, Vol. 1 (1966): 11–20.

In/Formation: Black Revolutionary Newspaper. [Ed. by Amiri Baraka] Totem Press, Pre-publication copy, January 1965. The Berg Collection of English and American Literature, The New York Public Library, Astor, Lenox and Tilden Foundations.

Ismaili, Rashidah. *Onyibo and Other Poems*. New York: Shamal Books, 1985.

Ismaili, Rashidah. 'Slightly Autobiographical: The 1960s on the Lower East Side'. *African-American Review*, Vol. 27, No. 4 (Winter, 1993): 585–92.

Johnson, James Weldon. *God's Trombones: Seven Negro Sermons in Verse*. New York: Viking Press, 1927.

Jones, Charles E., ed. *The Black Panther Party Reconsidered*. Baltimore: Black Classic Press, 1998.

Jones, Hettie. *How I Became Hettie Jones*. New York: Grove Press, 1990.

Jones, Patricia Spears. 'Thinking in Words: A Talk about Lorenzo Thomas'. Presented as part of the Passwords Series at Poets House on 16 May 2006. Available online: http://www.tribes.org/pjones/essays/thomas. Accessed 20 November 2012. Link no longer available.

Kane, Daniel. *All Poets Welcome: The Lower East Side Poetry Scene in the 1960s*. Berkeley: University of California Press, 2003.

Karageorgos, Konstantina M. *Beyond the Blueprint: African-American Literary Marxism in the Period of the Cold War, 1946–1969*. PhD dissertation, unpublished, University of Michigan, 2015.

Kelley, Robin D.G. *Freedom Dreams: The Black Radical Imagination*. Boston, MA: Beacon Press, 2002.

Kent, Leticia. 'No Meeting of Minds: LeRoi Jones Found Guilty'. *The Village Voice*, 9 November 1967: 3.

Kilmer, Joyce. 'Trees'. *Poetry*, August 1913: 160.

Klein, Melanie. *Love, Guilt and Reparation and Other Works*. New York: Macmillan, 1984.

Kim, Daniel won-gu. 'In the Tradition: Amiri Baraka, Black Liberation, and Avant-garde Praxis in the U.S'. *African-American Review*, Vol. 37, No. 2/3 (Summer–Autumn, 2003): 345–63.

King, Woodie, ed. *Black Spirits: A Festival of New Black Poets in America*. New York: Random House, 1972.

Koch, Kenneth. 'Fresh Air'. In *The New American Poetry, 1945–1960*. 1960. Ed. by Donald Allen. 424–5. Berkeley: University of California Press, 1999. Reprint. 229–36.

Krämer, Sabine. 'Nefertum'. *The Encyclopaedia of Ancient History*. Available online: http://dx.doi.org/10.1002/9781444338386.wbeah15299, Wiley, 2012. Accessed 13 July 2014.

Kupferberg, Tuli, ed. *Birth*, No. 3, Book 1, Autumn 1960.

Lacey, Henry C. *To Raise, Destroy, and Create: The Poetry, Drama, and Fiction of Imamu Amiri Baraka* (LeRoi Jones). Troy, NY: Whitston Publishing, 1981.

Lask, Thomas. 'LeRoi Jones, Talk-in Attraction, Inveighs in Poetry & Prose'. *New York Times*, 4 October 1966: 51.

Lopate, Phillip, ed. *Journal of a Living Experiment: A Documentary History of the First Ten Years of Teachers and Writers Collaborative*. New York: Teachers and Writers Collaborative, 1979.

Luciano, Dana. 'Passing Shadows: Melancholic Nationality and Black Critical Publicity in Pauline E. Hopkins' *Of One Blood*'. In *Loss: The Politics of Mourning*. Eds. by David L. Eng and David Kazanjian. 148–7. Berkeley: University of California Press, 2003.

Lurker, Manfred, 'Lotus'. In *The Gods and Symbols of Ancient Egypt*. Trans. by Barbara Cumming, rev. by Peter Clayton. 77–8. London: Thames and Hudson, 1980.

Mackey, Nathaniel. 'Sound and Sentiment, Sound and Symbol'. In *Discrepant Engagement: Dissonance, Cross-culturality, and Experimental Writing*. 1987. 231–59. Cambridge: Cambridge University Press, 1993.

MacLeish, Archibald. 'Ars Poetica'. *Poetry*, June 1926: 126–7.

McWhorter, Susan. *Carry Me Home: Birmingham, Alabama, the Climactic Battle of the Civil Rights Revolution*. New York: Simon & Schuster, 2001.

Magee, Michael. 'Unlocking the Chain: Lorenzo Thomas' *Extraordinary Measures*'. *Sagetrieb*, Vol. 18, No. 1 (Spring, 1999).

Magistrale, Anthony S. 'Calvin Hernton'. In *Dictionary of Literary Biography, Vol. 41: Afro-American Poets since 1955*. Eds. by Thadious M. Davis and Trudier Harris. 139–47. Detroit: Gale Research Co., 1985.

Major, Clarence. *Black Slang*. London: Routledge & Kegan Paul, 1971.

Major, Clarence. *Juba to Jive: A Dictionary of African-American Slang*. New York: Penguin, 1994.

Mance, Ajuan Maria. '"The Same Old Danger/But a Brand New Pleasure": The Black Arts Movement in the Twenty-first Century'. In *Free at Last?: Black America in the Twenty-first Century*. Eds. by Juan Jose Battle, Michael Bennett and Anthony J. Lemelle, Jr. 207–26. Newark, NJ: Transaction Publishers, 2006.

Margolies, Edward. *Native Sons: A Critical Study of Twentieth-century Black American Writers*. New York: Lippincott, 1968.

Marriott, David. *On Black Men*. Edinburgh: Edinburgh University Press, 2000.

Marx, Karl and Friedrich Engels. *The Communist Manifesto*. 1888. Trans. by Samuel Moore. London: Penguin, 2002.

Maxwell, William J. *F. B. Eyes: How J. Edgar Hoover's Ghostreaders Framed African-American Literature*. Princeton, NJ: Princeton University Press, 2015.

Mercer, Kobena. 'Decolonisation and Disappointment: Reading Fanon's Sexual Politics'. In *The Fact of Blackness: Frantz Fanon and Visual Representation*. Ed. by Alan Read. 114–31. London: ICIVAs. 1996.

Middlebrook, Diane. 'David Henderson's Holy Mission'. *The Saturday Review*, 9 September 1972: 38–40.

Mingus, Charles. *Mingus in Wonderland*. New York: United Artists, 1959.

Mingus, Charles. *Oh Yeah!* New York: Atlantic Records, 1962.

'Mobs Rampage around World in Lumumba Protest: Screaming Demonstrators Riot in United National Security Council'. *Lodi-News Sentinel*, Thursday, 16 February 1961: 1.

Moore, Marianne. 'Poetry'. In *Others for 1919: An Anthology of the New Verse*. Ed. by Alfred Kreymborg. New York: Nicholas L. Brown, 1920.

Moten, Fred. *In the Break: The Aesthetics of the Black Radical Tradition*. Minneapolis: University of Minnesota Press, 2003.

Mullen, Harryette. *Recylcopedia: Trimmings, S*PeRM**K*T, and Muse & Drudge*. Saint Paul, MN: Graywolf Press, 2006.

Mullen, Harryette. *The Cracks between What We Are and What We Are Supposed to Be: Essays and Interviews*. Tuscaloosa: University of Alabama Press, 2012.

Mumford, Kevin. *Newark: A History of Race, Rights and Riots in America*. New York: New York University Press, 2007.

Murray, Albert. *The Omni-Americans: Some Alternatives to the Folklore of White Supremacy*. New York: Vintage, 1970.

Murray, Sunny. *Sonny's Time Now*. (Rec. November, 1965.) Jihad 663, 1967. LP.

Neal, Larry. 'The Development of LeRoi Jones'. 1966. In *Imamu Amiri Baraka (Leroi Jones): A Collection of Critical Essays*. Ed. by Kimberly Benston. 23–8. Englewood Cliffs, NJ: Prentice-Hall, 1978.

Neal, Larry. 'The Black Arts Movement'. *The Drama Review*, Vol. 12, No. 4, Black Theatre (Summer, 1968): 28–39.

Neal, Larry. 'Any Day Now: Black Art and Black Liberation'. *Ebony*, August 1969: 54–8, 62.

Neal, Larry. 'Conquest of the South'. [Rev. of *The Free Southern Theater* by the Free Southern Theater.] *The Drama Review*, Vol. 14, No. 3 (1970): 169–74.

Nelson, Cary. *Repression and Recovery: Modern American Poetry and the Politics of Cultural Memory, 1910–45*. Madison: University of Wisconsin Press, 1989.

Nelson, Cary. *Revolutionary Memory: Rediscovering the Poetry of the American Left*. New York: Routledge, 2001.

New York Art Quartet. *New York Art Quartet*. (Rec. November, 1964.) ESP-Disk 1004, 1965. LP.

Newfield, Jack. 'LeRoi Jones at Arms: Blues for Mr Whitey'. *Village Voice*, Vol. X, No. 9 (17 December 1964): 1, 12.

Newton, Huey P. *Revolutionary Suicide*. 1973. New York: Writers and Readers, 1995. Reprint.

Nielsen, Aldon Lynn. *Black Chant: Languages of African-American Postmodernism*. Cambridge: Cambridge University Press, 1997.

Nielsen, Aldon Lynn and Lauri Ramey, eds. *Every Goodbye Ain't Gone: An Anthology of Innovative Poetry by African-Americans*. Tuscaloosa: University of Alabama Press, 2006.

On Guard Committee for Freedom. *Constitution*. N.d. [1961] The Berg Collection of English and American Literature, The New York Public Library, Astor, Lenox and Tilden Foundations.

Oren, Michel. 'A '60s Saga: The Life and Death of Umbra'. *Freedomways*, Vol. 24, No. 3 (1984): 167–81 [Part I], and Vol. 24, No. 4, 1984: 237–54 [Part II].

Oren, Michel. 'The Umbra Poets' Workshop, 1962–1965: Some Socio-literary Puzzles'. In *Studies in Black American* Literature, *Vol. 11: Belief vs. Theory in Black American Literary Criticism*. Eds. by Joe Weixlmann and Chester J. Fontenot. 177–223. Greenwood, FL: The Penkenvill Publishing Company, 1986.

Oren, Michel. 'The Enigmatic Career of Hernton's Scarecrow'. *Callaloo*, Vol. 29, No. 2 (2006): 608–18.

Oxford English Dictionary, Third Edition. Online. Oxford University Press, June 2016. Available online: www.oed.com. Accessed 13 June 2016.

Panish, Jon. '"As Radical as Society Demands the Truth to Be": *Umbra*'s Radical Politics and Poetics'. In *Don't Ever Get Famous: Essays on New York Writing after the New York School*. Ed. by Daniel Kane. 50–73. Champaign, IL: Dalkey Archive, 2006.

Patterson, Raymond. *26 Ways of Looking at a Black Man*. New York: Award/Tandem, 1969.

Patterson, Raymond. *Elemental Blues: Poems 1981–1982*. Merrick, NY: Cross-cultural Communications, 1989.

Peery, Nelson. *Black Radical: The Education of an American Revolutionary*. New York: The New Press, 1997.

Perlstein, Rick. *Nixonland: The Rise of a President and the Fracturing of America*. New York: Scribner, 2008.

Pisano, Claudia Moreno, ed. *Amiri Baraka and Edward Dorn: The Collected Letters*. Albuquerque: University of New Mexico Press, 2013.

Porambo, Ron. 'What Really Happened with LeRoi Jones in Newark'. *The Realist*, No. 82 (September 1968): 5–10, 14.

Poulos, Jennifer. 'Lorenzo Thomas'. In *The Concise Oxford Companion to African-American Literature*. Eds. by William L. Andrews, Frances Smith Foster and Trudier Harris. 391–2. Oxford: Oxford University Press, 2001.

'Protests in Several Nations'. *New York Times*, 17 February 1961: 3.

Quarless, Benjamin, ed. *Blacks on John Brown*. Champaign: University of Illinois Press, 1972.

'*Race Riot*: Sale 2847, Lot 23'. *Christie*'s Auction Results: Post-war and Contemporary Evening Sale, 13 May 2014. Available online: http://www.christies.%20com/lotfinder/paintings/andy-warhol-race-riot-5792521-details.aspx?from=%20salesum mary&intObjectID=5792521&sid=b4369e0f-8d10-4417-9e4a-bb78%2063e1815d. Accessed 27 November 2014.

Raines, Howell. *My Soul Is Rested: The Story of the Civil Rights Movement in the Deep South*. London: Penguin, 1983.

Rambsy, Howard, II. *The Black Arts Enterprise and the Production of African-American Poetry*. Ann Arbor: University of Michigan Press, 2011.

Ramey, Lauri. 'Calvin C. Hernton: Portrait of a Poet'. In *The Heritage Series of Black Poetry, 1962-1975: A Research Compendium*. Ed. by Ramey. 117-22. Aldershot: Ashgate, 2008.

Ramey, Lauri, ed. *The Heritage Series of Black Poetry, 1962-1975: A Research Compendium*. Aldershot: Ashgate, 2008.

Randall, Dudley and Margaret Burroughs, eds. *For Malcolm: Poems on the Life and Death of Malcolm X*. Detroit: Broadside Press, 1966.

Records for the Calvin C. Hernton Collection at the Robert E. and Jean R. Mahn Center for Archives & Special Collections, Ohio University. Available online: www.library.ohiou.edu/archives/mss/mss014.pdf. Accessed 22 February 2015.

Reed, Ishmael. 'If I Were Icarus, Come Down Crashing'. *Liberator*, Vol. V (1965): 20.

Reed, Ishmael. 'I Am a Cowboy in the Boat of Ra'. In *The New Black Poetry*. Ed. by Clarence Major. 109-11. New York: International Publishers, 1969.

Reed, Ishmael. *Conjure: Selected Poems, 1963-70*. Amherst, MA: University of Massachusetts Press, 1972. (1972A)

Reed, Ishmael. *Mumbo Jumbo*. New York: Scribner, 1972. (1972B)

Reed, Ishmael. [Rev. of David Henderson, *De Mayor of Harlem*]. *Black World*, April 1972: 88. (1972C)

Reed, Ishmael. *Flight to Canada*. New York: Random House, 1976.

Reed, Ishmael. *Conversations with Ishmael Reed*. Eds. by Bruce Dick and Amritjit Singh. Jackson: University Press of Mississippi, 1995.

Reed, Ishmael. 'Another Day at the Front: Encounters with the Fuzz on the American Battlefront'. In *Police Brutality: An Anthology*. Ed. by Jill Nelson. 189-205. New York and London: W. Norton, 2000. (2000A)

Reed, Ishmael. *The Reed Reader*. New York: Basic Books, 2000. (2000B)

Reed, Ishmael. *New and Collected Poems, 1964-2007*. New York: Thunder's Mouth Press, 2007.

Reed, Ishmael. 'Ishmael Reed on the Miltonian Origin of the Other'. *The East Village Other*, January 2012. Available online: http://eastvillageother.org/recollections/reed. Accessed 6 March 2018.

Reed, Ishmael. 'LeRoi Jones/Amiri Baraka and Me'. *Transition*, No. 114 (2014): 13-29.

Reed, Ishmael. 'The Black Arts Movement and Its Influences'. [JR Varley interviews Reed] San Francisco Bay View, February 2014. Available online: http://sfbayview.com/2014/02/the-black-arts-movement-and-its-influences-conference-hits-uc-merced-feb-28-march-2-an-interview-with-writer-ishmael-reed/. Accessed 26 March 2018. (2014B)

Riesman, David. 'The Fate of the Union: Kennedy and After'. *New York Review of Books*, 26 December 1963: 3.
Rigaud, Milo. *Secrets of Voodoo*. 1953. Trans. by Robert B. Cross. San Francisco: City Lights, 1969.
Riley, Clayton. 'Living Poetry by Black Arts Group'. *Liberator*, Vol. V, No. 5 (May 1965): 19.
'Riot in Gallery Halts U.N. Debate'. *New York Times*, 16 February 1961: 1:5, 10.
Robinson, Cedric. *Black Marxism: The Making of the Black Radical Tradition*. 1983. Chapel Hill: University of North Carolina Press, 2000.
Rogers, Norma, ed. 'Lower East Side Feature'. *African-American Review*, Vol. 27, No. 4. Lower East Side Retrospective (Winter, 1993): 569–98.
Ronda, Bruce A. *Reading the Old Man: John Brown in American Culture*. Knoxville: University of Tennessee Press, 2008.
Rothenberg, Jerome. *A Book of Witness: Spells and Gris-Gris*. New York: New Directions, 2003.
Sanchez, Sonia. *We a BaddDDD people*. Detroit: Broadside Press, 1970.
Sanchez, Sonia. *It's a New Day. Poems for Young Brothas and Sistuhs*. Detroit: Broadside Press, 1971.
Sanchez, Sonia. *A Blues Book for Black Magical Women*. Detroit: Broadside Press, 1974.
Schneck, Stephen. 'LeRoi Jones or, Poetics & Policemen, or Trying Heart, Bleeding Heart'. *Ramparts*, 13 July 1968: 14–19.
Sell, Mike. *Avant-Garde Performance and the Limits of Criticism: Approaching the Living Theatre, Happenings/Fluxus, and the Black Arts Movement*. Ann Arbor: University of Michigan Press, 2005.
Shaw, Lytle. 'Baraka's Newark: Performing the Black Arts'. *National Poetry Foundation Mesh*, 2008. Available online: http://vectors.usc.edu/thoughtmesh/publish/177.%20 php. Accessed 30 May 2013. [Earlier version of Shaw, below.]
Shaw, Lytle. 'Baraka's Newark: Performing the Black Arts'. In *Fieldworks: From Place to Site in Post-war Poetics*. 89–115. Tuscaloosa: University of Alabama Press, 2013.
Simanga, Michael. *Amiri Baraka and the Congress of African People: History and Memory*. New York: Palgrave Macmillan, 2015.
Sloan, Cle. dir. *Bastards of the Party*. Fuqua Films/HBO, 2005. Film.
Smethurst, James. *The New Red Negro: The Literary Left and African-American Poetry, 1930–1946*. Oxford: Oxford University Press, 1999.
Smethurst, James. *The Black Arts Movement: Literary Nationalism in the 1960s and 1970s*. Chapel Hill: University of North Carolina Press, 2005.
Smethurst, James. 'A High Note'. *Massachusetts Review*, 1 November 2014. Available online: https://www.massreview.org/node/315. Accessed 28 November 2014.
Smethurst, James, ed. with Sonia Sanchez and John H. Bracey. *SOS – Calling All Black People: A Black Arts Movement Reader*. Amherst: University of Massachusetts Press, 2014.
Smith, Dale. *Poets beyond the Barricade: Rhetoric, Citizenship, and Dissent after 1960*. Tuscaloosa: University of Alabama Press, 2012.

Smith, David L. 'Amiri Baraka and the Black Arts of 'Black Art''. *boundary 2*, Vol. 15, No. 1/2 (Autumn, 1986): 235–54.

Snyder, Gary. *Turtle Island*. New York: New Directions, 1969.

Sollors, Werner. *Amiri Baraka/LeRoi Jones: The Quest for a Populist Modernism*. New York: Columbia University Press, 1978.

Spicer, Jack. *My Vocabulary Did This to Me: The Collected Poetry of Jack Spicer*. Eds. by Peter Gizzi and Kevin Killian. Middletown, CT: Wesleyan University Press, 2008.

Spillers, Hortense. "'All the Things You Could Be by Now, If Sigmund Freud's Wife Was Your Mother': Psychoanalysis and Race'. In *Black, White, and in Color: Essays on American Literature and Culture*. 376–427. Chicago: University of Chicago Press, 2003.

'State of New Jersey, v. Everett LeRoi Jones, Defendant'. Superior Court of New Jersey, Essex County Court, Law Division – Criminal. Decided 21 April 1969. New Jersey Superior Court, Appellate Division – Published Opinions: Decisions, 1969, 496–505.

'Statements by Stevenson, Zorin and Hammarskjold in U.N. Debate on the Congo'. *New York Times*, 12, Thursday, 16 February 1961: 2–3.

Stanford, Max. 'The World Black Revolution'. *Black America*, Fall 1964: 11–12.

Stepto, Robert. *From behind the Veil: A Study of Afro-American Narrative*. Urbana and Chicago: University of Illinois Press, 1979.

Story, Ralph D. *Master Players in a Fixed Game: An Extra-literary History of Twentieth-century African-American Authors*. PhD dissertation, Unpublished, University of Michigan, 1984.

Sullivan, Robert, ed. *Life: 100 Photographs That Changed the World*. New York: Life Books, 2003.

Szwed, John F. *Space Is the Place: The Life and Times of Sun Ra*. New York: Pantheon Books, 1997.

Tande, Dibussi. 'France's Dirty War in Cameroon: The Assassination of Félix-Roland Moumié'. In *Scribbles from the Den: Essays on Collective Memory and Politics in Cameroon*. Bamenda and Buea, Cameroon: Langaa RPCIG, 2009: 60–64.

Teague, Robert L. 'Negroes Say Conditions in U.S. Explain Nationalists' Militancy: Negroes Explain Extremist Drives'. *New York Times*, 2 March 1961: 1.

'The Magic Word Was "Prison"'. *New York Times*, 7 January 1968: 6.

Thomas, Lorenzo. 'A Tale of Two Cities'. *Umbra* I, Winter 1963: 36–7.

Thomas, Lorenzo. 'The Unnatural Life'. *Lines* #1, September 1964: n.p. Reprinted in *TB*, 17.

Thomas, Lorenzo. 'Embarkation for Cythera'. *Liberator*, Vol. V, No. 5 (May 1965): 21. Reprinted in *TB*, 23–4. (1965B)

Thomas, Lorenzo. 'Modern Plumbing Illustrated'. *East Side Review*, January/February 1966: 62.

Thomas, Lorenzo. 'The Bathers'. 1970. *Southern Exposure*, Vol. 3–4. Institute of Southern Studies, University of Michigan, 1975: 73–5. Reprinted in *TB*, 59–62. (1975A)

Thomas, Lorenzo. 'Poems'. In *Jambalaya*. Ed. by Steve Cannon. 25–54. New York: Reed, Cannon & Johnson, 1975. (1975B)

Thomas, Lorenzo. 'Two Crowns of Thoth: A Study of Ishmael Reed's *The Last Days of Louisiana Red*'. *Obsidian*, Vol. II, No. 3 (1976): 5–25. (1976A)

Thomas, Lorenzo. 'Statement'. In *None of the Above: New Poets of the U.S.A.* Ed. by Michael Lally. 193–4. New York: The Crossing Press, 1976. (1976B)

Thomas, Lorenzo. 'The Shadow World: New York's Umbra Workshop and Origins of the Black Arts Movement'. *Callaloo*, Vol. 4 (1978): 53–72.

Thomas, Lorenzo. *Chances Are Few*. Berkeley, CA: Blue Wind Books, 1979.

Thomas, Lorenzo. *The Bathers*. New York: I. Reed Books, 1981. (*TB*). (1981A).

Thomas, Lorenzo. '"Between the Comedy of Matters and the Ritual Workings of Man": An Interview with Lorenzo Thomas'. 1978 interview by Charles Rowell. *Callaloo*, No. 11/13 (February–October 1981): 19–35. (1981B).

Thomas, Lorenzo. 'Annotated Bibliography of the Umbra Workshop, 1962–1982'. Umbra Poets Workshop Oral History Transcripts, Schomburg Center for Research in Black Culture, New York Public Library.

Thomas, Lorenzo. [Interview by Michel Oren, 31 July 1983.] Umbra Poets Workshop Oral History Transcripts, Schomburg Center for Research in Black Culture, New York Public Library.

Thomas, Lorenzo. 'Tom Dent'. In *Dictionary of Literary Biography, Vol. 38. Afro-American Writers after 1955: Dramatists and Prose Writers*. Eds. by Thadious M. Davis and Trudier Harris, 86–92. Detroit: Gale Research Co., 1985.

Thomas, Lorenzo. 'Alea's Children: The Avant-Garde on the Lower East Side, 1960–1970'. *African-American Review*, Vol. 27, No. 4 (1993): 573–8.

Thomas, Lorenzo. *Extraordinary Measures: Afrocentric Modernism and Twentieth-century American Poetry*. Tuscaloosa: University of Alabama Press, 2000.

Thomas, Lorenzo. 'Memoir'. In *Angel Hair Sleeps with a Boy in My Head: The Angel Hair Anthology*. Ed. by Anne Waldman and Lewis Warsh. 604. New York: Granary Books, 2001. (2001A)

Thomas, Lorenzo. 'Knowledge Is Power: Frederick Douglass and the Roots of Literacy'. In *The Teachers and Writers Guide to Classic American Literature*. Ed. by Christopher Edgar and Gary Lenhart. 15–21. New York: Teachers and Writers Collaborative, 2001. (2001B)

Thomas, Lorenzo. 'Kindred: Origins of the Black Avant-garde'. *Tripwire: A Journal of Poetics*, Vol. 5 (Fall 2001): 57–64. (2001C)

Thomas, Lorenzo. 'The Pleasures of Elusiveness: What Is in and around Ron Padgett's Poetry'. In *Don't Ever Get Famous: Essays on New York Writing after the New York School*. Ed. by Daniel Kane. 288–302. Champaign/London: Dalkey Archive Press, 2006.

Thomas, Lorenzo. *Don't Deny My Name: Words and Music and the Black Intellectual Tradition*. Ann Arbor: University of Michigan Press, 2008.

Thompson, Robert Farris. *Flash of the Spirit: African and Afro-American Art and Philosophy*. New York: Vintage, 1984.

Tinson, Christopher M. *Radical Intellect: Liberator Magazine and Black Activism in the 1960s*. Chapel Hill: University of North Carolina Press, 2017.

Touré, Askia (Rolland Snellings). "Cry Freedom". *Liberator*, Vol. 3, No. 5 (May 1963): 9–11.
Touré, Askia (Rolland Snellings). 'The Long Hot Summer'. *Black America*, Fall, 1964: 13–14.
Touré, Askia (Rolland Snellings). 'Afro-American Youth and the Bandung World'. *Liberator*, Vol. 5, No. 2 (February 1965): 4–7, 68. (1965A)
Touré, Askia (Rolland Snellings). 'Keep on Pushin': Rhythm & Blues as a Weapon'. *Liberator*, Vol. 5, No. 10 (October 1965): 6–9. (1965B)
Touré, Askia (Rolland Snellings). 'A Letter to Ed Spriggs: Concerning LeRoi Jones and Others'. *Black Dialogue*, Vol. 3 (Winter, 1967/68): 304.
Touré, Askia (Rolland Snellings). 'Jihad!' *Negro Digest*, July 1969: 10–17.
Touré, Askia (Rolland Snellings). *From the Pyramids to the Projects*. New York: Africa World Press, 1990.
Touré, Askia (Rolland Snellings). 'Rudy Interviews Askia Touré'. *Chickenbones: A Journal*, December 2004. Available online: http://www.nathanielturner.com/rudyinterviewsaskiaTouré.htm. Accessed 12 March 2018.
Tyson, Timothy B. 'The Civil Rights Movement'. In *The Oxford Companion to African-American Literature*. Eds. by William L. Andrews, Frances Smith Foster and Trudier Harris. 147–52. Oxford: Oxford University Press, 1997.
Tyson, Timothy B. *Radio Free Dixie: Robert F. Williams and the Roots of Black Power*. Chapel Hill: University of North Carolina Press. 1999.
United States Department of Justice. 'F.B.I Records for Calvin C. Hernton, 1955–1969'. (Assorted documents dated 14 March 1955 to 29 August 1969. Internal case file no. 100-417598.) In *F.B. Eyes Digital Archive: FBI Files on African-American Authors and Institutions Obtained through the U.S. Freedom of Information Act (FOIA)*. Ed. by William J. Maxwell. Washington University Digital Gateway. Available online: http://omeka.wustl.edu/omeka/exhibits/show/fbeyes/hernton. Accessed 30 October 2017.
'U.N. Rioting Laid to Pro-Africans'. *New York Times*, 16 February 1961: 11.
Van Newkirk, Allen, ed. *Guerrilla: Free Newspaper of the Streets*, Vol. 2, No. 1 (1968).
Vanderborg, Susan. *Paratextual Communities: American Avant-Garde Poetry since 1950*. Carbondale and Edwardsville: Southern Illinois University Press, 2001.
Vincent, Ricky. *Party Music: The Inside Story of the Black Panthers' Band and How Black Power Transformed Soul Music*. Chicago: Lawrence Hill Books, 2013.
Waggoner, Walter W. 'LeRoi Jones Jailed in Manacles after Outburst in Jersey Court'. *New York Times*, 24 October 1967: 30.
Waggoner, Walter W. 'LeRoi Jones Jailed for 2½ to 3 Years on Gun Charge'. *New York Times*, 5 January 1968: 33.
Waldman, Anne. 'Blues Cadet'. In *Journals and Dreams*. 75–6. New York: Stonehill, 1976.
Walker, Alice. 'Advancing Luna – and Ida B. Wells'. In *You Can't Keep a Good Woman Down: Stories by Alice Walker*. 85–104. New York: The Harcourt Brace Jovanovich, 1981. (Orig. *Ms.*, 6, July 1977: 75–9.)

Walmsley, Anne. *The Caribbean Artists Movement, 1966–1972: A Literary & Cultural History*. London: New Beacon Books, 1992.

Wang, Jackie. *Carceral Capitalism*. New York: Semiotext(e), 2018.

Ward, Jerry W., ed. *Trouble the Water: 250 Years of African-American Poetry*. New York: Penguin, 1997.

Watts, Jerry Gafio. *Amiri Baraka: The Politics and Art of a Black Intellectual*. New York: New York University Press, 2001.

'What Means Independence in the Congo'. *On Guard*, Vol. 1, No. 1 (February 1961): 1

Williams, Robert F. 'Urban Guerrilla Warfare'. *The Los Angeles War Cry* (1964): 6. (1964A)

Williams, Robert F. 'USA: The Potential of a Minority Revolution'. *The Crusader*, Vol. 5, No. 4 (May–June 1964): 1–7. (1964B)

Williams, William Carlos. *Collected Poems, Vol. 1, 1909–1939*. Ed. by A. Walton Litz and Christopher MacGowan. San Francisco: New Directions, 1986. (1986A)

Williams, William Carlos. *Collected Poems, Vol. 2, 1939–1962*. Ed. by Christopher MacGowan. San Francisco: New Directions, 1986. (1986B)

De Witte, Ludo. *The Assassination of Lumumba*, trans. by Ann Wright and Renée Fenby. London: Verso, 2001.

Wood, Eben W. *Black Abstraction; The Umbra Workshop and an African-American Avantgarde*. PhD dissertation, unpublished, University of Michigan, 2004.

Woodard, Komozi. *A Nation within a Nation: Amiri Baraka (LeRoi Jones) and Black Power Politics*. Chapel Hill: University of North Carolina Press, 1999.

Wolfenstein, Eugene Victor. *A Gift of the Spirit: Reading the Souls of Black Folk*. Ithaca, NY: Cornell University Press, 2007.

Wright, Jay. *Death as History*. New York: Poets Press, 1967.

Wright, Sarah E. 'The Lower East Side: A Rebirth of World Vision'. *African American Review*, Vol. 27, No. 4 (Winter, 1993): 593–6.

Wyden, Peter. *The Passionate War*. New York: Simon and Schuster, 1983.

X, Malcolm. 'Not Just an American Problem'. In *The Last Speeches*. Ed. by Bruce Perry. 153–83. London: Pathfinder Press, 1989.

X, Marvin. *Fly to Allah*. Fresno, CA: Al Kitab Sudan, 1969.

Ya Salaam, Kalamu. (as Val Ferdiand) 'On Black Theatre in America: A Report from New Orleans'. *Black World*, April 1970: 28–31.

Ya Salaam, Kalamu. 'Black Arts Movement'. In *The Oxford Companion to African-American Literature*. Eds. by William L. Andrews, Frances Smith Foster and Trudier Harris. 70–4. Oxford: Oxford University Press, 1997.

Ya Salaam, Kalamu. *The Magic of Juju: An Appreciation of the Black Arts Movement*. Chicago: Third World Press, 2016.

Index

A
Abdul, Raoul 26, 175
Abraham, Nicholas and Maria Torok 168, 172
Academy, academics 15, 75, 79–80, 108, 173, 185–6, 200, 220–1
Addison, Lloyd 1, 4, 22
Africa
    African-American solidarity with 37, 40–2, 52–3, 56–7, 61, 64–5
    Cultural connection to 82, 90, 101, 118, 145, 160, 165–6, 170, 172, 180, 185–93, 202, 212, 217, 222, 225
Afrocentrism 9, 12–13, 19, 40, 53, 163, 178, 212, 216–17, 220
Afro-Futurism 115
Ahidjo, Ahmadou 51
Ahmad, Muhammad. *See* Stanford, Max
AIDS 223
alchemy 74
Algeria 42, 74–5
Allen, Donald 9
Allen, Walter 14
ambivalence (Psychoanalysis) 161, 166
American South 4, 6–7, 9, 15–18, 22–7, 33–4, 36–7, 40–2, 56, 62, 83, 100–1, 107, 126, 128, 133, 138, 144, 151–73, 175–89, 193–5, 197, 199–203, 221–2, 224–5. *See also* Hernton, Calvin; Dent, Tom
Amidon, Bill 130
Angelou, Maya 36, 38, 40–1, 44
anti-imperialism 20, 31, 36, 40–2, 48–50, 53–8, 61–4, 70, 105, 109, 117, 137
Anti-University of London 126
apocalypse 56, 59, 137, 206
appropriation 53–4, 65, 103, 112, 134, 152, 160, 209, 215
Armageddon 61, 136–7
Ashbery, John 92
Asia 41–2, 65, 110, 118–19, 225

Asilomar Negro Writers Conference 70–2, 95
Association for Women of African Heritage 19, 38, 44
Audubon Ballroom 104, 111, 124
Auschwitz 121, 130
avant-garde 14, 19–20, 23–4, 72, 76, 176

B
Bahir, Mustapha 58
Baldwin, James 10, 40, 58, 71
Bambara, Toni Cade 145
Bamileke 51
Bandung 40–1, 55, 61, 115, 132, 225
baptism 134, 208–10, 213, 216
Baraka, Amiri, 99–102, 108, 110, 114–16, 121–3, 125–8, 131–4, 136–7, 143, 145–9, 151, 160, 163, 171–2, 176, 179, 182, 184, 188, 195, 197, 206–10, 219, 222–4
Anti-Semitism 88, 90
on Charles Mingus 53
and On Guard for Freedom 23, 35–8, 40–3
Poetry of 25, 27–8, 31–3, 69–97
trial of 90–7
and Umbra Poet's Workshop, 1–15, 69–71, 77–8, 84, 89, 93, 95
works by
    'American Sexual Reference: Black Male' 83, 87
    'Answers in Porgress' 3, 93, 100
    The Autobiography of LeRoi Jones/ Amiri Baraka 2–3, 10, 12, 35, 42, 55, 66, 89, 91–2, 97, 108, 148, 172, 208, 223–4
    'Black Art' 79, 84–90
    'Black Dada Nihilismus' 32, 69–74, 76–7, 79–84, 89–90, 92, 123, 171, 204
    'Black People!' 90–7, 114
    Blues People 2

'The Changing Same' 32, 115, 210
'Cuba Libre' 41
'Dada Zodji' 219
The Dead Lecturer 70–6, 80–3, 85, 87
Dutchman 69, 90, 121
Madheart 146, 149
'Philistinism and the Negro Writer' 71–2
'A Poem for Black Hearts' 123–4
'The Screamers' 83, 188
BART/S 5, 12–13, 22, 27, 29, 36, 43, 56–7, 65, 69, 84, 88–9, 91, 93, 102, 117, 126, 149, 158, 173, 181–2, 224
Bay of Pigs 13, 42
bebop 64, 106–7
Bechet, Sidney 188–9
Before Columbus Foundation 46, 221, 225
Benston, Kimberly 95
Berger, Art 1, 11, 21, 25–6, 45, 57, 126, 209, 233 n.3
Berke, Joseph 126–7
Berrigan, Ted 19, 77, 104, 197
Bibbs, Hart LeRoi 5, 27, 101, 147
Bigart, Homer (journalist) 15, 50–3
Birmingham, Alabama (Civil Rights Campaign) 6, 9, 30, 34, 202–17
Black Arts Movement (BAM) 1, 4–6, 8–10, 12–13, 20, 23, 28–33, 36, 46, 54, 56, 66–7, 76, 118, 122, 125–8, 145–6, 150, 160, 173, 181, 184, 186, 200, 208, 219, 222–5
Black Fire: An Anthology of African-American Writing 56, 76, 81, 84, 99, 101, 107–12, 114–16, 131–3, 137–8, 140–1, 146–7, 149, 208
Black Nationalism 5, 12–14, 25–9, 31, 38–9, 43, 50, 54–9, 65–6, 88–90, 109–10, 178, 180, 182, 193, 207–8, 211–12, 219, 222
blackness 72, 74, 78, 84, 140, 150, 154, 178
Black Panther Party 38, 59, 94, 110, 136, 149–50, 201, 222
Blake, William 46, 127, 177
BLKARTSOUTH 181, 225
blues 62–4, 104, 122, 153, 160, 170
Bobbs-Merrill 184
Boggs, James 4
bohemianism 9, 15, 23–5, 67, 102–3, 120–1, 129–30, 199

Bond, Julian 22
Bonney, Sean 70, 73–4
Brathwaite, Edward Kamau 126, 186
Breman, Paul 45, 140, 168
Browder, Earl 25
Brown, John 50–3

C
California 4, 46, 70–2, 100–1, 199, 220–1, 225
Callaloo 34, 179, 184, 186, 189, 200, 225
Cameroon 49–52, 64, 78
cannibalism 164–9, 206
Cannon, Steve 1, 11, 127, 225
capitalism 15, 112, 136, 150, 213
Caribbean Artists Movement (CAM) 127
Carmichael, Stokely. *See* Ture, Kwame
Castaneda, Carlos 160
Castro, Fidel 22, 36, 39–41, 65, 85, 102, 107
Césaire, Aimé 77–8, 198
Chaucer, Geoffrey 167
childhood, children 6, 153, 156–7, 172, 203, 209
China 56, 64
Christianity 73, 78, 134, 164, 170, 202–12, 216
CIA 15, 18, 35, 38, 42, 50, 123, 135–6
Class Politics 23, 31, 58, 71, 158, 178, 193–4, 221
Cleaver, Eldridge 76, 137, 149, 201
close-reading 6–7, 9, 30, 32–3, 91, 97
COINTELPRO 67, 144, 150
Coleman, Ornette 101
collective unconscious 142
collectivity, collectives 4–8, 27–31, 41–3, 84–5, 107–9, 115–17, 124–6, 128–31, 133–43, 147–50, 192–4, 199–207, 213–14, 216, 222–5
colonialism 47, 49, 51–2, 57–9, 74–5, 84, 112, 190
Coltrane, John 62, 85, 122, 176
commodification 107, 187
Communism 13, 15–16, 25–7, 39–40, 43, 57, 61, 65–6, 132, 211
Communist Party USA (CPUSA) 25–7, 36–7
Congo 2, 13, 35, 37–40, 50, 61–2, 65–6, 73, 78

Connor, Theophilus Eugene 'Bull' 203-4
conservatism 14-15, 19, 25, 58, 147, 154, 214
contradiction 8, 14, 46, 125, 199, 219, 222
Corbett, John 27
Cortez, Jayne 66, 145
counterculture 20, 24, 27, 99, 117-19, 126, 131
Crawford, Margo Natalie 101, 176
Crimp, Douglas 223
Cruse, Harold 12, 36, 41-3, 65, 67, 84
Cruz, Victor Hernandez 101, 187
Cuba 13, 36-7, 41-3, 56-7, 65, 85, 105, 110, 143, 149
cults 10, 70, 73-5, 81, 83-4, 122

D
Damballah 82-3, 171
'Dancing in the Streets' (Martha and the Vandellas) 61, 112, 132
Davis, Angela 205, 211-12
Davis, Miles 22, 176, 179
Deadwyler, Leonard 211
defeat 27, 30, 33-4, 61, 63, 82, 139, 149, 166, 197, 199, 202, 219, 222-5
Delany, Martin R. 110
demetaphorisation (Psychoanalysis) 168
demons, demonic 139-42, 199
Dent, Tom 1-2, 4, 6-13, 19-20, 22-4, 26, 28-34, 36, 41, 43, 45-6, 99-100, 102, 126, 129-30, 138, 145, 151, 154-6, 158, 162, 173, 175-95, 197, 199-200, 212, 221-5
  works by
    Magnolia Street 186-7, 189
    'Nightdreams – Black' 177, 179
    'Return to English Turn' 34, 173, 175, 178, 189-90, 192-3, 222
    Southern Journey 186-7, 193-4
    'Ten Years after Umbra' 28-30, 34, 227-30
détournement 58, 73, 85, 168, 208
dialectics 46, 141, 205, 211-12, 223
Dialectics of Liberation Conference 127
diaspora 34, 101, 107, 126, 128, 222-3, 225
Dickens, Charles 49-50
Diouf, Sylviane A. 163
di Prima, Diane 92

disguise 95, 103, 105, 116, 121
'Dixie' (song) 15, 53
Dolphy, Eric 144, 176
doo-wop 55
Dorn, Ed 4, 14, 75, 80, 171
double-consciousness 138
Douglass, Frederick 37, 52
Dragonette, Ree 1, 144-5
Du Bois, W.E.B. 19, 37, 41, 52, 125, 137
Dunbar, Paul Laurence 152
Duncan, Robert 82
Durem, Ray 1-2, 8, 13, 19, 22, 25, 31, 61-6, 100, 179
Durkheim, Émile 141

E
Ebony 4, 71
Egypt (Ancient) 27, 74, 81, 160, 202, 208-9, 213, 216, 222
Eliot, T.S. 167, 220
Ellison, Ralph 10, 18-19, 25, 27, 58-9, 71, 103, 105, 121
Engels, Friedrich 61, 214
Enlightenment 52, 73
ensemble 31, 49, 60, 73, 82-3, 89, 117, 119, 122, 149, 171, 202, 213
Evergreen Review 20, 41, 70, 76, 84, 90, 99, 126
Evers, Medgar 179

F
Fabio, Sarah Webster 10, 145, 187
Fanon 74-5, 128, 131, 137, 149
FBI 15-19, 66, 90, 122-3, 126, 136, 150
Feelings, Tom 58
Feminism 31, 148
Ferlinghetti, Lawrence 63
Fields, Julia 100, 144, 158
Filreis, Al 14-15
folk culture 152, 159-60, 163, 170-1
form, literary 8, 14, 19, 22, 30-1, 62, 81, 85, 93, 159
framing 214-15
Free Southern Theater (FST) 100, 181-4, 190, 225
Freud, Sigmund 166, 168, 172
friendship 7, 11, 29, 59, 99, 102, 145, 151
Front de Libération Nationale (*FLN*) 42, 70, 75

Frost, Robert 130
Fuck You: A Magazine of the Arts 99, 122, 134
Fuller, Hoyt 10, 71–2
future, futurity 14, 30, 160, 165, 193–4, 211, 213–14, 219, 222–3

G
Garvey, Marcus; Garveyism 22, 26–7, 90
gender 25, 33, 36, 43–4, 139, 143–9, 159, 169, 222, 231, 233 n.1, 234 n.3
gentrification 103
'ghetto' (African-American) 14, 57–8, 93–4, 101, 103–5, 107–8, 112, 115–17, 131, 133–4, 137–8, 152, 177, 183, 187, 204
Gilroy, Paul 163
Ginsberg, Allen 19, 92, 177–8
Giovanni, Nikki 145
Greenwich Village 102, 129
Grier, William and Price Cobbs 147
griot 160, 189–90
gris-gris 163–4, 166, 171
guerrilla warfare 50, 64, 82–4, 119, 122, 139, 142–4, 146, 149, 225
Guevara, Che 119

H
Haiti 53, 83, 160
Hampton, Fred 149
Harlem Renaissance 26–7, 32, 102, 117, 132, 156, 159
Harlem Riots 6, 9, 17–18, 22, 30, 32–3, 40, 66, 97, 101, 104, 107–16, 122, 125–8, 131–3, 203, 219
Harwood, Edwin 147
HARYOU 91
hashish 50, 52–3
Haynes, Al 1, 5
Haywood, Harry 25, 110
Henderson, David 1–5, 7–13, 20, 25–8, 31–3, 45, 55, 64, 97, 99–128, 131–2, 134, 138, 152, 154, 178–9, 197, 219–22, 225
    works by
        De Mayor of Harlem 22, 100–1, 104–6, 111, 114–16, 121
        Felix of the Silent Forest 22, 103–6, 118, 120, 122–3
        'Keep on Pushing' 22, 33, 99, 107–16, 121, 131–2
        'Neon Diaspora' 101, 107
        'Psychedelic Firemen' 121
        'They Are Killing All The Young Men', 111, 118, 122
        'Yin Years' 33, 105, 114, 116–17, 119, 121–2
Hendrix, Jimi 101
Hermes Trismegistus 69, 73–4, 81
Hernton, Calvin 1–12, 15–18, 20, 22–4, 27–34, 44–5, 53–5, 62, 84, 99–100, 102, 108, 176, 178–9, 182, 189–90, 197, 202, 209–11, 219–20, 222–5
    and American South 151–73
    'Existential Negro' 133, 138, 141
    and Grandmother 17, 55, 126, 156–8, 161–4, 166, 168–72, 192, 202, 211
    Violence in 125–50, 155, 159, 166, 168, 171
    works by
        'An Unexpurgated Communiqué to David Henderson – London 1966' 127–8
        'Chattanooga Black Boy' 17, 33, 156–8, 172
        'The Debt I Owe' 159, 162
        'Dynamite Growing out of Their Skulls' 17, 33, 57, 125–6, 131, 136–8, 140–3, 146, 148–50, 164
        'The Gift Outraged' 22, 129–30
        'Jitterbugging in the Streets' 17–18, 22, 33, 125–6, 131–3, 142
        'The Lynchers' 16–17
        Medicine Man 22, 128–30, 134, 139, 144, 154, 158, 161–2, 165, 167–8, 172, 192, 205–6, 210
        'Medicine Man' (poem) 28, 30, 33, 150, 154, 158–62, 164, 166, 168–9, 171–2, 190, 192–5, 202, 211, 222
        'The Mob' 134–5
        'Remigrant' 15, 154, 194
        Scarecrow 12, 17, 30, 33, 126–7, 139, 148–9, 157–8, 204
        'Terrorist' 205–6, 209
Hicks, Calvin 23, 26, 35–9, 41–3, 46, 57, 65–6, 175
Hicks, Nora 11, 41, 233 n.2, 233 n.3

Higashida, Cheryl 31, 36, 44, 234 n.3
Holiday, Billie 82
Homophobia 88
Hoodoo 33, 159, 163, 211, 222
hooks, bell 147
Horus 208–9
Hotel Theresa 22, 36, 39–40, 102, 107
Houen, Alex 235 n.2
House Un-American Activities Committee (HUAC) 16, 91
Howard University 75
'Howl' (Allen Ginsberg) 177
Howlin' Wolf 122
Hughes, Langston 25–7, 32, 45, 100, 102, 104, 106–7, 175–6, 179
humanism 74, 225
Hungary (Soviet Invasion of) 25

I
I Ching 117–18
immigrant communities 23–5, 129, 198
imperialism 23, 25, 38, 40, 42, 48, 54, 58–60, 69–70, 74, 77, 79–81, 110, 118–19, 136, 150, 168, 225
Impressions, The 108–9, 113, 115
In/Formation 13, 65–6
insurrection 7, 9, 33–4, 61, 64, 74–6, 97, 114, 119, 125, 129, 131–2, 134, 136–44, 150, 173, 219
internal colonialism 59, 234 n.1
internationalism 4, 7, 20, 31, 34–6, 38, 41, 44, 54, 56, 61, 65–7, 89, 104, 109, 128, 178, 182, 201, 222, 225
Invisible Man (Ellison) 58–9, 105, 120–1, 124, 204
Islam 12, 56, 91, 105, 202
Ismaili, Rashidah 1, 24, 33, 39, 66, 78, 103, 145–6

J
jazz 5, 27, 31, 49, 52–3, 61–2, 64–5, 85, 99, 104, 122, 126, 131–2, 176–7, 186–7, 191, 200
Jocko (DJ) 113–15
Johnn, Susan, 144
Johnson, Joe 1, 11, 20, 41, 126–7, 168, 225
Jones, Hettie 99, 116
Jones, Patricia Spears 200
Jung, Carl 142

K
Kane, Daniel 4, 62, 80
Kapp, Leon (Judge) 92, 96–7
Karageorgos, Konstantina 42, 65
Karenga, Maulana Ron 28, 66, 149
Kaufman, Bob 100
Kelley, Robin D.G. 25, 37, 65, 110, 144
Kennedy, John F. 13, 15, 100, 123, 130, 134, 207
Kgositsile, Keorapetse 186–7
Khrushchev, Nikita 22, 25
Kilmer, Joyce 69, 85–6
King, Martin Luther 115, 137, 203, 206, 212
Klein, Melanie 168
Koch, Kenneth 79–80, 89
Ku Klux Klan 57, 78, 153, 157, 202, 205–6
Kupferberg, Tuli 19, 50, 52–3

L
labour 37, 100–1, 111, 130, 155, 171, 190–1, 193, 197, 213–14
Lacey, Henry C. 94
Laing, R.D. 125–6, 139
law 90, 97
liberalism
 liberals 15, 21, 41–3, 88, 96, 103, 130, 133, 137, 143, 182, 209, 213, 225
Liberator 3, 5, 20, 31, 36, 39, 41, 54–7, 77, 84, 126, 198, 203, 205
Lincoln, Abbey 37–8, 41, 60, 65
looting 73–4, 93–4, 96, 109, 139
Louisiana 100, 187, 189–90, 200
L'Ouverture, Toussaint 37, 82
love 78, 84, 87, 89, 168
Lowen, Marilyn 144
Lower East Side (LES) 20, 22–7, 30, 32–3, 101–3, 109, 121, 126, 128–9
Lumpenproletariat 12, 83
Lumumba, Patrice 2, 6, 31, 35–42, 45–50, 53–4, 58, 61–3, 65–6, 70, 73, 82, 84, 123, 203
lynching 16–17, 37, 42, 62–3, 76, 78, 159

M
Mackey, Nathaniel 168
MacLeish, Archibald 69, 85–6
Madhubuti, Haki 10

madness 85, 112, 137, 139–40, 142, 165–6, 168
Magee, Michael 217
magic 69, 83, 90–1, 94–7, 163–4, 171
Major, Clarence 95, 234 n.2
Makeba, Miriam 60
Mallory, Mae 57
Mance, Ajuan Maria 76
'manhood'
    masculinity 33, 76, 87, 106, 137, 143–9, 164 (see also gender)
Mao Tse-Tung
    Maoism 53, 55, 64, 119, 198
Marcoux, Jean-Phillipe 4, 6, 115
Mardi Gras 155, 186, 188, 191
Margolies, Edward 70
Marriott, David 150
Martha and the Vandellas 61, 112, 115, 132, 134
Marx, Karl 61, 214
Marxism 25, 27, 39, 50, 56, 65, 149, 163, 219, 222
Masses and Mainstream 20–1, 26, 57
maternal 154, 160, 164–5, 202, 211
Mau Mau 53, 64, 71
Maxwell, William J. 19
McCarthyism 14–15, 18–19, 25, 27, 223
McLucas, Leroy 1, 4, 12, 22, 41, 58, 66
McWhorter, Susan 203, 209
Meade, Matthew 58–60
melancholia 30, 34, 159, 161, 166–8, 171, 173, 223
memory 30–4, 150–8, 188–93, 195, 197, 202, 219
Mercer, Kobena 149
middle-class 70, 73, 75, 77, 103, 138, 141, 144, 155, 170, 175–7, 183, 194
Middle Passage 80, 158–9, 165, 167, 186, 219
migration 122, 154, 162
Mingus, Charles 49, 53–4
minstrelsy 53, 79, 82, 108
misogyny 30, 76, 88, 146–7
Mississippi 56, 129, 162, 179–80, 182, 184, 187, 189, 194, 222
modernism 9, 14, 19, 22, 26, 47, 80, 107, 160, 220
money 92, 94, 112
Monk, Thelonious 176

Monroe 36, 48, 57, 83
Moore, Charles 34, 203, 207–9, 213, 215, 217
Moses, Gilbert 182–4
Moten, Fred 83, 233 n.8
Moumié, Félix-Roland 49–51
mourning 27–8, 30, 61–3, 149–50, 159, 163, 166, 168, 171–2, 197, 202, 211, 222–3
Moynihan, Daniel Patrick 33, 147
Muhammad Speaks 77–8, 234 n.1
Mullen, Harryette 200
multiculturalism 4, 23, 46, 101–2, 104, 109, 193, 221, 225
Murray, Albert 160
music
    Amiri Baraka and 83, 85, 93, 97
    Askia Touré and 54–61
    Calvin Hernton and 130, 132, 160
    David Henderson and 99, 101, 107–24
    and Internationalism 61–5
    Lorenzo Thomas and 49, 52–4, 198–201
    Tom Dent and 176, 181, 184, 187–92
    Umbra Poets' Workshop and 4–5, 8, 22–3, 25, 27, 31–2
mysticism 26, 32, 120, 197, 210
myth 12, 27, 56, 81, 157, 159, 165, 168, 197, 202–4, 209, 213, 216, 222

N
NAACP 19, 26, 45, 70, 179–82
Nation of Islam 12, 26, 77–8, 133, 208, 222
Neal, Larry 5, 10, 19, 32, 55–6, 84, 91, 99, 108, 115, 125, 136, 160, 184
Négritude 77
Negro Digest (*Black World*) 56, 76, 99, 126, 133, 224
Neo-HooDoo 46, 52, 160, 164, 172
Newark Rebellion (1967) 3, 6, 14, 18, 30, 32–3, 40, 69–70, 80, 90–7, 100, 104, 134
New Orleans 6, 8, 12, 33–4, 100, 151, 154, 173, 175–9, 181–3, 186–91, 193–5, 221, 225
Newton, Huey P. 137, 149, 201
New York. *See also* Harlem
    Amiri Baraka and 66, 73, 77–80, 84, 92, 97

Bowery 115–18, 120
    Calvin Hernton and 125–38, 145,
        151–7, 173
    David Henderson and 99–124
    Downtown 9, 32, 43, 102, 108, 116–17,
        132, 198
    On Guard for Freedom and 38–41, 43,
        46, 48–50, 52, 55–8, 62
    Lorenzo Thomas and 197–201, 203,
        215
    Poetry scenes and racial politics 22–7
    Tom Dent and 175, 178–9, 181–7,
        193–4
    Umbra Poets' Workshop and 1–4,
        6–7, 9–11, 13–15, 17–19, 30, 32–5,
        222–5
    Uptown-Downtown Split 101–4, 152
Nielsen, Aldon Lynn 4, 158, 213–14
Nietzsche, Friedrich 125, 140
Nkombo 34, 181, 184, 186, 225
non-violence 13, 73, 78, 84, 133–4, 138,
    141, 143, 202, 207, 209, 215
Nuyorican Poets Café 99, 225

O
O'Hara, Frank 77, 104
O'Neal, John 180, 182–3
On Guard for Freedom
    and UN protest 35–41
    after UN protest 41–6
    and Umbra poetry 46–67
    and Umbra Poets' Workshop 2, 13,
        18–20, 23, 31, 102, 109, 117, 123,
        175–6
Oren, Michel 4–5, 44–5
Organization of Young Men 2, 13, 35, 38,
    41, 65
orisha 208, 210, 213

P
Pan-Africanism 12, 27, 63, 84, 90
Panama 197, 201
pastoral 119–20, 153, 159
pathology 33, 78, 139–40, 142, 146–7
patriarchy 145, 148
Patterson, Charles 1, 5, 11, 66
Patterson, Raymond 1–2, 4, 8, 10, 12, 28,
    31, 44, 108, 122, 175
    works by

'Lumumba Blues', 61–3
Peery, Nelson 16, 38, 66, 119, 143, 211
Percikow, Henri 25, 99, 197
performance 5, 54–5, 107, 122, 126, 184,
    191
performative language 95–7
Pitcher, Oliver 1, 28, 231
plebiscite 110
Poggioli, Renato 15
Poindexter, Jane 145
police 17–18, 35, 51, 67, 83, 85, 88–92, 95,
    97, 106–11, 116, 118–25, 130–5, 143,
    147, 153, 188, 202–3, 206–11, 215
populism
    populist modernism 14, 22
post-Fordism 67
Pound, Ezra 46, 73
poverty 23, 130, 138, 155, 158, 187, 194
Powell, James (Harlem Riots) 109–10, 132
primal scene 165
Pritchard, N.H. 1, 11, 84, 126
prostitution 86–7
psychoanalysis 140, 159, 166–7, 187
psychology 12, 128, 139–40, 142–3, 147,
    153, 155–7, 212
Puerto Rico 24, 129

R
Ra, Sun 27, 93, 101, 115
`radio 46, 79, 94, 104, 108, 113–15, 200–1
Rahman, Yusuf 100, 147
Raphael, Maryanne 1, 11, 144–5
Reed, Ishmael 1–5, 8, 10–11, 17–18, 22,
    31–2, 36, 38, 52, 56, 61–2, 77, 92–3,
    100, 108, 126–9, 154, 160, 163–4,
    166, 200, 203–4, 206, 216–217,
    219–21, 225
    Works by
        'badman of the ghost professor'
            220–1
        'The Ghost in Birmingham' 203–5
        'If I were Icarus, Come Down
            Crashing' 17–18
        'Neo-HooDoo Manifesto' 160, 164
        'Patrice' 46–8, 54, 62
        'Time and the Eagle' 46
reparations 37
Republic of New Afrika (RNA) 12, 37, 110
revenge 75, 78, 139, 206–7

Revolutionary Action Movement (RAM) 5, 20, 37, 41, 55, 91, 143–4, 150, 181
Rexroth, Kenneth 79
rhythm and blues 99, 107–15, 123, 132
Riesman, David 15, 18
Riley, Clayton 5, 158
Rilke, Rainer Maria 177
riot 6, 9, 17–18, 22, 30, 32–40, 48, 52–4, 58, 61, 66, 74, 84, 89–93, 97, 101, 104–105, 137, 139, 141–3, 147, 153, 179, 184, 203, 206–7, 209–11, 215, 219. *See also* Harlem Riots; Watts Rebellion
Roach, Max 37, 53, 60, 65
Robeson, Paul 37, 175
Robinson, Cedric R. 27, 39
Rogers, Norma 4, 23
Rollins, Sonny 85
Rukeyser, Muriel 100
Russ, Tom 37, 82, 171

S
St Mark's Poetry Project 24, 100, 198
Sanchez, Sonia 10, 56, 93, 145, 208
Sanders, Ed 19, 122, 133
Sartre, Jean-Paul 74–5, 92, 131
Scalapino, Robert 113
SCLC 202–3, 206–7
Scottsboro Boys 17, 25, 37, 157
Seale, Bobby 66
self-determination 25, 37, 85, 89, 119, 212, 214, 225
Senghor, Leopold 77
shamanism 160–1
shame 82, 161, 166, 171–2, 216
Shango 82, 159, 164–5, 167, 192
Shepp, Archie 1, 4, 26, 41, 65–6, 175–6
silence 73, 80–1, 83
Sixes and Sevens (Anthology) 45, 140, 168
slavery 37, 52, 82, 121–2, 155, 161–71, 184, 186, 188–92, 204, 212, 219, 222
Smethurst, James 5, 7–9, 25–6, 29, 31, 36, 40, 67, 102, 104, 197, 224
SNCC 19, 26, 45, 56, 71, 179, 181–3
Snellings, Rolland. *See* Touré, Askia
Sollors, Werner 14, 70, 72, 81, 85, 91
Southern Agrarians 15
Spellman, A.B. 41, 66
Spicer, Jack 69, 86

Spillers, Hortense 165
spirituals 60–1, 170, 172
Stanford, Max 5, 143–4, 150
Stepto, Robert 162
stereotype 46, 50, 53–4, 65, 70, 76–81, 83, 112–13, 125
Stevenson, Adlai 23, 35, 38, 112
surveillance 15–16, 18–19, 66, 125–6

T
Tambellini, Aldo 20, 126
Tambo, Oliver 37, 82
Taylor, Cecil 1, 4
Teachers and Writers Collaborative 100, 221, 225
Thomas, Cess 207
Thomas, Lorenzo 1–7, 9–13, 15, 19, 21–8, 58, 61–2, 64–5, 75, 84, 86, 88–9, 92–3, 99–100, 104–5, 125, 128–9, 134, 151, 158–9, 163, 176, 184, 186, 189–90, 219–20
 works by
  The Bathers 77–8, 198–9, 202, 208, 210, 212–14, 216
  'The Bathers' (poem) 27–8, 30, 34, 134, 195, 197–217, 222–3, 225
  'Broadway-Lafayette Espadrille' 198
  Chances Are Few 199–200, 217
  Dracula 198, 213
  Extraordinary Measures 4–5, 9, 12, 22, 25–7, 55, 57, 66, 92–3, 112, 115–16, 151, 158, 159, 167, 186, 197, 200, 212, 220
  'A Tale of Two Cities' 15, 19, 48–54
  'The Unnatural Life' 32, 77–9, 81, 208
  'Wheeling' 200–1
Thompson, James 1, 11, 13
Till, Emmett 13, 37
Toomer, Jean 159
Torok, Maria 168, 172
Touré, Askia 78, 84, 89–91, 108, 110, 115–16, 121, 126, 132, 143, 146, 154, 175, 206–8
 and Activism 36, 45, 179–81
 Poetry of 31–3, 54–63, 151–2
 and Umbra Poets' Workshop 1–5, 8, 10–12, 14, 20, 26, 219–20

works by
'Afro-American Youth and the Bandung World' 41, 55, 61, 115, 132
'Cry Freedom' 54–61, 64, 106, 110, 121
'Floodtide' 22, 151–2
'Keep on Pushin': Rhythm and Blues as Weapon' 56, 115
Trade Unions 25, 106
transmutation 73–4
trickster 115, 160
Triggs, Nann 144
Ture, Kwame (Stokely Carmichael) 110, 127, 201
Turner, Nat 37, 82

U
Umbra (Magazine) 2, 4, 6–7, 11, 13, 18, 20–2, 26, 32, 48, 55, 99–101, 144–5, 220, 223–4
Umbra Poets' workshop
  Afterlife of, 219–22
  and Amiri Baraka, 1–15, 69–71, 77–8, 84, 89, 93, 95
  and Birmingham 202–7
  and Gender 144–6
  and Mourning, 27–30
  and New York, 22–7
  and On Guard for Freedom 35–6, 40, 44–5
  and the Politics of form, 14–22
  and the South 151–6, 181–2
  Split 1, 5, 13, 29, 66, 100, 149, 179, 224
underground (artistic / political) 22, 24, 27, 105, 121–2, 124, 144
Underground Railroad 122
Union des Populations du Cameroun (UPC) 49–53
United African Nationalist Movement (UANM) 39
universalism 60–1, 108, 204, 212
utopianism 94–6, 149

V
Vesey, Denmark 37, 82, 204
Vietnam War 18, 34, 56, 89, 105, 116–19, 124, 134, 195, 219, 225
  and Lorenzo Thomas 198–201, 207, 215

violence 32, 43, 46, 49–50, 52–4, 179, 184, 222–3
  in Amiri Baraka 69–90
  in Calvin Hernton 125–50, 155, 159, 166, 168, 171
  in David Henderson 95, 104, 106–7, 110–11, 113
  in Lorenzo Thomas 200, 202, 207–8, 210, 214–15
Voodoo
  vodoun 49–50, 52, 82–83, 160, 163–4, 186, 208

W
Walcott, Brenda 1, 145
Waldman, Anne 198–9
Walmsley, Anne 126–7
Ward, Clara 49, 53
Ward, Jerry 6, 158, 184, 225
Warhol, Andy 215, 217
Watts, Daniel 38–9, 84
Watts, Jerry Gafio 36, 43, 70
Watts Rebellion 105, 115–19, 124–5, 128, 134–5, 207, 210–11
Weatherly, Tom 101
Wilkins, Roy 138, 144
Williams, Robert F. 4, 21, 36–8, 41, 57, 83, 119, 143–4, 149–50
Williams, William Carlos 85, 160
Wood, Eben 4, 12, 37, 39, 41, 54, 66
Woodard, Komozi 36, 43, 90, 110, 137, 149
Working-class 39, 92, 115, 176, 182, 187, 215
Wright, Richard 10, 18–19, 25, 27, 45, 100, 121
Wright, Sarah E. 36–41, 42–4, 62, 65–6

X
X, Malcolm 22, 44, 46, 55–6, 60, 66, 84, 110, 134, 137, 149, 181, 208, 234 n.3
  Death of 12, 31, 62, 102, 104, 111, 122–4
X, Marvin 208

Y
ya Salaam, Kalamu 20, 31, 45, 149–50, 184, 186
  on The Black Arts Movement 4, 8, 149, 219–20, 225
  on Tom Dent 154, 179, 190, 221
Yūgen 10